TURNING MEMORIES INTO MEMOIRS

A Handbook for Writing Lifestories

Since 1988, Denis Ledoux has helped thousands of people get started on their memoirs.
—*Time Magazine*

Very beneficial…helps writers get off to a great start.
—American Library Association *Booklist*

Ledoux makes big promises… and he achieves them.
—Portsmouth [NH] *Herald*

Contains countless helpful suggestions…
—*Down East Magazine*

An excellent book…
—*New Haven Sunday Register*

Turning Memories Into Memoirs is lively, entertaining, and practical.
—*Yankee Magazine*

Ledoux's book will be immediately useful for anyone about to embark on writing personal history.
—*Maine Sunday Telegram*

If you've ever thought of putting your story into book form…be sure to look into Denis Ledoux's *Turning Memories Into Memoirs*.
—*The VVA Veteran*

Turning Memories Into Memoirs is a guide that brings one's past alive and helps one to share it with others in a way that will capture interest.—*Wisconsin Bookwatch*.

Writing your memoirs may be the next best thing to reliving life…
—*New York Times*

Anyone intent on writing a family history should read *Turning Memories Into Memoirs*.
—*Baltimore Sun*

A satisfying way to preserve experience and pass along information to another generation.
—*Christian Science Monitor*

Fun to read, filled with practical tips and stimulating ideas.—Quincy [MA] *Patriot Ledger*

A step-by-step manual to writing successful memoirs even for those who think they don't know how to write.—*West Hawaii Today*

…offers step-by-step instruction, lots of examples, a fine appendix and a detailed index, making it a useful reference over time…
—Cincinnati *Post*

PRINTED IN THE USA
THIRD EDITION, FIRST PRINTING

BOOK & COVER DESIGN: Martha Blowen

Art work pages 144, 145 © Martha Blowen. *Here. This is for You*, handmade paper, 1992. *Eye in the Soup*, encaustic on board, 2005

SOLEIL PRESS
95 GOULD ROAD #200, LISBON FALLS, MAINE 04252
Tel: 207-353-5454 ■ memoirs@turningmemories.com
Visit us on the web at www.turningmemories.com

Soleil Press is the publishing division of Soleil Lifestory Network, an international company dedicated to helping people to write personal and family stories through workshops, editing and coaching, teacher training and certification, co-authoring, and book production services. Please visit our web site for a current listing of programs and services, upcoming workshops and teleclasses led by Denis Ledoux, and a roster of Turning Memories® teachers in eight English-speaking countries around the world.

PUBLISHER'S CATALOGUING IN PUBLICATION DATA
Ledoux, Denis
    Turning Memories Into Memoirs /A Handbook for Writing Lifestories
    1. Creative writing.– 2. Self actualization (psychology).– 3. Autobiography.
    I. Title
    ISBN 0-9742773-4-7

ACKNOWLEDGEMENTS: ■ The workshop teachers of the Soleil Lifestory Network have given us feedback and inspiration over the years—many thanks. ■ Original development of the Turning Memories into Memoirs® workshops in 1988 was made possible in part by grants from the Maine Humanities Council. ■ We are grateful to Bob Feeman and Sally Lunt, Soleil staffers who worked on this revision at the outset of the project. ■ We are indebted to Winnie Easton-Jones and Debb Hill who provided helpful edits of the manuscript in process, and to Chris Madsen, dear friend and consummate literateur, who executed a skillful penultimate edit. ■ Special thanks to Zoé Blowen-Ledoux who, in addition to appearing in several photos in this book, proofread the ultimate copy: *Merci beaucoup, tout le monde!*

TURNING MEMORIES INTO MEMOIRS

A Handbook for Writing Lifestories

Denis Ledoux

SOLEIL PRESS

Author's Note

Except for the photographs which accompany lifestories and the images from my workshops which illustrate later chapters, all the pictures in this book come from the personal collections of my family and that of my partner in Soleil Lifestory Network and in life, Martha Blowen, who designed and co-edited this book.

One hundred-plus years of the Franco-North American and Yankee New England communities in which our particular families lived are thus well-illustrated here.

But these images of our ancestors, our childhoods and our own family life necessarily represent a limited ethnic and cultural diversity.

As our workshops, coaching and editing clientele and book production projects have proven over the years, access to the rewards and challenges of lifestory writing is in no way restricted to any specific gender, ethnicity or religious, philosophical, social, educational, economic, geographic, lifestyle, sexual-preference or national group.

Only your interest and your skills can keep you from enjoying the benefits of writing your lifestories. I hope this book will empower you to nurture both.

—Denis Ledoux

Dedication

for those who started our stories—
Albert and Lucille (Verreault) Ledoux and Arthur and Ladora (Davis) Blowen

and for those who will carry them on—
Zoé and Maxim

—D.L., M.B.

By the Same Author

scrapbook journaling
> The Photo Scribe: A Writing Guide, How to Write
> the Stories Behind Your Photographs

companion lifestory writing workbooks
> The Lifewriter's Memory Binder
> The Photo Scribe's Memory Binder
> The Genealogist's Memory Binder

manuals for memoir teachers and personal historians
> *(part of the Soleil Affiliate Teaching Packages)*

> The Turning Memories Into Memoirs® Presenter's Manual
> The Turning Memories Into Memoirs® Curriculum Manual
> The Personal History Practice Planning Manual

fiction
> What Became of Them & Other Stories from Franco-America
> Mountain Dance & Other Stories

memoir
> Marie Bilodeau Ledoux: A Lifestory
> William Ledoux: A Lifestory
> Here to Stay: My Ancestors in 17th Century New France
> Simply Bucksport: A Seminary Education

as editor
> Lives in Translation, An Anthology of Contemporary
> Franco-American Writing

Table of Contents

Introduction

There is power in storytelling, and that power is accessible to you. *Turning Memories Into Memoirs* will initiate you into the process of writing your personal and family lifestories and will help you make decisions on what to write as well as on *how* and *why* to write your stories. Soon, you will find yourself working the magic of lifewriting for yourself and for your family.

"The telling of your stories is a revolutionary act."
—Sam Keen
writer

This book has evolved from my memoir work. Since 1988, I have guided thousands of people in the process of remembering and writing their stories—first through local and national workshops and now also through editing, coaching and telephone conference-call classes.

One day in 1988, I read to a group of Foster Grandparent volunteers from my first collection of short stories. Several dozen men and women, sitting at long tables, many smiling in recognition of elements in the stories I had just shared, said in one way or another, "These are people just like us!" They seemed to recognize the child climbing the apple tree at the edge of the meadow or to glimpse once again their own parents in the tired women and men trudging through the tenement district on their way back from the textile factory.

"My life might seem ordinary to others, but it wasn't to me. I made a good life for myself."

—Workshop writer

After I read my stories that day, my listeners began to tell me their stories. These were set in a number of countries around the world and in a variety of cultures within the US. As people spoke, some grew animated while others exuded peace. Some spoke with pride; others, with sorrow. All, however, seemed to need to tell the stories of their lives and of their families.

"Those were terrible times. I survived both Hitler and Stalin. My children need to know what it was like to live in a time when devils walked the earth."

—Workshop writer

"I was taught that if I couldn't write like a pro, I shouldn't write at all! That attitude held me back for years. Now I'm going to move ahead. If I've learned anything in my life, it's that not much is perfect—and that's quite okay."

—Workshop writer

Once again, storytelling had "primed the pump" of memory to enable personal and family stories to pour out. After my reading that day, I left for home feeling justified in my faith in the primal function of storytelling to affirm and reaffirm meaning in our lives.

Soon, I read again from my collection of stories to a second group of Foster Grandparent volunteers. Afterwards, the state director of the program phoned me at home. "Both groups of volunteers you spoke to would like to write their lifestories," she said. "Would you like to work with them?"

"Yes!" was my immediate response to this opportunity to help people gain access to the power of their stories. The proposal the director and I wrote for a lifewriting project eventually received two major grants from the Maine Humanities Council.

This book is based on the success of those Turning Memories Into Memoirs® workshops and of the many I have presented since then.

Don't lose your stories!

Your stories—about the time you woke in the night to see flames engulfing the barn, about the cross-country trip your mother's family took during the Depression years to look for work, about how your grandparents met in Lithuania—these are the stories that have shaped you and your family.

We might even say that we are the stories we tell, and we are the stories that members of our family tell about themselves and about us.

You intend to record your personal and family stories, of course—someday. For now, though, you tell yourself, writing these stories will have to wait. There are so many of them. Where do you start? What do you do after you've started? And you're busy—you know how it is! You don't have the time to figure out how to go about writing and organizing your stories.

You tell yourself you're better off relegating the task to another time—or to another person.

Remember how your great-uncle, or perhaps it was your aunt, told marvelous stories about your people back in Mexico—or was it Sweden? But now the family storyteller is gone and where are the stories? Gone too? Lost? Not just the general information ("Our family came from the city of Bratislava in Slovakia") but the details of history and humor, of success and disappointment that flesh out a story and make it real. ("Because I walked to grade school and back every day for six years, I knew the neighborhood well. I always stopped on the Grimes' stone wall for a rest, and if Mrs. Naughton was home, I'd linger near her house, hoping she'd invite me into the kitchen for a cookie.") Many of these details that explain so much about how you and your family were shaped are lost because the family storyteller didn't take the time to write them down—or perhaps, was intimidated by the very idea of writing.

And you—all these years—you've been a housewife, or an insurance agent, or a computer technician, or a math teacher. You haven't done much writing—and high school or college English class was so long ago. How can anyone expect you to write your stories!

> "If you start well, you will write all your stories."
>
> —Natalie Goldberg
> poet

> "Because it was on paper, I was at peace. My wife's memory would last. It would not end with me."
>
> —Workshop writer

Write your stories—now!

This book will lead you through a step-by-step process that will enable you to produce your personal and family stories—one at a time, one after another. In the Turning Memories Into Memoirs® workshops, hundreds of people—"just like you"—have written thousands of pages of memoirs for themselves and for their families. Even those who insisted they couldn't write and declared they had never written anything before the workshop have composed dozens of stories, sometimes adding up to hundreds of pages—and the pages have resulted in coherent, interesting and rewarding accounts of their lives.

Like all long-term projects, lifestory writing will have its ups and downs. When you experience a "down," take a moment to remind yourself that what you are undertaking is meaningful and important and that the rewards for you and your family will be great!

With the help of *Turning Memories Into Memoirs*, writing your stories won't be as arduous as you might think.

■ *Turning Memories Into Memoirs* will increase your ability to remember more vividly the details of the stories you want to tell.

■ *Turning Memories Into Memoirs* will offer concrete suggestions for fleshing out your writing with proven storytelling techniques. Not only will you remember your story, you will learn to record and share it in an interesting and meaningful way both for yourself and for your reader.

■ *Turning Memories Into Memoirs* will teach you the skills to gain access to your life's deeper, inner meaning—to the realm of your spirit. Using the simple writing and memory-recall techniques you will learn, it will be possible for you to achieve a new understanding of your lifestory and of your family history.

How to read this book.

■ **First, read the two initial chapters.** They will create the context from which to understand the chapters that follow.

■ **Then, either read the rest of the book in the order presented or flip through it to the sections that seem to be the most helpful** to you at your stage of writing. In the Turning Memories Into Memoirs® workshops, I generally present material in the order set in these pages. However, individuals will often interrupt the workshops to ask for specific help or information—and I respond to those questions as they arise, not when they are scheduled to be presented.

Approach this book in the same way. Familiarize yourself with the table of contents and read first the chapters that will help you the most. Then go on to read the rest of the book.

There is ample blank space in the margins. Use it to make notes or write your own marginal quotes. This is your book. Make it work for you!

■ **Read the lifestories that follow each chapter and those gathered together in Appendix A.** These are stories written by people "just like you"—people who, one day perhaps much like today, decided to write their lifestories. Many have written full-length memoirs they then published.

These writers stood at the place where you now stand, at the beginning of a rewarding exploration of their personal and family pasts or perhaps at the threshold of a new stage of understanding and acceptance.

Let these stories be your support and encouragement: **you too will succeed in writing your lifestories.**

■ **Read the book again and again.** As you acquire more and more experience with memoir writing, you will come to understand parts of the book which may not have held much meaning for you before.

It's okay to start with the writing skills you have now. As you write, you will learn more about writing and your skills will increase. If you wait until you know everything—well, you might never get to write at all!

Tools you'll need in lifewriting.

You probably already have everything you'll need to write your lifestories. Here's what I recommend you use:

■ **A three-ring loose-leaf binder.** This sort of notebook allows you to add to or delete from your collection of printed stories at any time. Seeing your stories accumulate will be very encouraging.

■ **Manila folders.** These are useful for keeping discarded stories and fragments to recycle into your text later—or to refer to during your rewriting. Folders are also handy for organizing interview and research notes, photocopies of articles and letters, etc.

■ **A computer.** While some people write finished stories by hand, I can't recommend this. Computers (and basic computer instruction) are so readily available that *not* using one is a terrible waste of your time. Computers make corrections and changes easy. Computer printouts are much more readable. Look for an adult education class that will make you comfortable with and skilled at using this important tool. (See Chapter 7, Section 1, for more on computers.)

The Lifewriter's Memory Binder is a companion to this book. It is a three-ring binder with sections for every step of the process. It includes additional prompts, exercises and tips, and many forms that will help you to organize your source material and keep your writings organized as you work.

Chapter One—As You Prepare to Start

A. Tell me a story!

B. You, too, can be a storyteller.

C. What moves you to write your stories?

D. The payoff for you and your family.

E. Scope: what's right for you?

F. Make a schedule for success.

LIFESTORIES FROM THE WORKSHOPS:
   The Price of Happiness by Gillian Hewitt

A. *Tell me a story!*

Stories fascinate us all our lives. As children, we loved to be told fairy tales and to hear, time after time, the tales our parents told us about what we did and said when we were babies, as well as the stories about their own childhoods. As soon as we were old enough, we told stories about ourselves for our parents and for our friends.

As adults, we speak in stories at work, at family get-togethers, at class reunions, at town meetings, at the post office when we meet our neighbors. In fact, stories are such an important medium for us that even the numerous stories we tell and hear daily are not enough to satisfy our enormous appetites—we consume additional stories by reading novels, seeing movies, and watching dramas on television.

What is the meaning behind telling (and listening to) all of these stories? Obviously, stories entertain us, but our need to be entertained doesn't fully account for our great hunger for stories. A more satisfying explanation of the power stories hold for us is that they provide rehearsals for life: they furnish us with the reassurance and the guidance we need to become adults who live full, happy lives.

Let's see if this idea holds true when we examine a story we all know: Hansel and Gretel. In this story, the children are abandoned by a wicked stepmother and a weak-willed father. The children rescue themselves by killing the witch. In the end, in spite of his initial lapse, their "true" parent (the reformed father) welcomes the children back and promises to protect them against overpowering adult forces (the stepmother and the father's own weaker side).

This chapter will help you to understand the larger context of your writing before you start.

It will also help you to feel confident and comfortable about telling your stories.

This chapter will support you in establishing writing-friendly behaviors and environments that will lead to success.

"I needed to live, but I also needed to record what I lived."

—Anaïs Nin
diarist

We learn a lot about people by the stories they tell. One person, for instance, is always the butt of her own jokes, while another never tells a story that doesn't illustrate how cleverly he got the better of some poor, unwitting adversary.

Does this story provide reassurance and guidance? It certainly does. The story reassures children that there is always hope of a happy ending no matter how bad things get and that their true parents do love them in spite of their weaknesses. It also reassures children that, although they themselves are weak and vulnerable, they are capable of working out solutions to help themselves. It is Gretel, after all, who pushes the witch into the oven.

Grown-ups tell their stories and listen eagerly to the stories of others for the same reasons. We, too, are looking for order and meaning in the chaos of our lives. When we say, "After the house burned down, she went to pieces. She forgot she had a family to live for," we are telling a story that contains reassurance and guidance about order. We are saying that, in spite of the calamity, this woman could have found comfort and meaning in her relationships. It provides a clear guiding message to both the listener and the speaker: tragedies can either be compounded or overcome—it's up to us to choose.

We read novels or watch movies for the same reason we tell stories: we want both reassurance that we can succeed in this journey called life and the guidance to do so. We want to see and hear how others have been successful in the struggles of their lives. We want to know the meaning of the decisions they took: did finishing school afford them a better job? was putting off marriage a sensible thing to do? what were the consequences of following or deviating from the patterns their families had set for them?

We want stories to reassure us that the inner strength we can muster will be sufficient against self-doubt, loss, grief, and disappointment. (People may exaggerate in their stories not to aggrandize themselves or to boast, but to rehearse the strength and meaning that may be missing in their lives and, by doing so, to acquire the strength and meaning they need.)

It's not out of idle curiosity that your children and grandchildren want to know about you and your life. What is more natural than for them to turn to the stories of their own parents and family for reassurance and guidance? Your stories have this power and, if they are preserved, they can offer meaning and direction for your children and grandchildren—just as they can for you.

When you tell your personal and family stories, you are filling a need that exists not only in your family but in the larger human community to receive reassurance and guidance. Every year, as more and more once-tightly-knit groups in our society unravel and our access to our rightful inheritance of family stories is threatened, telling and writing your stories becomes increasingly important.

"How can the arts overcome the slow dying of men's hearts that we call progress?"

—W.B. Yeats
poet

e x e r c i s e 4

Warm up to writing by recalling stories and recording details.

■ Recall a family story you heard when you were a child. This story may be a fragment—in fact, that's how many family stories are handed down.

■ Now, write a list of the details you remember about the story (or fragment). When you make this list, use short sentences, phrases, or even just single words. At this stage, you are not writing a narrative, just making a list. The following might be included: the names of the people in the story; their relationships to each other and to you; what they did for pleasure and work; what the story's context was (physically—the place and event; spiritually—the ideas and emotions; culturally—the attitudes and the ways of doing things); what the conflict (the action that leads to a crisis) was; and how it was resolved.

■ Be as specific as you can with the details you put on your list ("auburn hair braided into a coil"; "a scar from beneath his left nostril to just under his left ear lobe"). Make every effort to remember what people might have worn ("high, lace-collared dresses"), or sayings they might have used ("as dark as the inside of a pocket"), etc.

■ Using this list (which should considerably stimulate your memory), generate a rough first draft of the story you wish to write. Since writing is a different medium from speaking, you may feel yourself less fluent in writing than in speaking the story. Don't let this bother you. It is a natural reaction, and over the long run, the practice of writing will provide you with the fluency you seek.

■ Keep this story draft in your three-ring binder. You can develop it into a more polished story later.

B. *You, too, can be a storyteller.*

This section suggests
features that make
stories interesting to
hear or read.

Some people come to lifewriting with a natural facility for storytelling. Don't despair if you aren't one of them. To a great extent, this is a facility which can be learned. It's a matter of acquiring both **technical skills** and **belief in yourself** and in your role as storyteller.

1) **You can learn to make effective use of a variety of technical skills to write successful stories.** I will mention only a few here. In other sections of this book, you will learn more about these and other elements.

"Nothing you write,
if you hope to be
any good, will ever
come out as you
first hoped."

—Lillian Hellman
dramatist

■ **Successful stories usually have a recognizable** *beginning* ("It was the year I was nine that my father fell sick"); a *middle* that tells what happened in the story ("He took to bed; my mother went to work; my grandmother came to stay"); and an *end* that reveals how the story concludes ("Finally, in the fall, he died, and slowly Mother pieced our lives back together again").

■ **Successful stories have *characters* who are recognizably human.** Don't let your loved ones come off as "stick characters" in your stories. Even if you are writing about people you do not like and would prefer to show only their faults, write about some of their positive qualities or habits. Otherwise, your readers will not feel the humanity of your characters and may dismiss not only what you say about those persons, but also whatever it is you want your story to convey (see Chapter 5, Section D).

■ **Successful stories have *action*.** Action is often presented as a conflict (the clash of opposing or contradictory desires, or an unfolding of events) that is resolved before the end—see Chapter 3, Section A. ("Afternoons after school, Janie and I would take turns sitting next to his bed, reading aloud, enticing him to drink a little tea or listen to the radio. I willed him to be distracted from his illness and return to being the dad I used to rough-house with in the backyard.")

■ **Successful stories are full of** *sensory details* (colors, shapes, textures, smells, sounds, flavors—also in Chapter 3, Section A). When your stories portray a world ("three sweet-scented roses") rather than a vague one ("some nice flowers"), you make it easier for readers to take the leap of faith into the world of your writing.

If your story has abstract and vague wording like "After a while absence from home made fidelity difficult for him and he committed adultery...," your readers will be less interested in (and less swayed by) what you have to say than if your narration is filled with concrete and details such as "One evening, four months after he left his wife, he went into a bar. He had worked in the sun all day building houses and he was very tired. Somebody played a love song on the jukebox, and he began to ache with loneliness. A waitress with piercing black eyes asked him how he was doing, and he told her a story. He made it into a funny story because he didn't want her to know how lonely he really was. When he had finished, she laughed, and her laughter rang in his ears. He had not talked to a woman in this way in a long time and..."

The details above not only make this story more vivid but transform this lonely man into an Everyman.

The Greek myth of the Labyrinth illustrates the need for and material details in stories. The Labyrinth was a maze of passageways at the center of which lived the Minotaur, half man/half bull. In the story, a young man, Theseus, entered the Labyrinth to slay the Minotaur. Many young men had entered the Labyrinth before him only to become lost in the maze and perish. Theseus, however, connected himself to the outside world by a material detail: he used a string. After slaying the Minotaur, he followed his string to retrace his steps out of the Labyrinth and thus re-entered the outside world.

The Labyrinth story provides not only entertainment but guidance and reassurance for us as lifewriters. As lifewriters, we enter a literary maze at the center of which is "the truth"

Your three-ring binder will prove to be a flexible tool.

Because you can remove and insert text anywhere within your binder, it is easy to change your text as new ideas for its content and format occur to you. As the number of finished pages increases, so will your sense of accomplishment and confidence.

You will see your book of lifestories become real day by day!

about our lives. If we are not to get lost in the psychological and emotional labyrinth of characters and events, we and our readers must be connected to the world by sensory and material details just as Theseus remained connected to the outside world by a string.

2) **You can acquire the belief in your role as storyteller that is so necessary to transmit your stories effectively.** If you write your stories as honestly and as thoroughly as you can, you will come to believe in the rightness and importance of this work. This belief will lend your stories moral authority, and in its own way, your lifestory will transport the reader just as the ancient legends and epics do.

Storytellers (and modern artists) are at their best when telling a story—not just because they entertain and dazzle us with their virtuosity but because they are aware that stories play an inherent role in guiding us to live life meaningfully and in reassuring us this can be done.

Being a storyteller is a calling. Even if you don't understand or accept it now, you, too, are responding to this calling as you undertake to tell your story. (See *At the Workshops*, page 29.)

■ **You will also begin to understand and accept your role as a storyteller** as you do more and more lifewriting and become better with the technical skills (telling the how and the what).

"I go...to forge in the smithy of my soul the uncreated conscience of my race."

—James Joyce
novelist

At the Workshops

Tom was from the Azores. He sat in the front of the room, a dark man among the paler Franco-American and Yankee faces, and he listened attentively to my presentation on lifewriting.

When I asked for comments, Tom said, "Where I come from, there are older people who tell the stories of our islands. They know all the stories—even the stories that took place before people living there now were born.

"Whenever we get together, the storytellers tell these stories. As they speak, they look around to see who's listening—especially the children. There'll be some of the kids—most of them really—who don't take too long to start fidgeting, you know. They want to be someplace else, anywhere else. 'Who's that by the river?' and 'What's that noise over there?' These kids leave as soon as they can.

"There's another group of children who are so-so interested and they listen a while longer, but soon they've had enough and they wander away, too. The storyteller has more to tell than these kids want to know.

"But, then there are the others who don't walk away—maybe just a few, one or two even. They listen to the storyteller's every word. It's as if they can't hear enough. It's not because they're being polite or someone told them to listen. It's because they need the stories the way other children need to run and play.

"The storyteller knows there are kids like these—probably he was one himself—and he makes sure he tells them all his stories. He knows these kids will be the storytellers for the island when he is gone.

"Don't you have this here, too? You should tell people that all their children need to hear some of their stories and that some of their children, the ones who are really listening even if they're only one or two, these kids need to hear all the stories. Who else will give these children their stories unless you do?"

Tom paused a moment and then he said, "People have to tell their stories. The new generation needs them."

exercise

Assess how you view your role as a storyteller.

■ Recall a storyteller you have known or observed and some of his/her memorable stories.

■ Make a list of the elements that made these tales memorable. Was it plot, or character development, or setting? Was the storyteller adept at the technical details: creating drama? reproducing dialogue? setting a scene? Did the subject matter interest you? (Remember: the drama of the subject is not enough by itself. We've all known people who have bored us to tears as they narrated "exciting" elements of a divorce, lawsuit or accident, etc.)

■ How did this storyteller see himself as a storyteller? Was he, and the tale, memorable because of his perception: the depth of insight? his conviction or compassion? Was it his moral authority (i.e., sense of the importance of the story's message)? What relationship did the teller have to the story: was he an active participant or an observer? was he sympathetic to or disengaged from his subject? was he humorous or dramatic? How did this relationship affect the stories?

■ Of the qualities you identified above, which ones do you possess? Which ones do you think you can acquire?

■ Did you know another storyteller whose stories were less successful? What was it that was missing—or present in the wrong proportions? (Sometimes we can learn a lot from what doesn't work!)

C. *What moves you to write your stories?*

This section explores some of the reasons that motivate people to be successful at lifestory writing.

You will need to be motivated to write your memoirs. The following are motivations that have inspired participants in past workshops.

1) **Many people tell a story because they derive pleasure from the telling itself.** They enjoy the unfolding of the tale, the discovery inherent in creating a story. They are enlivened by a connection with the past which telling their stories provides. These people have reasons like:

—I need to share the pleasure these stories have given me.
—I want to memorialize people and events of my past.
—I want (or need) the energy of storytelling in my life.
—I want to participate in something larger than myself.

These lifewriters are lucky: they have a workable and pleasurable starting point because they are grounded in their own need to express themselves. Such a motivation, combined with various supports mentioned elsewhere in this book, is likely to see these writers to the end of their project.

2) **Some people come with an agenda of troubling memories to be soothed and eventually resolved.** Their untold stories seem to threaten them from deep inside, and as Theseus did with the monster Minotaur, they may wish to "slay" their memories. These lifewriters may have reasons to write such as:

–I need to understand my life.
–I want to see which family patterns reveal themselves as troublesome across the generations of my family.
–I want to work through some blocks I have in relation to myself and my family or my past.

If this second set of thoughts describes your motivation to write your personal and family stories, you, too, are in luck: lifewriting is often successful in expelling personal demons. Writing to heal is often not easy. However, as telling your story frees you of anger or fear or anxiety, you will be strongly motivated to continue because lifewriting will bring you peace and comfort.

Lifewriting is often therapeutic, but therapy is not always easy. Some workshop participants have found themselves overwhelmed with the pain of their memories and have sought the support of a therapist or a group. If you feel overwhelmed and fear you can't continue alone, it may be time to seek out the help of a professional to lead you through your memories. But, for many writers, the writing itself will be enough.

3) **Others approach lifewriting from a less successful perspective.** They are likely to come up with reasons such as:
–I ought to do it.
–It's a good thing to do.
–My children want me to do it, and I want to please them.

"I love the start up phase. That's when I feel most like a god inventing the universe."

—Workshop writer

"That a man may be free of his ghosts, he must return to them as to a garden."

—Maxine Kumin
poet

Sometimes, when you feel guilty planning writing time "just for yourself," that guilt can masquerade as an overwhelming sense that your memoir writing is not as important as all the other things you could be doing that day.

These last reasons won't, by themselves, provide a solid foundation for your lifewriting project. They are based on meeting someone else's needs instead of your own. Rather than motivate writers, these reasons are more likely to slow them down by making them feel guilty. To ease their consciences, these writers will eventually have thoughts such as:

–It's important work, but I'm just too busy right now!
–I just didn't have time this week!
–I really don't have anything to say.

People motivated by "I ought to" and "it's good to" are usually not successful memoir writers.

4) Everyone needs to ask, "Is lifewriting an effort I *need* to make?" This is not the same question as, "Is lifewriting an effort I feel capable of making?" If you enjoy storytelling or if lifewriting is something you must do to meet an inner need, then you will find yourself more willing to show up to write on a regular basis. Being more willing, you will commit yourself to the effort needed to acquire the habits and skills to succeed. Haven't you already succeeded at many difficult tasks because you were motivated to do them (perhaps it was raising a family, nurturing a career, or supporting a parent or mate through a difficult illness)? You are not unacquainted with responding to a challenge.

"Leap and the net will appear."

—Julia Cameron
creativity guru

The task of lifewriting will not require more work and energy than you are capable of, but writing your lifestories will require some sacrifice—especially if you haven't done much writing before.

Remember: when you start from your own needs, you are much more likely to succeed.

Lifewriting is important. Believe in your stories enough to commit yourself—today, tomorrow, and the day after—to write them down for yourself, your family, and possibly the world.

exercise

Make a memoir-writing mission statement.

■ What motivates you to write your memoirs? Compile a list of reasons (e.g., "I've had an interesting life and I want to share my experience"; "I need to understand why I was always attracted to jobs that I would fail at."). Does this list include reasons that will motivate you to keep writing?

■ Now place the items from your list of motivators in a mission statement. This statement can begin with "I am dedicated to writing my lifestories because…"

■ This mission statement, which will list benefits you foresee in taking on this project, is likely to change as you pursue lifewriting and become more and more aware of its possibilities. What's important now is that your statement expresses your motivation and that referring to it helps to keep you writing.

■ Review your statement periodically. Change it or add to it as you need to, but always articulate what motivates you to write.

D. The payoff for you and your family.

As you write your lifestory, you will benefit from the experience in many ways. Let these benefits also motivate you to write.

1) **You will develop a record of your personal and family stories.** This record will be a permanent one to hand down as a legacy to succeeding generations of your family. You will have the satisfaction of knowing that you have fulfilled your responsibility of preserving your family's past. Your children and grandchildren will be very grateful for this written legacy.

2) **You will enjoy the sense of celebration that comes from sharing a "tale well told."** Merely telling stories brings many people great satisfaction. Even if you have never felt it before, you will surely experience pleasure in celebrating your life experiences through storytelling.

3) **You will gain insights into yourself and your family.** As

> This section lists benefits you will derive from memoir writing.

> A lifestory is a gift one generation bestows upon another, a legacy people have been handing down from the beginning of time.

you view parts of your life in relation to other parts (and also begin to view it as a whole), you will undoubtedly perceive patterns and choices that facilitated or restricted growth for you or for other members of your family. This may challenge how you have previously understood your life or your family. Rather than continue to insist that things are "just the way they are," you may now appreciate the help you have received or see past difficulties not as fate but as symptoms of unresolved personal or family dynamics.

Although most of us spend no more than 20 or so years living with our families, we remain bound in various ways to family culture for the rest of our lives: what we need from relationships, the way we use money, how we view leisure time, etc., may still be influenced by how our families taught us. In addition, no matter how supportive or loving our parents were (and certainly not all parents are), no family is perfect in its ability to nurture and cherish each individual child. Sometimes family attitudes (e.g., views of sexuality) or unfulfilled childhood longings (e.g., to be loved for one's self) have constricted a writer's life. These limiting emotional residues are concealed by overlays of false beliefs ("we love all our children equally in our family!"). Although these practices and beliefs may have up until then remained unexamined, they have been—and possibly still are—powerful in their ability to shape or limit your life.

Your children are also products of your extended family and its history. The families we form with our mates can be dominated by tensions and struggles that originate from our birth families and the generations before us. Writing about *what* happened and *why* is one way you can break these repeating cycles of difficulty.

The task is not an easy one, but understanding your nuclear and extended family cultures will often help empower you to be more detached from any negative hold they have on you—whether you are 20 or 40 or 60 or 80!

Sometimes people will say, "But, shouldn't these unpleasant

(or horrible) things just be forgotten? Why stir up bad memories?" The answer is clear—*our families may forget the past, but the past will not forget our families.* The "sins" of our ancestors reveal ethical and spiritual traits that can pass in the family from generation to generation. Who would think it admirable for parents to hide from their children that kidney or lung or sight problems run in the family? Knowledge of such diseases is necessary for our children to seek the care they need to compensate for or overcome such inherited physical shortcomings. Clearly, most of us would agree that silence is unconscionable and unethical.

On the moral and spiritual planes, the same is also true. When we hide the shortcomings of our ancestors from our children, we may make it impossible for them to compensate for or overcome hereditary ethical or spiritual problems. By not telling certain stories, we may condemn them to repeat generational cycles of pain and loss.

4) **You may have insights about your mate's family.** Tensions that affect you and your children may originate from patterns in your spouse's family. Lifewriting can be the means for you to articulate and explore—the first steps in facilitating the resolution of these tensions. Revealing and discussing the past with trust and respect can be healing.

5) **Lifewriting often promotes family unity by initiating exchange.** The discussions you will have with your children about your writing will also be a primary means of transmitting your stories. Many workshop participants have reported that their commitment to writing has created occasions for them to sit and speak with their children or their parents in a way they had not done in a long time.

Your children will ask you many questions and may even take exception to some of your insights. Just as they will reap rewards from your efforts, you, too, will benefit from their input. Because they are one generation removed from your parents and two from your grandparents, they may not be as emotionally involved as you are in the dynamics of those people's lives.

It's not too late, and you are not too old to take a more proactive role in your own life.

"The gods visit the sins of the fathers [and the mothers] upon the children."

—a paraphrase from *Phrixus* by Euripides

"By the creative act, we are able to reach beyond our own death."

—Rollo May
psychologist

"He who knows others is wise. He who knows himself is enlightened."

—Lao Tzu
philosopher

In this section, you will be challenged to think about how broad you want your writing to be.

This emotional distance may provide a perspective you don't have on your own.

6) **Lifewriting often leads to personal growth** because writers feel empowered by the insights they derive from writing their stories. Some lifewriters have even said that the experience has liberated them. *The insights you derive from writing will not leave you untouched.*

■ **Lifewriting can provide meaning and order as you deal with hidden fears and failings.** However, like all long–term projects that are not quickly accomplished, there may be moments as you pursue personal growth through lifewriting when you will doubt both your ability to accomplish the task and even whether it is worth doing at all. At such moments, I urge you to reread the mission statement you articulated in the previous section (Section C, page 33) and to reaffirm your belief in the value of what you are undertaking—for you, for your family, and perhaps for the world.

E. Scope: *what's right for you?*

How much time and energy are you willing to give to lifewriting? The more honest and insightful you are in answering this question, the more pleasure you will derive from your writing and the greater the satisfaction you will find in preserving your stories.

The scope of your writing ambition is likely to change over the next months (often in favor of more rather than less time and energy). If you can formulate a realistic writing goal for yourself (*underpromise* and *overdeliver!*), doing so may well save you frustration and disappointment later.

1) **Do you have a definite range of experiences you want to write about?**

– my experiences in Army bootcamp.
– my children's birth stories.
– funny stuff that happened when I was a kid.

If this type of list reflects your thinking, then you have a clear set of parameters in mind to work within. It may be possible for you to write your limited number of stories in a few short months with the help *Turning Memories Into Memoirs* can give you.

When people get "hooked" on lifewriting, they often find they expand the scope of their lifewriting ambitions.

2) Do you want to write about something more comprehensive?

> – my life and its sociological, historical, cultural context.
> – my family's life and its historical context.
> – my community's history (social, economic, psychological).

If this interests you, you should plan to continue working for many months or even years. You will need a long time to research your material and write about it extensively.

3) Pacing the project is important. If you overreach (attempt a too extensive project), you may be exhausted by your ambition. Instead of being a joy and a challenge, the work may feel full of demands and responsibilities. You'll grow to resent or dread the writing, and you may even feel like a failure. You'll be very susceptible to giving up.

On the other hand, if you underreach (set too easy a goal for yourself), you may find the job not challenging enough to continue. If you don't go deep enough into the why of your history, if you avoid the difficult issues and events, if you record just facts and not feelings, you'll find lifewriting unsatisfying. The demands of your life—work, relationships, responsibilities—will rightly seem more worthy of your attention, and you'll soon abandon your writing project.

The best choice is to approach lifewriting as you might approach gardening: make your project the right size for your energy, neither too large to accomplish nor too small to satisfy, keep it where it can give you regular, daily pleasure (collect your stories in an accessible three-ring binder), fill it with the "flowers" you find most beautiful and the "vegetables" you

"Work inspires inspiration. Keep working. If you succeed, keep working. If you fail, keep working. If you're interested, keep working. If you're bored, keep working."

—Michael Crichton
novelist

most love to eat (your self-exploring, self-expressing stories). Your project will be nurtured on a regular basis. You'll be rewarded with the many benefits of lifewriting and will eagerly maintain your commitment to turn your memories into memoirs.

4) **Regularly assess your work to maximize success.** From the start and continually throughout your writing project, ask yourself if the scope of your ambition and the shape your work is now taking are appropriate for you. I have seen many writers wander away from their goals and lose their enthusiasm as their projects either grow out of bounds or remain superficial. *Be willing to do what it takes for the project to continue to be the right size for you.*

F. *Make a schedule for success.*

This section has guidelines for getting the most writing out of your days!

You've already taken several steps in lifewriting. You have begun to read this book and you have done some of the exercises. Now you need to take another step by establishing a writing schedule for yourself.

Rather than think in the general terms of "I'll write as much as I can" (who are we kidding here!), base your writing schedule on a specific time or a page quota.

1) **Decide how much time per week you want (or have) to devote to lifewriting.** You may come up with a vague idea like: "Oh, five hours." If you don't push yourself to be more specific, you are likely to fail at putting in your five hours. If you want to succeed, be specific. Break your hours down to precise times on certain days. Write this schedule down where you will see it and be reminded of your commitment.

Here's an example: "I have five hours a week to devote to lifewriting—two hours on Tuesdays and Thursdays, 8 to 10 AM and one hour on Fridays from 4 to 5 PM."

With that schedule, you are less likely to have to confess: "Time got away from me, and I didn't write at all this week!"

Eventually, as your writing schedule becomes a habit, the

pages will accumulate, and you will feel encouraged to continue lifewriting. It will get easier and easier to do.

Sometimes people find it useful to set a date for finishing their work: a holiday, a family reunion, an anniversary. Many writers report that a deadline (but keep it flexible!) helps them to stick to their schedules. It works even better if people expect your lifestories by your deadline!

2) **Or, determine how many pages per week you need to produce to make some progress and achieve your goals.** This is an alternative to the above. Let's say you want to turn out five pages per week. Estimate how many hours it will take you to do that. (Eventually, with practice, you will have a sense of how many pages you can generally write in a given time.) Suppose you write roughly a page an hour. It will take five hours to meet your five-page quota. Now assign those five pages to five hours on specific days. Your schedule might look like this: two pages during the two hours on Tuesday from 8 AM to 10 AM and two pages during the two hours on Thursday from 8 AM to 10 AM and one page during the hour on Friday from 4 PM to 5 PM.

You can do that, can't you? But the rub here (which makes it different from the first suggestion) is that *you must continue to write past 10 AM on Tuesday or Thursday or 5 PM on Friday if you have not met your page quota!* Conversely you may get up early from your writing desk to do something else once you produce your five pages (but I'm not encouraging you to do that—why not write additional text that day?).

■ **Whether you budget writing by time or by pages, you do not have to write accomplished, sophisticated stories at any sitting.** Many lifewriters begin by producing short, even journal-like, entries they place in their loose-leaf binders. After a while, they collect and rework these entries until what they have is a more and more satisfying story. Eventually, the story is finished and it can take its place in the writer's memoir. This bit-by-bit method keeps you producing while you develop both

Do you want to be successful at lifestory writing?

■ create a writing schedule.
■ establish routines and rituals.
■ set and meet. your deadlines.
■ tell others what you are doing (going public makes you accountable).

Keep fragments and stories that don't seem to belong anywhere in one section of your three-ring binder.

Don't throw away your bits and pieces! You may decide to rework them, or you may eventually revise parts to include in new writing. You may even grow to like them as they are and see where they can fit in!

Inch by inch,
it's a cinch!
Yard by yard,
it's hard!

"I write a certain number of pages per week. The hours during which I write are negotiable, but the output is not. I find that as Thursday approaches, I feel a certain pressure to meet my personal quota by the week-end. I begin to "make more time" to write."

—Coaching client

the regular habit of writing and your skills as a writer.

3) **Either way—approaching the task by the time or by the page—be creative.** A schedule can maximize your chances for success. Both laxity and rigidity will work against you.

If you need to "borrow" time from your writing schedule on any one day, remind yourself to "pay back" before you allow yourself to "borrow" again. Being lax with this "credit" system will set you up for discouragement, and you could quickly feel overwhelmed (how easily and enjoyably can you "pay back" 30 hours?) or you'll find that you are kidding yourself—you're no longer writing at all.

Rigidity will also work against you. If your thoughts are flowing, continue writing even if you've met your page or time quota for the day. Stopping in the middle of your creative process—just because you've met your quota—doesn't make sense.

Pursue writing step by step, day by day. Make decisions that contribute to your success.

Remember: the work you are doing is important.

e x e r c i s e

Create a writing schedule.

■ Create a weekly and monthly writing schedule. Be specific about dates, days, and hours.
■ Write this schedule on your calendar and advise members of your household. (Be willing to negotiate or to offer something in exchange for their cooperation and support.)
■ Pin the schedule to your family bulletin board or refrigerator so that they—and you—will be reminded of it.

LIFESTORIES FROM THE WORKSHOPS

The Price of Happiness
by Gillian Hewitt

In 1953, we moved into a three-bedroom flat above a hardware store in the small town of Tottenham, Ontario. There was no central heat nor hot water, but I thought it was a palace compared to the tiny basement apartment we had left.

The center of activity was the huge kitchen, where a massive Findlay woodstove kept us warm in the winter months. Pale green cabinets sprawled along the opposite wall. They came to an end at the four-burner Frigidaire range.

Every week, my mother would get down on her hands and knees and apply a coat of Johnson's paste wax to the green-and-white-checkered linoleum floor. When we arrived home from school, my brother Stephen and I would delight in wrapping old rags on our feet and "skating" over the floor, bringing it to a glossy sheen. This was my mother's Tom Sawyer act, and it worked every time.

Off the kitchen was a large bathroom with a huge claw-footed tub, a pedestal sink, and enough room for our wringer washer and laundry tubs. The bathtub was never used, as hot water was a precious commodity. To conserve hot water, Mom washed us in the wringer washer! She heated water on the range or woodstove and carried it into the bathroom to fill the washer. Removing the agitator, she lifted Stephen and me into the washer. What great fun we had in that "tub!"

In the winter, we brought our pillows and our flannel pajamas out to the woodstove and placed them high up in the warming oven. When they were heated through, we would get dressed for bed beside the stove, snatch our pillows, and race down the hall to our bedrooms. It would take no coaxing to get us into bed, as we wanted to be snuggled in and off to sleep before the warm pillows cooled down. In the morning, we would reluctantly pull down the blankets to see our breath frozen in the air and witness Jack Frost's canvas on the icy window.

On my way to Tottenham Elementary School, where I attended Grade One, I used to pass by a grocery store on Queen Street. Out in front were baskets of fruits and vegetables, and each

Gillian Hewitt, is a certified Soleil Lifestory Network teacher. In this story, she accomplishes what so many lifewriters seek to do: she tells a simple story that fully captures her ordinary childhood days. Gillian offers Turning Memories® workshops and lifewriting services in the Toronto area.

day I would linger in front of some of the biggest, shiniest apples I had ever seen. They were five cents each. I told my mom about them but never dared to ask her for the five cents. I knew we had little money, and we were saving every penny to buy a house of our own.

One morning, she surprised me by slipping a shiny nickel into my hand. "Go buy yourself a nice apple for lunch," she said to me. Just then, I was sure she was the best mom anyone could have.

That day, I skipped my way along the street, pink plastic skipping rope in one hand and my precious nickel in the other. Arriving at the grocery store, I stood there, surveying the apples, trying to decide which one to choose. Shifting the skipping rope into my nickel hand, I reached toward the basket to claim my prize.

The coin dropped out of my grip onto the sidewalk. Before I could bend down to retrieve it, a large, grimy shoe stamped down on top of my nickel. I looked up into the eyes of Susan McMahon.

Susan was a nasty girl with stringy blonde hair. Her family lived in a squalid, ramshackle house on "the other side of the tracks." No one liked the McMahons.

"That's my nickel," I said. "Take your foot off it."

"It's mine now. Get outta here."

One look at her face told me I wasn't going to get that nickel back. She bent down, took my nickel, and was gone.

My lip started to quiver; I felt tears burning my eyes. I turned back towards home and ran.

Wailing and sobbing, I stumbled up the steps to our flat. Mom met me halfway down. I managed to get my story out. Instead of scolding me for losing the money, she took out her little turquoise change purse and handed me another nickel.

"You want that apple really bad, don't you? Put this in your shoe and don't take it out until you give it to the grocer." With that, she dried my tears and sent me off again.

I bought the apple but it didn't taste as good as I had thought it would. All I could think of was how much of a sacrifice my mom had made for me.

Chapter Two—Getting Started

A. The backbone of writing: Memory Lists.

B. Prime the pump of your memory.

C. Write your "up front" stories first.

D. More ways to jog your memory.

E. Work with or through pain.

LIFESTORIES FROM THE WORKSHOPS:
   The Phone Call by Jean Travis

A. *The backbone of writing: Memory Lists.*

People who attend Turning Memories Into Memoirs® workshops will sometimes say, "I want to write my stories but I have forgotten so many details. Is there any way I can get them back?"

There is one tool above all others that makes the experience of lifewriting successful. That tool is the **Memory List**. No other exercise opens up the process of lifewriting as quickly and as surely as the thoughtful and thorough compilation of the Memory List. It's simple, and as a first step, it's crucial.

In this section, I will talk about the Memory List (a general term for your list of memories), the *Extended Memory List* (its widest, most all-inclusive version) and the *Core Memory List* (the list refined to the ten most important memories).

Your Memory List is always a work in process because the more you remember and jot down, the more you'll recall. You will return to and rework your Memory List again and again as you write your lifestories.

1) **The Extended Memory List consists of short memory notes** (three to five words is sufficient) of people, events, relationships, thoughts, feelings, things—anything—from your past. The list is usually random and always uncensored. Each line lists a different memory. When you write a different memory, start a new line. Do not feel compelled to write in full sentences. (In fact, I urge you not to write in full sentences!)

■ **Let the logic of creating a Memory List be internal.** Do not force yourself to be chronological ("everything I did when I was sixteen") or thematic ("my father"), and do not strive for cause-and-effect relationships ("because this happened, that followed…") unless the memories come that way spontaneously.

> This chapter will help you identify the stories of your life. Then it will guide you in the initial stages of writing them.

> "I spent a whole week making lists! Was that lifestory writing?"
>
> *work in progress.* —Workshop writer

■ **Do not censor your memories.** As soon as you find yourself thinking something like "Is this really important enough?" you are censoring your memory and compromising your Memory List. Censoring can result in a list that is less comprehensive—and therefore, less useful to you as a lifewriter—than it would be if you allowed yourself to be free-flowing and uncensoring. Let yourself go where your imagination takes you.

■ **A Memory List includes both BIG items and small ones.** Any of the following are "on target" for a Memory List:

- brother Stan died.
- green wallpaper—stage coaches and buttes.
- Sister Marie Gertrude fell on stairs.
- my parents divorced.
- blue Schwinn bicycle.

The list is for you, and you're the only one for whom it needs to have meaning. No one else will see it unless you share it. Include enough data to make the notes understandable to you at some future time. Don't fall into the trap of writing something cryptic like "cap." In a month's time, you may not remember which "cap," or whose, you were remembering. But, if you wrote "Bob's Red Sox cap/1970," it is likely you will have enough of a cue to recall what you meant.

■ **The Extended Memory List ought to be fairly long.** It is not unusual for a writer to spend two or three weeks or even months compiling it. You will find yourself adding to it regularly in the months ahead as more and more memories come to you.

This Extended Memory List will go in your three-ring binder. It will serve as your source of writing inspiration and be a tremendous time saver. Whenever you sit down to write, you won't need to spend time coming up with a topic. All you have to do is pick an item on the list and write about it. (Write everything you remember about the "blue Schwinn bicycle" you

mentioned on your list.) With your Memory List, you need never again have writer's block. With an extensive list of memories to pick from, you will always have a ready prompt.

2) **The Core Memory List is a list of the crucial relationships and events which have shaped your life.** It contains just ten or fewer items.

This is because Core Memory Lists are about the relationships and events which, *had they not occurred,* your life (or your mother's or father's, etc.) would have taken a different turn, and you would absolutely have become a different person from the one you are.

If life teaches us anything, it's that we don't have inexhaustible energy and time. It is perfectly possible to run out of both before we get all our stories written. With this in mind, because you have compiled the Core Memory List, you can identify your most important lifestories—the ones about the prime relationships and events of your life—and concentrate on writing these first. These few core memories serve well as the backbone of your longer lifewriting project. The peripheral stories can be dealt with later—as time and energy permit.

What kind of items will appear on the Core Memory List? The answer is: only big items. Here are a few Core Memory List possibilities:

"Writing comes more easily if you have something to say."

—Sholem Asch
writer

- a major illness or a death in the family.
- the arrival of a sibling.
- the community—the town or neighborhood, the ethnic, religious or social group you grew up in.
- a significant fire, flood, car accident or historic event.
- a formative relationship with an older person or a peer.
- a failure or success at school—scholarships, sports or arts awards, a decision to go or not go to the university, conflict with a teacher, having to leave school for work.
- boyfriends/girlfriends, deciding to marry or to not marry.
- marriage/relationships.
- children and family life.
- career choices and changes, successes, failures.
- religious and spiritual quests and experiences.

■ **Limit your Core Memory List to ten items.** Limiting yourself to ten—admittedly an arbitrary number—forces you to evaluate and select the most significant material to start writing about.

The items on your Core Memory List are almost never splashy events: not the time when you met someone famous briefly and superficially (e.g. Elvis Presley kissed you goodbye on the cheek when you both happened to be at the same airport in 1965!) but something essential like deciding (or deciding not) to move away or marry, or like winning a scholarship and going to the university instead of going to work at the mill (or vice versa).

One way to create a Core Memory List is to analyze the Extended Memory List you have already compiled. You may notice that a number of seemingly separate items are really part of a single category and might be grouped together into one story. Instead of scattering, or listing separately, the names of the men (or women) you dated from your eighteenth to your twenty-fourth year, you might cluster these relationships under a Core Memory List heading like "Getting ready to meet my husband/wife." In this category, you might make a sublist of the more significant relationships you had. This would create a natural occasion for you to write about how your understanding of what you needed in a mate matured over those years as you dated each of these people until you were finally ready to marry. By grouping Extended Memory List items, you can discover core stories and make it easier for the reader to understand or evaluate your experience.

Compiling a Core Memory List will make it easier for you to organize your material early in the writing process and assure that you write your most important stories first.

By identifying core influences in your life, you can focus on them quickly in your lifewriting. In this way, you will develop a body of stories that depict the person you are and have been. If your time and energy is limited, you will not squander either one on writing about secondary events in your life. Perhaps you and your friends were impressed, at the time, that Elvis kissed you at the airport, but how has this influenced your development as a person?

If you have the interest and the time, later on, you can write about the secondary events in your life. Otherwise, you may find yourself having "run out of wind" on the unessential stories before you commit your core stories to paper.

"Writing is most of all an exercise in determination..."

—Tom Clancy
novelist

exercise

Start your Memory List now.

■ Write down at least twenty memories to start off your Memory List (fifty would be better, and a hundred preferable).
■ Place these pages in your three-ring binder.
■ Every day, continue to add memories to your list. Do not stop until you have five hundred items. (Yes, five hundred!)
■ Take your time to mull over your Memory List. Add or delete, combine or expand until you have a list that represents your life.

B. Prime the pump of your memory.

Creating your Memory List ought always to be the first effort you make to prime the pump of your memory. It is the most easily accessible tool to compile and then use. Following close in utility as a memory jog is the process of writing itself. Writing will help you remember more and more! Like water flowing from a hand pump that has been primed, memories will begin to flow once you prime them by writing. As you write, from somewhere you may have thought you had no access to, memories will come. The more you write the more you will remember: how it was to have a new sibling to share

Read the next sections in any order. You may want to re-read them as you work.

Section B will help you structure the content of your writing. *Section C* will help you write stories you have told before. *Section D* will help you to generate "new" memories.

your parents' attention…how your grandparents looked at each other across a room, their eyes full of love for one another…how insecurity tormented you at your first school dance. These memories, and many more, will flow once you prime the pump of your memory.

1) **Write a lot and write frequently.** Don't worry about whether or not your writing is "good enough!" As you write, be comfortable with letting first drafts be first drafts: rough, incomplete, contradictory. Thinking in terms of "good enough" is a trap that will prevent you from writing a lot or writing frequently. It will inhibit your ability to remember.

Unfortunately, we all have an inner censor judging our actions. It is the inner censor who asks if our writing is "good enough." Our censor causes us to hold back, instilling fear that we will look silly.

Only the inner censor expects you to write elegant prose on your first attempts—so tell your inner censor to relax! You are not competing for the Nobel Prize in Literature: you are merely "priming the pump" of your lifestory writing.

If you haven't already written some of your memories, stop right now and select an item on your Memory List—preferably something from your Core Memory List. Turn your computer on or pick up a pen. Do it now. Don't continue reading this book until you've composed at least one page of memories!

Writing is a different skill from that of remembering, but developing skill with one will enhance the other. The more you write, the more easily your memories will return to you.

2) **Write vignettes, scenes, and/or dialogues that are prompted by your Memory Lists.** Don't stop to figure out how these snippets may eventually fit together into a story. These bits and pieces will accumulate as you recall more and more and continue to write them down. Giving yourself permission to write in small, separate segments (vignettes, scenes, dialogues, etc.) is a great way to start writing. Because there will always be your Memory List of things to write about, you will

never experience "writer's block!" Fitting these pieces together to craft a polished story will come later, in the rewriting stage. *Right now, it's important to get text—any text—down on paper.*

If you start by writing on paper, here is a suggestion to make this early stage easier: *write on the backs of scrap paper cut into half sheets*—this will help free you from any obligation you may feel to fill whole blank pages! Feeling obligated to write can quickly make a drudgery of what ought to be pleasurable.

Put these half pages of vignettes, scenes, and dialogue in any order that makes sense to you at the moment. Don't belabor making sense of things at this stage. Write more vignettes, scenes, or dialogue as they occur to you.

When it feels appropriate, go through your individual stories and create an order for them as seems best. As you re-read them, note where you need to fill in gaps in your emerging memoir or make transitions ("…and because Uncle Boris came to America, my mother was able to…"). These transitions will connect the separate components to each other. What were disparate vignettes, scenes, and jottings at first (and perhaps for a long time even as you continued to write) will add up to readable, informative stories when you add fillers and transitions. (Eventually many of these stories will take their places in the chapters of your memoir.)

After you have many pages of text, the time will come for you to decide that this is better than that, to expand on this piece that now seems too short or to make more concise what had once already seemed economical prose. This is editorial work, and it has its proper place in lifewriting—but you are not yet at that stage of writing! Right now, you are priming the pump with first drafts. Let first drafts be first drafts.

3) **Free yourself, once and for all, from the sense of obligation to write "from the beginning."**

■ **Start writing your story from anywhere** you want to start writing, and write for as long as you wish to write.

■ **Don't fret about how to start your story**—if you do, you'll

> Having "writer's block" may be a way you legitimize the fact that you are not allowing your unconscious thoughts to surface. Linger more with your writing. Trust your intuition—don't block it from informing you and your story.

> Your writing itself will always be your most important teacher.

People often wonder, "Am I starting to write at the correct place?"

The fact is: any place you start is right! Where is not as important as starting.

get bogged down at this stage. **Remember:** it is the reader's experience of a story that starts at the beginning, not the writer's.

■ **Compose the beginning of your memoir during the final stages of writing.** The beginning sets the tone for a story, but until you have written the story and have come to understand its storyline and its meaning, you may not be able to establish the tone the beginning needs.

4) Each stage of your writing will provide its own rewards and challenges. Perfection is something to strive for later—but not at this early stage of lifewriting. For now, retire the inner censor and strive for volume.

e x e r c i s e

Don't let your inner censor carry the day!

■ If you are anxious about writing, it may help to write about your early writing experiences. Did school, a particular teacher, or a relative make you too sensitive to the inner censor, too critical of yourself?

■ Write about learning to write, about the history of your experience of writing. Might it have been penmanship or theme composition that closed you off? Did you face such constant criticism that it seemed impossible to have anything you wrote accepted by a critical teacher—or was that the harsh voice of your own inner censor protecting itself? Become aware of your writing history by writing about it. To paraphrase a well-known statement: those who ignore their personal writing history are doomed to repeat it!

■ Personify your inner censor. Imagine it as a little devil or a sprite. Tell this creature its presence is unwelcome and unnecessary. See (in your mind's eye) your inner censor turning away, disappearing, melting like the Wicked Witch of the West.

C. *Write your "up front" stories first.*

There are several categories of stories that new writers seem to gravitate towards. These stories need the least work to recall and so are good starting points.

1) **Some of these stories are the family stories you have often told and shared.** These are the stories you can write about first—because they are the easiest to write. As you write, the process may seem spontaneous, the prose slips from your pen or appears magically on the computer screen! You may even wonder how you can write so easily, you who may not think of yourself as a writer and have put off writing all this while!

This may be what has happened: over the years, you have rehearsed these stories in your mind. As you thought of them, you have pared these narratives down to their essential components and reshaped them for dramatic effect. Over time, as you told these stories, it was obvious that you got better reactions from your listeners if you mentioned a certain detail first and then built up to another detail with specific transitions, etc. Is it any wonder that you are writing these stories now with relative ease? Most of the prep work was done ages ago, and the stories are now highly polished!

These pieces may even prove to be the best writing you produce for a while. Enjoy the appreciation you receive from those with whom you share these "new" stories.

But beware. Pieces you write later may disappoint you by being much less polished than these first attempts. Remember that you will have spent only a few hours, rather than years, preparing to write the subsequent stories. Eventually, as you develop the craft of writing through repeated practice, you will write better stories earlier on in the writing process.

2) **A less happy group of stories are the ones that may lie just beneath the surface waiting to jump out at us.** Your first attempts at writing may also reveal memories you need to clarify or integrate into your life. Often, the memories we have not

"Which stories should I write first?" people ask me. This section offers the answer.

"This poem came with practically no effort, and all of a piece. I was not surprised, though, for I had been obsessed with the subject matter for several months."

—Joan Campbell
poet

resolved lie on the surface of our consciousness waiting for us to deal with them. When you sit down to write, these memories may jump out at you and insist you write about them rather than about something else.

Do you know people who tend to cry easily when they see something sad on TV? I don't think it's so much because they are more sensitive than others (although that may be true). It's more likely because they harbor unresolved memories of their own past sorrows. Sad stories are opportunities for them to mourn something in themselves they may not be fully aware of.

Lifewriting can be a healthy way to allow memories you have avoided to come to the surface. Committing them to paper may be a way to free yourself of their burdensome weight in your life.

εxεrcise

Write a family or personal memory that comes immediately to mind.

■ As you write, don't attempt to censor your production or channel it in certain directions. Let it go where it wants to go.
■ Is this an easy story or vignette to write? Why or why not?
■ What does this story or vignette tell you about yourself and your family?

D. More ways to jog your memory.

Don't believe you can't remember—it's all in there, every detail! These suggestions will help you access your memories. It really is true that the more you remember, the more you'll remember!

Besides doing the Memory List, here are a few additional "memory jogs" to get you thinking and especially *feeling* about the people and places of your past.

1) **Scrutinize your photo albums.** Who are the people in your photos? What were their names? What were their relationships to you and to each other? What was happening to you and to them at the time of the photo? What do you

remember about the place in which the photo was taken? Why were you there?

If you decide to preserve this information on the back of photos, use permanent ink felt tips to avoid making impressions or cracks in the surface of the photos. Allow at least a half hour for the ink to dry before you stack your photos together. Always write full names, full dates, and full locations. Never write just "Mary, Springfield, June," or "Jason, age 2." What is so obvious to you at the moment could be a mystery for generations to come! (For more information, see my book, *The Photo Scribe, A Writing Guide: How to Write the Stories Behind Your Photographs*.)

2) **Take an imaginary photo.** Go back in time and "take" the photo you wish you had. Who would be in it? How would they be posed? Describe the details: clothing, hair styles, setting. What would have happened right before this photo was taken? Right after? How would the people in the imaginary photo have felt about being photographed together?

3) **Look at photos and paintings of the time you want to remember and write about.** Study books and magazines on the history of fashions, of home decorations, etc. that deal with the relevant era. Also visit vintage clothing shops, take in old movies, browse at flea markets.

> "First, I had to work at remembering, but now the memories keep me up at night—they're coming even in my dreams!"
>
> —Coaching client

4) **Make lists of members of your family:** their names, birthdays, principal residences, the type of schooling they had, their marriage dates, the number of children they raised, their illnesses, jobs/careers, special events in their lives, circumstances surrounding their deaths, etc. You will find that focusing on finding this information for one member of your family will clarify facts about others—or suggest areas you should explore. For instance, as you determine that Aunt Marie made that trip to New York in June 1962, you'll realize that Uncle Eli couldn't have gone with her that summer because they didn't meet until two months later in August.

5) **Make lists from your past** of both the serious and the frivolous items: all your relatives; record albums you owned or

hit songs you liked; movies, favorite dance steps, special foods—anything in your past that interests you. Then, choose one at a time and write about the memories these items evoke.

6) **Make opportunities to talk about the past** with people who were there. Stay clear of nostalgia and sentimentality. Look for facts, try to detect patterns and compulsions. Remember the good times. (See Chapter 4 on interviewing.)

7) **Write "time-capsule" descriptions** of yourself and of anyone else you wish to include. These descriptions should contain physical, emotional, and spiritual considerations. Select various ages—for example, at 20, at 40, at 60. When did noticeable differences in appearance and character occur? Are these differences attributable to age, to sickness, to an accident, to a reversal of fortune?

8) **Learn the simple technique of visualization.** Visualization is a meditation-like experience in which a person calls forth ("visualizes") specific images of people, places, things. Through exercises, you can visualize the images of your ancestors, of places where you have lived, of experiences that were important to you. Visualization can provide information your conscious mind may not even be aware of.

Sometimes our sense of reserve keeps us from writing about others. Visualization can help you ask "permission" from departed loved ones to inquire into, and write about, their lives. For many lifewriters, receiving "permission" frees them of the guilt—or at least, the discomfort—they feel about probing into the lives of others.

However you choose to explain why visualization "works," it remains a useful tool for opening up your intuition to understanding another person, to making sense of what you may have repressed. Visualizations can be an enormously creative experience with many benefits. By all means, find books on visualization and undertake the practices suggested. (See Appendix B for reading suggestions).

9) **Write letters to someone—now alive or dead—you**

want to write about. Write as if you were composing a real letter. Ask specific questions. Ask for their thoughts and feelings and share yours. Now, answer your own letter as though your subject were writing back to you. Provide the answers to your questions, "share" his/her feelings and point of view. This "correspondence" may surprise you! Your intuition is tapping your subconscious to give you information and insight you didn't know you had.

These letters may also help you to recreate believable dialogue in your stories. The "letters" may contain favorite expressions and/or the diction (the style of speech) of a person you are writing about. Incorporating these into your stories will make your characters come alive.

10) **Become a journal writer.** The spontaneity and utter privacy of a journal entry helps the writer connect with her intuition and inner strength. The journal's honesty—after all, who are you kidding but yourself if you alter the truth in your journal?—can give you courage and practice in writing honest lifestories. The journal can also be an important source for lifewriting portraits and stories. Many people first explore issues and memories in the journal—sometimes making several attempts at recording them before transcribing sections into their lifestories.

> "Forcing the emotions brings errors; letting them come naturally is the way to make them clear."
>
> —Lu Chi
> philosopher

E. Work with or through pain.

Although delving into the past is a generally pleasant experience and promotes healing and growth, it can also be painful. In fact, sooner or later, pain seems to come with memoir writing. This pain, if not handled well, can inhibit—and even stop—you from continuing with your writing.

Sometimes painful memories (poverty, childhood humiliation, abuse, abandonment, addiction, etc.) you had "forgotten" will resurface. Or, you may be unwilling to evoke certain memories at all. Perhaps they are still too painful, or perhaps you are

> This section will provide strategies for dealing with your painful, difficult memories.

"I put my story away for a while. Writing about that time made me cry."

—Workshop writer

"I felt like I was a crazy person who had made it all up. Writing it down made me feel that it had really happened. Finally, I began to understand— it wasn't me who was crazy."

—Workshop writer

afraid you will not be able to handle the pain if it comes back.

You might say, "I put that behind me years ago. I don't want to relive it." No one wishes you to resume gratuitously the pain which once clamped down on your life. But, if a memory is so painful that you are still afraid of it, take this as an indication that you haven't gotten over it yet. If a memory is still sapping your emotional energy—whether you are consciously aware of it or not, lifewriting may be very helpful to you.

■ **The very act of writing about a painful experience can generate relief from that pain.** It works because your writing serves as an observant consciousness. In a sense, your paper or notebook becomes a confidant, an ideal listener. When your pain is witnessed and acknowledged by another person, then it is validated as being real and not a concoction. In the same way, writing provides an observer self, an effective way of assuaging your pain and sometimes of freeing yourself of it once and for all.

How many times have you heard people say: "I feel better having shared this with you." By sharing your pain with your writing—and with your reader (even if that reader is a future you and no one else), you can create relief for yourself.

■ **Begin to approach your pain by writing around it.** For instance, if the death of your spouse is still too difficult for you to write about, you might try writing about when you first became aware of the signs of illness, or about initial treatments when you hoped a cure was still possible.

When you feel ready, try writing your difficult stories. Eventually, as when you peel an onion layer by layer, you will come to the center of your grief—and to acceptance and understanding. Though the process may be difficult, it will lead you to a new relationship with the memory, one relieved of the pain that now surrounds it.

■ **Writing your lifestories is not intended to be emotional or psychological therapy, or a substitute for such work under the guidance of a professional counselor.** Yet lifewriting sometimes conveys benefits very similar to therapy and can do away with the need for such intervention.

People would be well advised, when writing about painful memories, to think of a time when they were at a dentist. I have sometimes had work done on my teeth without any painkiller being administered. I feel discomfort but no great pain. There have been other times, however, when I have started out without painkillers and then have ended up grimacing with pain. When the dentist asks if I'm ok, I cry out an emphatic "No! I need help."

In writing about painful memories, there's a time when you know you can handle the experience alone. But when it's clear you need some help, look for assistance from a professional therapist whose expertise will guide you safely and effectively through your quagmire of memories.

It's helpful to journal first after a traumatic event. Then as you begin to understand and accept, turn to lifewriting. It will contribute to the process of healing.

εxεrcise

Writing about painful experiences can be difficult.

■ Identify a past experience that continues to be painful to you—either because it was a loss or an unresolved interaction or because it caused you shame. Write a few sentences about the experience. Write more if you feel so inclined—but only for as long as you feel comfortable.

■ Now, on a different page, write a few sentences about what you will gain by exorcising this painful experience. Write about how it will feel to have your pain gone. Write about how much fuller your life will be.

■ What you are gaining by holding on to the painful experience? Write a few sentences about that on yet another page. Pain and a troubled past can serve as an excuse for not taking action to be happier in your life.

■ When it feels right, continue writing about the painful experience until you feel the need to stop again. Allow yourself to return to this subject whenever it comes up until you have laid it to rest.

At the Workshops

Roseanna had not spoken much during this workshop series except when I asked her a direct question, and then she answered with a simple *yes* or *no*. She had not yet written a story to share with other members of the workshop.

"I didn't go far in school," she explained, "and I've never done much writing."

We were now at the half-way point of the series. At age seventy-nine, Roseanna must have a lot of stories, but she wasn't sharing them. Why had she come? Were we simply an occasional afternoon's diversion for a lonely woman? I tried to think of ways to encourage her without putting her on the spot or pushing her further into silence. But I wondered, would today be another no-share session for her?

That day, when I asked for volunteers to read their lifewriting assignments, Roseanna's hand shot up first thing.

"Roseanna? You would like to read something?" I asked, hiding my surprise.

She reached into her voluminous purse and pulled out a handful of papers.

Slowly, she began to read her story. She read as though she had gone into another room by herself, as though if she looked up and saw us there with her, she would be startled back into silence. In her story, she was a little girl of four who lived in a small town. She told us about her life there and about her father who worked in the woods and made her little dolls when he was away in the lumber camps. She described her mother who had a beautiful voice and sang to the children at night. Then she told us that suddenly she had to be very quiet because her father needed to rest. He was very sick. Then she was no longer allowed into his room. Her grandmother came to stay because "Mama needed help to take care of us, she was so busy nursing Papa."

Then, one day, her papa died. She watched the neighbors move the furniture to make room to put his body in the living room. The house was full of people.

His body was to be transported to the family cemetery plot some one hundred miles away. "Mama and the baby accompanied his body. I stood with my brothers and Nana at the station as the train pulled away with my daddy. I wanted him so much."

Tears streamed down Roseanna's cheeks.

"Even after seventy-five years," she said, finally looking up, "it still hurts a lot."

We sat dazed, tears in our eyes. We were in mourning for the little girl whose papa's death was still so painful.

LIFESTORIES FROM THE WORKSHOPS:

The Phone Call
by Jean Travis

"Mom, can I move home?" asked Mark as soon as I picked up the receiver. I could hear the strain in his voice.

My heart sank as my mind began to whir. "Mark, what's wrong?"

"I can't live this way anymore," he said. "Kate and I are getting a divorce."

"Oh, Mark, you know you're always welcome here."

My mind was going numb. "We have to think this through. I don't think it would be wise to vacate your house. You sound like you need someone to hug you. Can I meet you somewhere? Do you want me to come to your house?" The questions tumbled out as my brain raced.

"Ya, I do. Could you come down?" he asked in a very small voice.

"Give me 30 minutes and I'll be there."

I had gone directly to my computer that morning without the usual shower and shampoo. I was a mess, but this was no time to dawdle. I quickly ran a brush through my hair, grabbed my keys, and left for Mark's house.

My mind flashed back to a scene years earlier when Mark's dad, Tom, and I had experienced an ugly confrontation, with Tom slamming the door as he left the house. Mark was four at the time. He and Beth, age six, and Andy, age two, had clung to me, crying. Beth had said, "Will we have Christmas?" And Mark had said, "I feel like my heart's been pierced by an arrow." Andy had just cried because everyone else was crying.

Later I had thought, *Pierced by an arrow.* How had Mark, my blond, curly-headed little cherub, even known those words that had summed up the situation so succinctly!

Now he was experiencing his own painful divorce saga. I knew he had vowed, like my other children, to avoid divorce if at all possible.

A sudden, painful development in her son's life makes Jean Travis's own painful memories vivid once again. Her story is about dealing with both. A certified Soleil Lifestory Network teacher, Jean lives in the Minneapolis area where she offers Photoscribe workshops for scrapbookers.

I thought of the house he and Katy had been so excited about buying right next to the University of Minnesota, where he could go to class and she could go to rehearsals at the theaters in the area. When he had called to tell me about it, he had been ecstatic.

"Mom, you're not going to believe the house we found. It's perfect for us. It's in a historic, restored area on Longfellow Avenue and all the houses are either brick or wood siding, turn-of-the-century, with front porches and gingerbread trim. They face a boulevard planted in flowers and trees. You'll think it is so cute."

It was cute. The exterior remained true to the turn-of-the-century, but the interior had been remodeled into two contemporary apartments, one on the first floor and one on the second and third floors. The third floor had been fashioned into a balcony area that featured a bedroom with skylights and a Jacuzzi bath.

Immediately after moving in, Mark had hung a large picture of him and Katy high up on the dining room wall spanning the two stories. The photo was a poster-sized replica of the front of their wedding invitation that had been cleverly designed as a cover of a romance novel. There, high up on the wall, the cowboy held the opera star in a dramatic pose under the title Sweet Betrothed. It had seemed a perfect place for the picture of a perfect couple.

I checked my speed going down 35W and thought, *Pay attention. Traffic gets crazy downtown by the university.*

At last, I parked in front of his house and ran up to the door. Mark, handsome and tall at six foot one, met me in the entry. I noted his red-rimmed eyes and the quiver in his voice when he said, "Thanks for coming, Ma."

We went up the stairs to his apartment. I was met by the dogs, Ginger and Mike, who jumped up on me with canine exuberance. *So much for the Christmas present,* Dog Training for Dummies, I thought.

First, I calmed the dogs down and then began to calm Mark down, a task I willed my numb mind to do. "Mark," I said, "I knew you were unhappy this summer, but I had no idea things were this bad. Let's go sit on the couch. You talk, and I'll listen."

We sat down, and the dogs joined us.

"In the spring," Mark began, "Katy told me she didn't think she wanted children—ever. And you know how I love children. Then she told me she didn't think she felt the same about me as she used to. You remember when you came with Uncle Pete to the Swingin' Sisters production?"

"Yes. That was in May."

"Well, after the show when we were all talking in the lobby, I noticed a guy hanging around eyeing Katy. That night she came home three hours later. Mom, I remember how you tried for eight years to make your marriage work with Dad. I just can't do that."

This piece of news struck a painful cord. Katy had seemed tired and aloof during the summer, and Mark was depressed at times. I had thought it was her awful schedule that was getting to the both of them.

But no, the very thing I had prayed would never happen to any of my children was happening to Mark, my sensitive middle son who bought roses for Katy's opening nights and supported her in her career. He had been in love with her from college days riding to Madison, Wisconsin, and back.

He went on. "I told her I would never ask her to, but I wanted to know that, if she had to, would she give up her career for me? I just needed to know I matter. I'm not a bad person."

"Oh, Mark, you're a beautiful person," I said. "And I'm not just saying that because you're my son."

My heart was breaking, and my head racing as I thought about the years I had lived with a wounded heart and a permanent lump in my throat. How could I help him deal with the ache in his own heart, the lump in his throat?

"I know it's hard for you to hear me talk about your dad and me, but I have to tell you that I finally realized in the middle of the agony back then that I could have been Gina Lollabrigida, Marilyn Monroe, and Bo Derek all wrapped into one and Tom still would have left to find someone else. His issues were far greater than "our" issues. It's not entirely you, Mark. I know we all have faults, but I know, too, that you have done your best."

We continued to talk, and Mark began to gain some control over his emotions. "I feel so much better just talking about it," he said. "I've been miserable and I just didn't want to tell you."

I could identify only too well with him as I thought about those years long ago when I had pretended everything was just fine, but my family had known something was very wrong.

It was nearing five o'clock. I didn't want to be there if Katy came home from her rehearsal at the Fitzgerald, where she was in a Shakespeare play. We had all been so excited to share with her when she landed that role.

I gave Mark another hug and told him I loved him—and that a whole lot of other people did too. We would all be there for him, no matter what the future would bring.

Chapter 3—Moving Your Stories Along

A. You can craft more effective stories.

B. How stories come together.

C. Edit your work.

LIFESTORIES FROM THE WORKSHOPS:
  Grandfather Harman by Pamela H. Daugavietis

A. *You can craft more effective stories.*

It is not enough *to remember* your stories well. You also need *to tell* them well. In the same way that carpenters and cooks use techniques to make their work easier and the results more attractive, writers, too, have techniques at their disposal.

Perhaps, like many lifewriters, you are passing your writing on to an innately-appreciative audience of relatives and friends. Naturally, your people want to encourage your efforts and tell you how wonderful your writing is. This appreciation doesn't absolve you, however, of the obligation to write well—for them and for the larger public you may wish to reach! Craft your stories as carefully as possible so that even strangers will shower you with accolades!

Learning to handle the following writing concepts and techniques will help you craft more effective stories.

l) **The people you choose to write about in your stories are your** *characters* (either you or someone else). Although they are people you've loved and known, your characters are often strangers to your children and grandchildren—and certainly to the larger audience you might aspire to.

You can make your reader "see" your characters by writing about them with *specific and striking details*: what did they look like (hair color, height, the style of their walk), what did they wear (colors textures, styles), how did they wear their clothing, how did they carry themselves? You can help your reader to "hear" these people whose voices perhaps still resonate in your ears: make extensive use of dialogue that was authentic to your people—favorite words and sayings, even phonetic transcriptions (writing according to

This chapter will help you use writing techniques and concepts to write better stories than you ever thought possible.

"No ideas but in things."

—William Carlos Williams
poet

"Pay attention. To everything...how [your characters] walk, talk, sing, eat, dress, dance, sleep, frown, twitch, yell, fight, cry."

—Marta Randall
novelist

Each new generation is a horde of barbarians that must be assimilated into the existing culture.

sound rather than grammar).

■ **Don't presume your reader will understand.** The people and the culture of your childhood are as foreign to your children or grandchildren as the people and culture of a far-away country! Don't take it for granted that anyone is familiar with the context of the story you are writing. Instead, assume no one knows anything. Portray your characters and their lives patiently and minutely with specific and striking details.

Here is an example of the lack of understanding that missing details can lead to. You write a piece for your grandchildren so they can appreciate how hardworking your own grandmother was on Monday washdays. You remember so clearly how the all-day job left her exhausted by evening. She would heat water for the wash, set out a variety of tubs for the different clothes, use a hand wringer propelled by muscle power, and hang everything out on a line—even in winter. You want your grandchildren to know about your grandmother, but let's say you have no patience with details and so you leave them out.

This is the summary you write so tersely as part of one of your lifestories: "My grandmother did the entire wash on Mondays when I was a child. It was a lot of work, and she was exhausted by the end of the day!"

Reading the story, your grandchildren conclude that Great-Grandma dropped the colored wash in the automatic washing machine, pressed a button, and then sat down to enjoy a soap opera on the radio (perhaps they know there was no TV then!). Forty-five minutes later, when the buzzer went off, she put the wash in the dryer, loaded whites into the machine, and then relaxed with more soap operas! "What's the big deal?" they want to ask—but resist because they don't want to hurt your feelings!

Unfortunately, the "big deal" is that you have presumed too much from your readers. As a lifewriter, you must suppose, instead, that your readers know nothing about your characters or the world they lived in! So, if you want them to appreciate your grandmother's hard work, provide the details. Go back to your Monday wash scene and describe heating water on the stove and setting the various tubs out on kitchen surfaces, etc. Don't tell us washday was a lot of work—show us by using specific and striking details. Lots of them.

2) **The *action* or plot of your story is what your characters do or what happens to them.** The action need not be dramatic (life's quiet moments make good stories, too) but it should be written so as to make your readers want to know what happens next (this is often achieved through *suspense*— hinting at something to come). You will make your readers turn pages, from one story to another.

It is **action** which gives drama to information.

The reader will want the action or plot to have a beginning in which the conflict is set up, a middle in which the conflict gets more complicated, and an ending in which the conflict is resolved or at least brought to a close.

■ **Start your action close to the *final crisis point* or climax.** This is the point (which you now know from hindsight) where things came together or fell apart for the people (the characters) in your story. Start writing your story close to the final crisis (climax) and proceed inevitably towards the ending. This will enable you to sustain the suspense needed to keep your reader "hooked." (One technique to achieve a bit of suspense is to use a sentence early on like "I didn't know it then but that day would change my life…")

Like any good detective solving a case, you must place one lifestory detail next to another to build a solid case for your story.

■ **Lead the reader to the crisis point by developing a few *episodes* that lead directly to the crisis.** An episode or vignette is a part of the story that cannot stand alone. What follows is a made-up story example of starting close to the crisis point and arriving there through the use of episodes.

If you were writing about your divorce, you wouldn't start with the first kiss you shared in high school. (That might make an interesting story, but for another piece with its own crisis point.) Instead, a divorce story could start with your awareness that you and your mate needed marital counseling after

umpteen years of unhappy married life. That would be episode one. Then, you might write a second episode about being in counseling and how those sessions seemed promising. There might be a reconciliation of sorts wherein married life seems more tenable. Subsequently, however, in a third episode, you would show how relations between you and your mate revert to how they had been. Perhaps you'd do an additional episode about proceeding (perhaps desperately) with counseling and about how that too ended in failure. Or perhaps you did not return to counseling but moved right on in your life to the crisis point—the point where things cannot continue as they are. The crisis point occurs in an episode when, after resisting once again the pain of acknowledging that this is a marriage that will have to end, you realize that you are bursting with tension— either you surrender your life or you surrender your marriage. You understand now that you cannot have both. This is the story's final crisis point or climax.

■ **The *turning point* comes when your character makes a decision that will change the story.** In the the divorce story I have been concocting to illustrate how to develop a story, you (the "I" character), having realized that it's you or the marriage, decide to go through with the divorce and face an uncertain future. After the turning point, things have changed. The character is no longer trying to save the marriage. The turning point episode might even include the legal proceedings.

■ **The ending is the conclusion of the story.** The ending of the divorce story used above may be as simple as stating when the divorce occurred. Resist the urge to recap your story in the last paragraph or to make a moralistic statement. Often, the easiest way to end is with a fact—*The divorce became final in May of the next year.*

3) **Show action, don't tell it.** This can not be overemphasized! The reader needs to "see" your characters in actions that will reinforce what you are saying about their personalities and temperaments. Don't tell readers your father was nurturing.

"Eventually, I realized that I recapped the whole story at the end of the piece because I lacked confidence in my ability to tell it right as I went along."

—Coaching client

Show him doing something nurturing in your story. You have to show us the action that supports the character you want to develop and the insight you want to convey. Skip your telling statements and just show the action! We can draw our own conclusion about your father. *When you tell rather than* show, *you take away from the drama of your story.*

■ **Convey the most important information in the form of action.**

a) The following example tells all the facts you want to relate to your reader.

> On our farm in 1939 we had three Guernseys, one Jersey, four Holsteins, six pigs, thirty-two chickens. Our house had two stories. We slept upstairs, and the rooms were not heated. My mother had an Atlantic stove. She made pancakes in the morning. I liked pancakes and oatmeal and waffles. The school was two miles away. We walked there with our family and friends. Our teacher was Miss Lindstrom. When I attended that school, I won a scholarship to attend the local academy.

b) This next example contains all the same facts, but it does something else that the first doesn't: it shows the facts in action form.

> We would wake up in the morning when my mother shouted up from downstairs, "Five-thirty!"
>
> The bedrooms were not heated so as soon as we opened our eyes we could see our breath congealed in the frozen air. We snuggled into our blankets, postponing getting up in the cold room for as long as we could.
>
> "Get up quick, boys," Mother would say. "Miss Lindstrom won't tolerate your being late, and Father needs help with the milking before you eat breakfast."
>
> We would run downstairs and dress next to the warm Atlantic stove. We left our clothing there at night to be warm in the morning.
>
> "When you get back, I'll have pancakes ready for you," Mother promised. Pancakes were my favorite breakfast, followed by oatmeal and waffles.
>
> We rushed out across the yard to the barn.
>
> "Do you think you'll find out today?" asked Jim.
>
> I had applied for a scholarship to our local academy, and Miss

"Tell a story! Don't try to impress your reader with style or vocabulary or neatly turned phrases. Tell the story first."

—Anne McCaffrey
novelist

"Let your story bring your characters to a different place (in body and/or soul) than where they started out."

—Catherine Breslin
writer

Lindstrom had said she thought she would have an answer for me that day at school. As my brother and I started with the milking, I fantasized what it might be like to study at the academy.

There were three Guernseys, one Jersey, and four Holsteins to milk so the chores took us a while to finish. My father was feeding the pigs. There were six as well as the thirty-two chickens…

The second example provides all the information you want to impart, but it does so in a more dramatic manner than the first because it uses salient details and is written in scenes. The second example transmits its facts through the action of a *typical* morning rather than an *actual* one. (You may not remember much of an actual day.) The rewrite also has an element of suspense. The reader will be kept wondering about the scholarship until he gets to the point at which Miss Lindstrom reveals the good news. The moment before she spoke, when you knew she was about to reveal something but did not know what she would say, would be the final crisis point or climax.

In this second story example, you convey a lot of information and create a successful story by making use of character, action/plot (beginning, middle, end), setting (see subsection #3 below for information on setting), and suspense.

■ **Choose a few of the clearest, most eloquent details to convey your ideas—***and always do it with action.* Demonstrate your point with three to five examples *at most*— better yet, put forth only two or three. More examples would be overkill—and potentially boring. If you simply must include more examples, go ahead and indulge yourself. After you've gotten them off your chest, however, eliminate all but the few best examples from your text, keeping only the most eloquent.

You must decide to write about the most important aspects of your life and to leave out a lot of peripheral material if you want to first engage and then retain your reader's interest. Effective lifewriting records the gist of your lifestories. **Sooner or later, lifewriters must accept that they cannot tell everything that happened to them**—the story would simply be too long both to write and to read.

Writing is like swimming. To do either well, you have to do everything together. But you can only practice one thing at a time. One day, you start doing several techniques at once and then all the techniques come together for you!

3) **The *setting* is the environment in which your characters live and in which your action occurs.** The setting includes the ***place*** (geography, buildings, interiors), the ***time*** (year, month, day, hour), and the ***atmosphere*** (mood, feeling, ethnic culture, religion, educational levels, etc.) Setting is crucial for interpreting character, but the particulars of a by-gone culture are often an inaccessible element for your younger readers. The details of the past, therefore, are a key element they need to interpret your story as you wish them to.

■ **Be specific in describing your setting:** avoid abstract words and phrases—especially when writing about physical settings. Because these kinds of words and phrases are vague, they conjure quite different images for different people. Specific and striking details, on the other hand, are more likely to mean nearly the same things to your readers as they do to you so they help your story to mean to others what it means to you.

Adjectives are especially troublesome. Take *rich*. It's easy to presume we all know what *rich* means—but we don't! Once a friend related how, when she was with a group of girls in college, one of them said, "I know you think I'm rich, but I'm not. I've never had a live-in maid. Ours always left in the afternoon." As my friend shared her own definition of *rich* with me, she laughed at the discrepancy. "I used to think people were rich," she said, "if they always had ice cream in the freezer!"

Don't use vague, abstract phrases either. Take *majestic mountain*. Be more precise in your observation. If the mountain is capped with granite and has two peaks, you might write: *twin, granite-capped peaks*. If the mountain is completely forested over with pines, you might write: *covered with pointed pines*.

Although it is true that the reader will always bring his own interpretation and experience to your writing, your details will guide his perceptions in a way that abstract words cannot.

■ **Make ample references to the senses.** We need to know what something *tasted* like, *smelled* like, *looked* like, *sounded* like, *felt* like. Again, avoid using abstract words (e.g., a *fragrant* odor)

"I have a diary my aunt kept on her trip back to the old country after the war. It would be a treasure if only she had written down what she was really experiencing.
'It was a nice flight. The flowers were lovely in the parks. It was great to see the old gang'—nice, nice, nice! Only at the end is there a hint of the real story of that trip. *'Sid drove me to the station,'* she wrote, *'but we didn't know what to say to each other. I cried all the way back to the States.'"*

—Frustrated family historian

in favor of very tangible, sensory ones (the odor of *wet pine* needles). References to the senses give your readers the illusion that the story is being lived as they are reading it, that they are part of the experience.

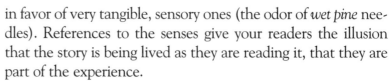

■ **Describe your characters' ethnic, religious, cultural (etc.) setting.** People have particular, intangible settings in which you must portray them if the reader is to understand "what made them tick."

A common mistake for lifewriters is to assume that what is true of their particular families is true for their entire ethnic group. If your family is musical, for instance, you may assume that your cultural group is musical. If your family did not value education, you may assume that was true of all families in your group. These assumptions don't help you to understand either your family or your cultural group.

The only way to give depth to your non-physical setting is to study your group's history and compare it to your family's. Generally, interviewing your relatives will not provide this information. Your relatives may know their family and personal history, but it's not likely that they are knowledgeable about the broader history of their culture. Most people aren't.

Another common mistake is tacking generic knowledge onto your ethnic group. For instance, most immigrants can be said to have responded in specific ways as they adapted to conditions in their new homeland. It is not enough to apply these generic responses to your family. You must learn about your own ethnic group's particular adaptations and then compare how your family was or wasn't typical. Were they following a pattern or charting a new course? You can then incorporate this information—rather than the generic responses— in your stories so that your portrait and your readers' interpretation can be more true to life.

4) **Focus your individual stories on only one set of characters, actions and settings.** Asides, or digressions, however scintillating they may be, change the focus and therefore sub-

"I thought we had no ethnic setting because we were Anglo-Americans. How wrong could I have been?!"

—Workshop writer

tract from the impact of a story. They tend to confuse because they include extraneous and complicating details or they tend to bore because they go on and on. Digressions are often "stories within a story." If they really are good stories, give them their own billing. Otherwise, cut them out.

5) **Your stories will have a** *point of view* **in addition to character, action, and setting.** Point of view is a technical term in writing. It refers to the "eyes" of the narrator from which the story is seen or perceived.

For example, if you are telling a story of when you were five from the point of view of the child you were then, your text will be written in "five-year-old" talk as if the five-year-old had written it or were speaking it. Obviously, the piece will contain different insights and vocabulary than the same story told from the point of view of the adult you are now reflecting on life back then.

■ **The point of view you select will help you to achieve certain effects.** The story of your childhood written from a child's point of view will have more intimacy and will elicit the reader's empathy but will necessarily lack the adult's understanding of life. However, if you tell the same story of your childhood from an adult point of view, although you will lose intimacy and empathy, you will be able to create a "bigger" picture that contains the consequences of what happened and your adult interpretation. For instance, an adult can write about the sources of a family's financial woes—misplaced ambitions, discord between the parents, conflicting values, etc.; a child can only write about the effects of those financial problems—screaming between the parents, not having enough food, moving to new apartments frequently.

Every story is told from a point of view: as a writer, you cannot avoid it and must be aware that you are always writing out of a point of view. If you don't consciously choose one, you will most likely write unconsciously from the point of view of an adult with an ax to grind. This may or may not be appropriate.

"I wanted to recapture the fear I felt then as a boy. I wanted my readers to experience how I felt so I wrote my story from a ten-year-old's point of view."

—Workshop writer

Style (in the sense of uniqueness) is something most writers think about too much. It's more useful to concern yourself with such elements as point of view and characterization than with style.

If you lose track of point of view—either forget to chose one or alter it within the story, you may write some things that don't make sense: like making an adult interpretation or using an adult vocabulary in what is a story told from a child's point of view. Choose and make consistent use of a point of view before you start writing—or, at least, as you re-write.

The choice between the adult or the child point of view is an obvious one, but you might also choose to write from the point of view of an angry daughter or wife, or the point of view of a long-suffering son or husband. The choices are endless. Only one thing is certain: whether you know it or not, you *will* be writing out of a point of view—so choose one that "works" for your story.

■ **The point of view will also help set the *tone* of your stories.** The tone is the story's emotional slant. It influences how the reader will feel about your story. Possible tones might include: pity, admiration, empathy. Besides being affected by the point of view, the tone is dependent on **vocabulary, images, metaphors,** and **organization of the text.** Often, when the reader does not feel what the writer hoped she would for a character, the problem is one of tone. For instance, it's difficult for the reader to feel empathy with a "hard-hitting gal" and easy to feel rapport with a "woman who faced life's challenges with hope and courage." The tone of the vocabulary changes the reader's feeling for the character.

■ **Your point of view (and consequently the tone) will also largely determine how the reader will interpret your stories.** Point of view is a powerful writing tool. Your sympathy or antipathy for your characters will dictate choice of detail, description, and action. It will ennoble or degrade your subject. Sometimes, the same characteristics and qualities can be presented as nearly opposites in their meaning—depending on the writer's word choices. For instance, a writer can say of a person who speaks a lot: "she foamed at the mouth" or "she was doing her thinking out loud." If the writer believes in the virtues of hard

"I still can't be detached enough to write about that turkey—so I'm just not going to!"

—A self-aware divorced workshop writer

work, she can write "Hard work helped my mother arrive at frugality"; but if she doesn't, she can write "Hard work bludgeoned my mother until she became a skinflint." An action that requires out-of-the-ordinary energy can be labeled either "courageous" or "foolhardy" depending again on the point of view.

Although we inevitably write from our own perspectives, it is possible to write without *imposing* an interpretation on others. For example, you can write:

> My mother was young and she found it difficult to fulfill her maternal responsibilities. When I was a little child, I wanted her to be more attentive to me.

instead of writing:

> Always forsaking her basic duties for her own selfish pleasures, my mother abandoned us emotionally. Everyone in my family felt lonely and resentful.

Although the first example clearly shows how *you* felt, one does not get the impression you are "throwing stones." The reader will therefore be comfortable accepting your interpretation.

The second example, however, is very judgmental and makes a sweeping statement that smacks of the need for revenge. Can readers be blamed for not wanting to be corralled to the writer's side against the mother's?

Abusing point of view (as in the second example) alienates the reader and is counterproductive to your goal: sharing your lifestories and your experiences with your audience and having others understand (and empathize with) what it was like to be you.

Choosing the right point of view will help you to achieve the effects you are striving for. In addition, remember that consistency in point of view strengthens the impact of your story whereas slipping back and forth from one point of view to another distracts the reader and weakens your story.

"I wanted to use lots of photos from my childhood in my book. When I look at them, it's like I'm there again. I experience the feelings I remember having when I was a child."

—Book production client

exercise

Evaluate character, action, setting, and point of view in the stories you have already written.

■ Are your characters described with sensory details? Do you describe what they looked like, what they wore, what they said, and how they said it?

■ Have you started your stories close enough to their climaxes?

■ Did you show the actions of your stories rather than tell them?

■ Have you focused your stories on one set of characters, actions, and settings (both physical and cultural, religious, etc.)? Have you avoided abstract words in favor of specific, descriptive ones?

■ Are you conscious of what point of view you have used? Is it the most effective point of view you could have chosen? Is it consistent throughout? Do you abuse the power of point of view by trying to get the reader on your side?

■ Have you chosen the right tone for each of your stories? Look at how your language may be value-laden in a way that will disturb the reader.

■ Make changes to improve your stories wherever you can. Remember: the time you spend rewriting is an opportunity for you to do your best work.

B. How stories come together.

I have urged you to write scenes, vignettes, and dialogues. This section shows how these can come together in your stories.

Earlier you were urged to write many stories and not to worry about how they come together.

1) **As you write—especially as you develop a manuscript, think in terms of *vignettes* or brief stories.** Don't worry about how to link these pieces. Instead, write as if you were creating separate movie takes. Each "take" is a discrete piece of the story with its own characters, action, and setting. In the making of a movie, these "takes" eventually get spliced together into a full-length product—the work of a film editor who organizes the separate scenes to make a whole. Your vignettes and brief stories will also be "spliced" together (by you!) into a satisfying and unified story—but that will come later.

■ **It is easier, and therefore perhaps more useful in**

achieving your writing goals, to begin by writing *many* stories rather than trying to write *long* stories. Don't let yourself be paralyzed by the fear of having to write many long stories. Frankly, *anyone* would be daunted by the prospect of a book project that entailed describing entire periods of one's life—or even one's whole life, but *everyone* can write a few pages about a first job or the birth of a child.

(As I undertook the writing of this book, for instance, I started by Memory Listing what I knew to be important. Then I jotted notes—a few lines, a half page, perhaps a full page—about various items on my Memory List. Eventually, I grouped what I had written on similar topics. This particular section, written on the backs of scrap paper cut into half sheets, was labeled "Writing Organization." At first, it consisted only of two half-pages.)

Eventually, two- and three-page vignettes and stories add up. If there are 20 or 30 of them, you will soon have 40 to 90 pages of text and, if there are 100 stories, 200 or 300 pages.

2) **You will have options in organizing your material**. Eventually, after you have written awhile and have amassed a pile of vignettes, story segments, and stories, you will want to group them together to make a statement, a bigger picture. How will you do it? Below are ideas for organizing stories.

Remember: These suggestions do not refer to the sequence in which the stories are written but rather to how they can be ordered after they have been written.

■ Chronology

If you choose a chronological order, you organize your stories in a way that most nearly replicates the sequence in which events happened. For example, what happened in your childhood is placed first in the narration and what happened in your youth is placed second and in your middle-age, third; what happened in the spring is placed first, in the summer, second, etc. If you organize all your stories in this way, there will be a natural continuum among them based on time connection.

Keep your work in the process stage for as long as you possibly can. If you call your writing "finished" too soon, you'll feel it can't—or shouldn't—be reworked. Most often, your story does need rewriting!

This is the way most people choose to link their stories and it is an easy organization for the reader to follow.

■ Subject

You might choose to put together everything about one person in one chapter and everything about another in a second chapter. This gives a clear account of your subject but omits interactions that might change the way we perceive a character. The collection of stories may seem disconnected.

■ Theme

You might write about a specific theme that is of interest to you. In this way, your story might be a story about labor unions or about dedication to art. Everything is chosen or omitted according to how it develops your theme. This can make for a very focused book.

The re-writing stage can be the most creative part of writing. Re-writing is often the time when you begin to understand what it is you are writing about. Re-writing is also the time when you may finally realize what it is you want or need to write.

Alternately, you can choose topics across the generations or among family members. These topics might include religion, careers, marriage, etc. For example, you might look at the relationship to work in your family during your childhood. You might write about your grandparents' and your parents' work attitudes and practices during this time. Then you can give your attention to other themes in their lives during your childhood: parenting, religion, etc.

Another possibility is to write about a theme in your grandparents' lives and then go on to its appearance in your parents' lives and then in yours and lastly in your children's. You can choose to give an internal chronological development to each of your themes: start with youth and proceed to old age or the present with each generation. Then start the whole process over again with another theme.

■ Both chronology and theme

Although you may begin to write your pieces chronologically or thematically, you may find yourself combining both of these elements in your final product. These approaches can easily be integrated into your lifestory as a whole.

3) **If you don't have the goal of writing a fluent, unified**

text (i.e., a full memoir) but you do want to create a collection of *stand-alone stories* with repeating elements such as characters and settings, you can simply *juxtapose* your stories in an order that makes sense to you. Transitions and links will be unnecessary.

εxεrcisε

Organize your stories and link them with transitions.

■ If there are stories you have written but have not printed, do so now and put them in your three-ring binder where they most seem to belong. Read all your stories with the eye of your eventual reader.

■ Re-organize your stories in your binder in the sequence that makes most sense to you now (either as you read or after the entire reading). What sort of order are your stories taking?

■ Where are there missing links between your stories? Do you need transition stories to fill the gap or just transition paragraphs or phrases to make the link?

■ Make a list of missing stories that you would like to include. items on this list may consist of just a few descriptive words or phrases to identify the missing info.

■ Take colored paper and write one paragraph or story description per sheet. Insert these sheets in the binder between the stories where those missing paragraphs or stories will fit. (If the missing part is inside a story, insert the sheet within the story.)

■ These colored sheets in your three-ring binder will give you a visual reminder of what you still need to write. You certainly won't have to worry about "writer's block" with a binder full of colored pages waiting to be filled!

■ Oh, yes—congratulate yourself for having done so much excellent writing!

C. *Edit your work.*

The secret to self-editing is to read your manuscript as your reader will—with fresh, observant eyes. This is another way of saying you need to develop a certain objectivity to edit your work effectively. How can you do this?

1) **Put your writing aside for a while.** After you have writ-

In this section, you'll learn techniques to act as your own editor so you can identify weak prose to improve.

"I put [the poem] away for a week or two until I have forgotten about it and can take it up as if it was something entirely fresh."

—Wallace Stevens
poet

"I understand my own pictures best six months after I have done them."

—Pablo Picasso
artist

Don't be discouraged if you see the need for changes in your lifestories. Most successful writers are persevering re-writers who see re-writing as an chance to do the real creative work of their project.

ten a story or a scene or a chapter of your lifestory, put it away. Time—two weeks, a month, six months—will give you the emotional distance to assess your work more objectively and will help you identify both its strengths and its shortcomings that call for more work. If your piece holds up to to this test, congratulate yourself! And keep writing.

I regularly put my work away for a while (for a week, a month, or even a year). I am always amazed at how much objectivity I have when I reread my work after a lapse of time. For a moment, I step into the unfamiliar role of the reader of the piece and out of the too-familiar role of the writer.

■ **Play the role of a reader.** Approach your manuscript from the point of view of someone who might be critical of your writing—like an editor or a reviewer, but not your inner censor who is more likely to criticize you than the work itself. Ad-lib something like: "Let's see, what have we here? Humph! A story by So-and-So. I wonder if it's any good?" Then read the piece from this critical perspective.

If the text doesn't pass muster, don't worry. Consider yourself lucky to have the opportunity to make the necessary changes to improve it.

2) **Show your manuscript to others for their constructive criticism.** Family members may be a good choice because they can add important information and details to your story.

But then again, they may not be a good choice. They may want you to write the story as they would have written it, and all their comments are aimed at changing your text to their point of view. They want to slant the story toward their interpretation of an event or relationship in order to substantiate their point of view rather than yours. (Let them write their own lifestory if they have something different to say!)

You also want to choose people who will critique the work itself rather than you. One form this takes is the following: someone says, "Why are you doing this hard work? Why don't you just enjoy yourself at your age!" (Conversely, the blindly-supportive "Isn't that nice, dear, I like anything you do!" response isn't at all constructive either!)

Most feedback can, however, teach you something. A disagreement with a relative about how a story ought to be slanted might tell you that you have not conveyed what happened with enough objectivity. Sometimes, you can do this by providing several sides to a story. You can write something like, "According to my brother John, our mother was a strict disciplinarian, but according to me, she…"

Others who are not relatives—trusted friends or colleagues perhaps—may be able to provide valuable feedback that is different than your relatives'. It may come in many forms. "I don't understand why your mother did this. It seems out of character according to the portrait you have drawn of her," one reader might note. "Why did your father say that? How can you see that as supportive? He comes across as very cold to me," another might add.

It is likely, however, that your portrait was a family-sanctioned view which you unconsciously superimposed on your own experience of events! (See Chapter 6, Section E.) Writing based on unexamined versions of events or relationships is almost always confusing or unsatisfying to others (who are not relatives with the same blind spot as yours). Perhaps a sudden realization may come from a reader's unexpected questions and comments. What seems so obvious to someone more detached and objective may be startling, challenging, dismaying or illuminating for you—in other words: unexpected treasure in the scavenger hunt for self-understanding!

■ **If you have to explain things to your reader, you probably need to re-write.** Your story must be so clear that it answers its own questions. Your childhood or youth culture (what life was like when you were young in your family and in your community) is perhaps foreign to everyone but yourself—and your siblings!

Remember: you will not be with the reader to answer

If you are like many people I have worked with, you will find it easier to rewrite a text than to create one. That's why it's so important to produce text early on—so you'll have something to work with.

Simplicity is often the key to clear communication.

> "Respect your reader. The niftiest turn of phrase, the most elegant flight of rhetorical fancy, isn't worth beans next to a clear thought clearly expressed."
>
> —Jeff Greenfield
> columnist

> "Speak your dialogue out loud. If it sounds like the way people talk, then write it down."
>
> —Tom Clancy
> novelist

questions every time your piece is read.

In a workshop or a coaching session, I will often ask a writer to explain to me what she meant by something she wrote. The most amazing thing then happens! Either because the writer knows that she must go into detail to be understood or because, in her speech, she doesn't search for the more literary words that she felt were necessary in writing, the writer will tell me in more complete and clear language what she meant to write in the first place. At that point, I will say the obvious, "You need to **write** what you **said** just now."

3) **If you don't have time to put your stories aside or to send them to someone who can do a critique, at least read them out loud—to yourself first and then perhaps to someone else.** Hearing your words will make you more objective about your text. Again, it will be as if you were your reader.

A variant of reading out loud is to read your stories onto a tape and then play the recording back to yourself. Hearing your story will enable you to put on the listener's hat. Switching roles, you can learn a lot about how effectively your writing communicates what you intended it to. This is especially useful for a writer who is in the early stages of learning to write.

Reading aloud, you will notice whether you are trying to use big words or flowery phrases. Sometimes people who are not experienced in writing feel that to achieve quality in their work they need to use "literary" words.

Sometimes, as you read aloud, you will notice yourself tripping over some of your sentences. Is this because you are using long or convoluted phrasing? As a rule, shorter sentences are better than longer ones. Shorter sentences are easier for the reader to read—and often for the writer to write. As readers, we don't like long, rambling sentences that require several readings to get through.

■ **After about 15 words, think of adding a period!** Otherwise, you'd better have a very good reason *not* to end that sentence soon!

4) **Work with an editor.** At a certain point, you may have done all you can with your manuscript and need a person with experience and training to get you beyond where you are now. In choosing an editor, the rapport between you is important. You will want someone who respects your story and your way of writing. In the end, you want the story to have your voice and not the editor's.

With today's tele-communications, living near your editor is no longer important. Manuscripts and notes can be sent via e-mail, and consultations can happen by telephone.

If you intend to publish your memoirs yourself and sell to the public, don't consider working with an editor to be optional. **On your own, you cannot do an adequate job of editing for publication.** (I speak from experience both as a writer and an editor here. This book has been edited by five professionals besides myself.) A sensitive editor is essential to fine-tuning your writing. The cost of editing a self-published manuscript will be a small part of the total cost of publishing your book and is money well spent. If you are publishing only for family and friends, you may certainly choose to dispense with an outside editor as your audience may be forgiving—but, on the other hand, what if it isn't!

A skillful editor will polish your manuscript subtly— without changing the voice or the tone of your text.

Exercise

Edit your own writing.

■ How do you currently edit your writing?

■ Do you keep the editing function for one of the last things you do when you write or do you edit as you go along? Perhaps a bit of both? Which way feels better? Which way keeps the inner censor quiet longer? Which brings better results?

■ Try each of the editing techniques outlined in this section. How does each technique feel? Which are you going to continue using?

■ Do you check all your facts—and your spelling?

Grandfather Harman

by Pamela H. Daugavietis

Pam Daugavietis is a certified Soleil Lifestory Network teacher living in Grand Rapids, MI. In this story, she uses a startling lead to introduce her grandfather. Later in her narrative, she returns several times to the lead event to create a satisfying symmetry.

In December of 1881, at the age of 13, my grandfather, Eber Hyde Harman, died of typhoid fever and his obituary, according to my Aunt Charlotte, keeper of family stories, appeared in the Columbus, Ohio, newspaper. His two sisters, Grace, 6, and Blanche, 4, also died, a week apart, as a result of drinking water from a contaminated well.

Grandfather had lived with his two sisters and his parents, Amos and Martha Hyde Harman, in a rented home on Starr Avenue. Aunt Charlotte told me that Grandfather slipped into a coma and was pronounced dead by the family doctor. His parents were so preoccupied taking care of Grace and Blanche, who were surviving him but were seriously ill, that they didn't immediately make an effort to remove his body.

Several days later, when the undertakers finally arrived in their horse-drawn hearse to collect not one, but three, bodies, the story of Grandfather's untimely death took an unexpected turn. As the undertakers lifted his body off the table in the front room, he raised his head, and in a weak but commanding voice, said, "Where are you taking me?"

Great-grandmother and Great-grandfather Harrman were overwhelmed with joy to have their son alive. Sisters Grace and Blanche did not revive, however, and were taken away to be buried in Union Cemetery in Columbus.

"Daddy told me that, when he was able to eat again, his mother gave him homemade biscuits and honey, and never again in his life did biscuits and honey taste as good as they did to him that day," said Aunt Charlotte.

Great-grandmother and Great-grandfather Harman had no more children, so Grandfather was raised as an only child.

Grandfather attended school in Columbus through the eighth grade. Then, he attended a business school in Columbus and eventually took a job as a fireman on a steam locomotive on the Hocking Valley Line and C & O, a coal freight train running from the southern Ohio coal fields to Toledo, Ohio.

In 1900, at about the time he met his future bride, my grandmother, Minnie Violet Broomhall, Grandfather was appointed examiner of stationary steam engineers for the Columbus District by Governor Nash. In this position, he also became a member of the Ohio Society of Mechanical and Electrical Engineers. His office was in the new State House in downtown Columbus.

Aunt Charlotte told me that one day while walking through the State House grounds, Grandfather met a man who had known his family years before.

"Why, Eber Harman," the man gasped, "I thought you were dead."

My grandparents met while attending the Third Avenue Methodist Church in Columbus. Their courtship lasted nearly 10 years. During that time, Grandfather gave Grandmother an opal "friendship" ring that later belonged to Aunt Charlotte.

In the spring of 1909, Grandmother received a diamond engagement ring from Grandfather. They were married on September 21 at the home of Rev. Good, with Grandmother's brother, Russell Broomhall, as witness. They honeymooned at a farmhouse near Bainbridge, about 15 miles southwest of Chillicothe. Grandfather was 41 and Grandmother was 34. Neither had been married before.

After their honeymoon, they returned to Columbus and moved into a newly-built home on East Norwich Avenue. According to Aunt Charlotte, the home cost $3,000, "fully furnished with curtains and all."

The following August 26, 1910, my father, their first child, was born at home on Norwich Avenue. In 1912, the year Hannah Eleanor, Daddy's first sister was born, the family moved to 1433 Jewett Drive in Zanesville, Ohio. It was the same year Grandfather was transferred to the Zanesville District as examiner of stationary steam engineers. Aunt Charlotte Maude was born in 1915.

"I was a love baby" Aunt Charlotte proudly shared with me one day, much to my surprise. "Mother told me, when I was old enough to know such things, she would always remember with great excitement the night I was conceived."

It was difficult to imagine my grandparents as lovers, especially my grandmother, a retired schoolteacher and strict disciplinarian. She was a devout Methodist, a large, imposing woman who wore no make-up, dressed modestly, and never left home without hat and gloves. Aunt Charlotte said it meant a lot to her to know that she was the product of a passionate marriage.

Grandfather Harman was also a lover of Indian lore and history and was especially passionate about arrowheads. He was fortunate in that his territory as examiner of stationary steam engineers included southeastern Ohio which held one of the richest deposits of flint in the state. Tribes of Native Americans, warring or friendly, had come there to get flint for making arrowheads. The area now contains the Flint Ridge State Park.

When my father was a little boy, he and Grandfather spent many hours searching, furrow by furrow, any field they could find in Muskingum, Licking, Perry, or Fairfield counties, that was freshly plowed after years of sitting idle. They would almost always be rewarded with at least one or two specimens to add to their collection, which I later inherited and passed on to my sons, John and Bob.

Grandfather had such an interest in these little, unique, wedge-shaped arrow tips that he learned to make them himself, using an old-fashioned buttonhook as a carving tool. His cousin, Eber Hyde, for whom he was named, had an extensive collection of flint arrowheads and other significant items, such as fiber bags and slippers, which are now a part of the permanent collection of Native American artifacts at the Ohio State Historical Museum in Columbus.

While Grandmother was serious and demanding, Grandfather was the opposite. My father and my aunts said their father's patience knew no end. Rather than complain while

waiting for Grandmother at the curb in front of the house, Grandfather became adept at playing *Yankee Doodle* on the clutch of his Model A Ford. While Grandmother and Grandfather were both devoted parents, it was Grandfather who broke into tears at the dining-room table on the eve of my father's departure for Ohio State University in Columbus, confessing deep sadness that the first of their three children was leaving the nest.

One of my few memories of Grandfather, a tall, slim man with silver-gray hair, was of him holding me on his lap as he slowly wound a little metal toy turtle, the only toy I remember playing with at their house. His hands and face were marked with the subtle aging spots that later also appeared on my father's hands and face, and that now appear on mine. As a two-year-old, I watched from the large, wooden front-porch swing as he mowed the lawn. The smell of freshly mown grass and the soft whirring sound of the hand-propelled blades helped to impress that memory in my mind forever.

On May 13, 1946, one day after my third birthday, Grandfather died again. This time it was fatal. He suffered a massive heart attack, at age 78, while mowing the grass.

My final memory of Grandfather is of his body, lying in the front parlor of the large white house where he and Grandmother lived, and where my father, Aunt Hannah, and Aunt Charlotte had grown up.

Chapter 4—Interviewing & Research

A. Before the interview.

B. At the interview.

C. Formal research.

D. Using the Internet.

E. Other kinds of research.

F. Taking research notes.

G. Accessing your research information

LIFESTORIES FROM THE WORKSHOPS:
  Searching for Poppa's Song by Marilyn Geary

Interviewing & Research

You may assume you can depend on your memory when you write your lifestories—but memory isn't always as reliable as you want it to be!

■ **Memory can fail you.** You simply may not be able to recall the information you need to write about another person—or yourself—with accuracy and detail.

■ **Memory can mislead you.** It can blur the negative role you may have played and cast another's positive role in the shadows. Memory does tend to be flattering to the rememberer. Conversely, it may elevate your having been "bad" to "really bad" when you were merely thoughtless or small in your actions.

■ **Memory can simply be wrong.** Time has ways of altering a memory. You may forget that you didn't know the facts at the time. You may confuse other people's accounts with your own experience of an event. It is also possible, because of your age or your needs at the time, that you had a partial or biased view of all that happened and why.

Interviews and research will stimulate, supplement and correct your memory. These activities will support and add to the facts and impressions you remember. They may also force you to reconsider what is true.

Interviews are basically guided conversations as you sit with people and talk to them. Research is information acquired from non-human sources.

This chapter provides you with the guidelines you'll need to conduct effective family interviews and to get the most out of your research.

"I remember my uncle as cold and uncaring, but he paid my college tuition. Why have I forgotten that?"

—Workshop writer

A. *Before the interview.*

1) Select whom you will interview. If your time is limited, or your family is large and offers many choices, it will be all the more important to identify a manageable number of knowledgeable relatives and friends to interview.

For example, Aunt Mary tends to talk endlessly—all afternoon if you let her. Her conversation seems to have little content as she wanders from one topic to another. Aunt Jane, on the other hand, is an incisive person whose intuition is always informing her about what things mean. Her many observations and reminiscences are usually interestingly told. Furthermore, they are consonant with your other research.

Can there be any doubt whom you will interview first—Aunt Mary or Aunt Jane? (Being nice to lonely Aunt Mary is a work of charity and it should not be confused with collecting information to write your stories.)

Another example: Cousin Luigi married into your Irish family. He is a dear old man and you love him very much, but his tales about his Italian family are irrelevant to understanding the history of your Irish ancestors. Cousin Luigi's are not the accounts you need to collect.

2) Make clear preliminary arrangements with the people you will interview. Be specific about the meeting time, the length of the interview, the place where it will occur, and the conditions necessary for its success. It is often effective and efficient to have the interviewee gather memory jogs (photos, clippings, mementos—see Chapter 2, Section D, as well as Section G of this chapter) that can be used as warm-ups.

Be very specific in your requests. Vague requests like "We'll need a good amount of time" can be interpreted so differently that they are useless in making arrangements. Instead say, "We'll need a two-hour block on Tuesday the fifth. Does 2 PM to 4 PM work for you?" If you say, "Is there a room in your house where we can talk quietly?" it is possible that your interviewee will say *yes* in spite of the fact that she knows someone will be watching television or working in that room. ("They'll just be watching their program!") You would do better to say, "We have to have a space where no other activity will be going on—no TV, no radio, no telephone conversations, no work." If your interviewee says there are no such rooms in house, perhaps you can suggest meeting at your place—if necessary, you can add, "I'll pick you up and bring you back." You cannot be too specific about the logistics. A detail left out of planning, or ineffectively decided upon, can sabotage your interview.

3) **Ascertain who else is likely to want to participate in the interview—and decide whether that person may or may not sit in.** An unexpected, or inappropriate, person can blur the focus of your interview.

For instance, your aunt by marriage, sitting in on the interview, may find what you are doing so interesting she begins to talk about *her* life experiences and, in doing so, may not allow your uncle (your mother's brother) much time to talk about his childhood relationship with your grandparents and your mother. Your aunt's experience, however interesting, will not provide the information you need to understand your grandparents and parents.

■ **Conversely, don't dismiss other people's input too quickly.** Their experiences can be valid for your family, too. By listening carefully to an articulate person talk about a general experience, you might learn a lot about your own family. For example, you are interviewing your mother's brother, and his wife (your aunt by marriage) begins talking about her family. It's likely you didn't know these people she's talking about and their lives don't fit into your story. As your aunt shares her stories, however, you realize how many of them are about work in and life around the mining towns of eastern Ohio and western West Virginia in the 1930s. Your family's experience in similar mining communities across the state line in Kentucky are not likely to differ widely from her family's. Use some of the infor-

mation provided by your aunt-in-law to flesh out your family's story ("In those days, many Polish miners used to…"). But do not get sidetracked on her niece's love story. At that point, the conversation is slipping into gossip and you risk losing the focus of your interview (*but* this story of a Polish niece in love with an "American" miner may reveal nuggets about relations between immigrants and "Americans" that could additionally round out the story of your immigrant ancestors).

■ **Sometimes, a observer at an interview can provide important coaching.** "John, why don't you tell about the time your mother confronted the company store manager?" or perhaps the other person will offer: "But, wasn't that before 1937—we were still living on Maple Street then. It wasn't until a month after Edward was born in January of 1938 that we moved to Elm Street!"

In fact, if you know of a person who might be good at prodding a significant but reluctant interviewee, ask that person to be present. But, again, be clear about what you are asking this person to do. "I'll be interviewing Uncle Alec about his childhood. Would you come along to encourage him to share his information with me? You might remind him of parts of the story you know when you notice he's overlooking them."

Clear communication and thoughtful preparation of your goals for each interview will heighten your chances of success.

ε x ε r c i s ε

Prepare for the interview.

■ List the missing information you need to write your lifestories.
■ Who are the people who might provide you with this information? Prioritize your list according to how knowledgeable your interviewees are likely to be about the information you need and how "interview-able" you feel each of these persons are.

■ Plan ahead. Set up interview times. Ask the interviewee to bring memory jogs. Anticipate problems you are likely to encounter from other people and from the location where you will be.

■ In what ways could other people contribute to the success of this interview? Think of who they are and invite them.

B. At the interview.

1) **Come to the interview with a list of questions.** If you prepare yourself carefully, you are more likely to leave with the information you need—and more likely not to forget to ask a crucial question.

This section will help you make the interview a success.

Before going on interviews for newspaper or magazine articles, I used to write down the questions that I needed answers to. Before the interview, I reviewed these questions so they would be fresh in my mind. During the interview, however, I did not refer to them much because I didn't want the interviewees to feel they were being directed toward supplying the "right" information or answer. Feeling prompted, interviewees may have rechanneled free-flow reminiscing into attempts to outguess me. This would have been clearly counterproductive.

Because you have listed the information you are looking for (what work conditions were in the textile mills in the early 1930s, what it was like to be a Catholic attending a public university in 1910, or how tenure was achieved in the 1940s, etc.), you can keep the interview on track. Toward the end, say fifteen minutes before the time you need to leave, check your list. Usually most questions will have been answered. Sometimes, however, key ones have not yet been broached, and you ought to focus the remaining time on getting answers to those questions. That's when you will be very grateful for the list I have encouraged you to prepare.

2) **Be specific with interviewees about what you are looking for.** "I want to know about the first years your parents were in this country. First, can you tell me the name of the town

"You're just like him," my aunt told me. "A lot of men in the family have his big eyes and that way of looking right into you!"

—Interview subject

"I wish I hadn't wasted time with my older relatives asking questions about my grandparents such as, "What were they like?" I got vague answers that tell me more about my aunts than anyone! I ought to have asked, "What did they do?" Then, I would really know what they were like!"

—Coaching client

in Norway they came from?" (Always be thinking of memory jogs. For instance, a map of Norway could be useful. The person might say, "I don't really remember, but it was not far from Oslo. Oh, yes, there it is! I remember now.")

Often, the interview is necessary to fill a specific gap in a story that you already have a lot of information about. While having an interviewee repeat information that you already know is often a waste of everyone's time, I let some wandering occur. In doing so, I am hoping to learn new details to flesh out my story.

If time is at a minimum, however, be decisive in asking the questions to fill the gaps in your information.

3) **Take notes during the interview.** There's nothing more frustrating and wasteful of everyone's time than returning home and not remembering significant details. At the beginning of the interview, tell interviewees you need to jot down their answers, but they should not try to interpret the importance you are attributing to various bits of information by the length of time you spend writing them .

If you are not comfortable writing notes, consider using a tape recorder to preserve the information for later retrieval.

4) **Be wary of asking for information that can be answered by a *yes* or a *no*.** These questions are called **closed-ended** and they do not deepen or extend the conversation.

> *You:* "Did you enjoy working on a cattle ranch?"
> *Interviewee:* "No."

Instead of the above question, which is reasonably but uselessly (for you) answered with a *no*, you might say:

> *You:* "Tell me something you liked about working on the cattle ranch and then something you didn't like about it."

This second example is an ***open-ended*** statement. "Tell me about…" cannot be answered by a *yes* or a *no*. An open-ended statement forces the interviewee to provide additional information—often very useful information.

5) Do not provide information or conclusions. If you were to say "Those were meaningful years for you!" you might be putting words into the interviewee's mouth. Her answers may then reflect not what she is thinking but her wish not to contradict you! Instead ask "Can you tell me what conclusions you have drawn from this experience?" This allows you to know how she interprets her own experience. (Haven't we all been surprised to find that another person viewed as positive what seemed to us clearly negative—and vice versa?)

6) **Do not rush your interview.** Tolerate silences and allow time for thinking. During these silences, it is likely that your interviewee could be arriving at new definitions of his experience. Or perhaps he is simply sorting his memories right on the spot. All of this takes time. People who are slow to speak could be shy or simply unused to sharing ideas and memories.

Here are three techniques to help you keep the interview flowing. These techniques can provide is a treasure trove of new information that gives insight into character and action in your family history!

■ **Repeat the interviewee's last words.** This can re-affirm your deep interest and help her feel comfortable. (This is not a summary statement, or an observation on your part—it is entirely different.) For instance:

> *Aunt Jeanette:* "Those were difficult times."
> *You, nodding your head in support:* "Mmm. ...difficult times."

This is the antithesis of saying, "Those must have been difficult times because wages were so low!" When the interviewer provides the "because...," she is *planting* information and could really end up quoting herself!

■ **Ask a question based on the interviewee's last words.**

> *Aunt Jeanette:* "Those were difficult times."
> *You:* "How were they difficult?" or "Why do you think they were difficult for you?"

■ **Remain silent after the interviewee has spoken.**

A tape recording of your interview can be more than just a means of checking information later. It becomes a permanent record of that person's voice—with all the unique intonations, modulations, vocabulary and distinct accent.

Videotaping can create a record of gestures, postures, general bearing, clothing, facial expressions, etc., which are valuable details to incorpate as you create character portraits in your stories.

Silence is sometimes the sound of some-one thinking what to say!

Aunt Jeanette: "Those were difficult times."

(Silence—even an awkwardly long one!)

Aunt Jeanette, who is wondering why you are not speaking, feels compelled to fill in the silence: "Well, those were difficult times because Uncle Hank was a union leader and he lost his job. It was around that same time that I had a miscarriage. I couldn't stand all day at the loom. I was still too weak to go back to work."

People often weigh the feeling of the moment—its sense of safety—before revealing unexpected or intimate things. Resist the urge to fill in the silence. You may be rewarded for your patience with information you could never have guessed would come your way.

I have found this "silent treatment" very effective in eliciting information beyond what an interviewee had originally thought to offer. To achieve this effect, however, you must not speak to break a silence as you would in a social situation where the silence might be understood as awkward. **Risk awkwardness for revelation!** Sit patiently. Do not distract the interviewee with fidgeting or with prompts. Silence will allow her time to synthesize, analyze—and share.

7) **End an interview with the question, "Do you have anything you want to add to what I have asked?"** I always say this, and often the interviewee will share unexpected, and potentially valuable, information. The new material is often prefaced by a statement like, "This may not be important but…" What you get then is often quite interesting, useful, and important.

8) **Plan enough time to be with your subject.** Elders move at a slower pace. Be aware that the fast tempo you take for granted may be exhausting and unpleasant for them. Your elderly interviewee may not have considered some of these memories for some time; it may be disturbing to relive the past. Allow for a "cool down" period—small talk as you put your materials away—that will ease your interviewee back to the present and give her a chance to re-establish her equilibrium. Ask, "Are you comfortable with my leaving now? Is there anything I can get for you before I go?" A phone call later to check in and thank your elder is both kind and comforting.

"I have so enjoyed revisiting those memories! I didn't think anybody cared anymore."

—Interview subject

exercise

Prepare questions for the interview.

■ In the previous exercise, you set up an interview. Now, based on the information you need, make a list of questions to ask during this interview.

■ If you intend to bring your tape recorder, use it at home first to ensure that you are comfortable handling it and that it works. Make sure you have enough tape for the allotted time of the interview—bring more blank tapes than you think you'll need.

■ Review your list of questions. If you are not used to asking open-ended questions, practice wording each one on your list as an open-ended one.

C. Formal research.

Interviewing family members and friends will provide a personal lode of information that will greatly enhance your stories—make them more accurate and more broad, but interviews alone may not be enough to give your stories the depth they require.

Perhaps you already know enough about the period in which you or an ancestor lived to write about it convincingly and fully. It is more likely, however, that you have only a sketchy knowledge of the context of your story. Your awareness, for instance, may be based on a child's limited perspective rather than the adult's broader, more insightful one. You may know what your family had by way of household items but not whether those items were commonplace in society at large or whether they reveal your family's special status (e.g., either more or less comfortable than society at large).

Even minimal historical research can help place your story in a context that will round out your tale not only for yourself but for your reader by helping you interpret the actions and attitudes of some of your characters.

If, for instance, your ancestors came with others from

> Your lifestory has a larger context. This section will help you find it and use it.

Serbia and settled in a Serbian-American (-Canadian) community, their experience is vastly different from a Serbian family that found itself without co-nationals in a totally "American" or "Canadian" setting. What are the ramifications of this history? If you have not thought about social history, give it some attention. Individual circumstances really do change a family's adaptation (e.g., learning a new language, intermarriage, and adopting new customs or forsaking traditions from the old country).

■ **Understanding history is a way of understanding the context of the everyday life of your subjects.** Our memories can change historical facts in order to protect us from the truth. For instance, I once heard a man in a radio interview explain why he had not gone to college In the late '60s, he said, fewer people got to go to school than today because there was little financial aid available. This struck me as inaccurate because I graduated from college in 1969! If ever there was a time when almost anyone who wanted to could go to college, it was the late '60s! There was an explosion in enrollments; universities in the U.S. were filled with first-generation students—I was one of them and used the abundant resources available from new government loan programs to finance the education my parents couldn't afford.

Why did this man resort to an historical fiction to explain his lack of education? The answer, of course, is complex and personal. It could be any of a number of reasons—shame, hesitancy, fear of the unknown or of bucking his family expectations, lack of ambition or academic ability. In his memory, however, *the cause remained outside himself* allowing his self-image to remain unchallenged. The point is clear: memory can play a supportive role to our unexamined and/or self-justifying views. Therefore, our own past requires historical research, too!

Here are suggestions for research:

■ **Read about the economic history of this continent.** Working in a sweatshop in Manhattan or a steel plant in

Pittsburgh is vastly different from working in an owner-run factory in a small northern New England town or on a ranch in Saskatchewan. You'll come to a different understanding of the energy it took one of your ancestors to make and carry out decisions if you understand the context in which those decisions were made.

■ **Read about the political, religious, and social climates in the old country as well as in the new.** It may be that you can make sense of your ancestors' decisions and actions only by understanding the larger context of your people's history.

Even your own life has a context larger than yourself and your immediate family. Writing that "a lot of people were out of work in the first years of the 1930s" is not as clear to your readers who did not live the experience as writing "one in three workers was unemployed or underemployed at the beginning of the 1930s."

■ **Read general histories of the period.** They give you a more accurate sense of what was happening and provide facts and dates and numbers to support your document. This research will create a framework on which to tell or reinterpret your story.

■ **Don't forget to read newspaper and magazine archives and historical society records for details on the area where your ancestors lived.**

■ **City and town tax records, military records and legal filings can also be very helpful.**

If your local library does not have all the material you need to conduct your research, you can borrow through the Inter-Library Loan (ILL) program or acquire a community borrowing card at your local university or college library. Your state, provincial or county library is a valuable resource, too. You should inquire about these.

"What I learned is that my grandfather purposely destroyed any photographs of his parents and siblings that revealed their working class origins. My generation's curiosity about our background couldn't be more different than his sense of shame! I have vowed not to destroy a single document my grandkids could use to learn more about me and my life!"

—Workshop writer

ɛxɛɾcisɛ

Use research to deepen and broaden your stories.

■ Go to your public library. Check out a history of your ethnic, religious, or cultural group. Read it carefully, looking for both statistics and for background details to increase the impact of your stories. Be ready to have your memories multiply as you encounter "new" phenomena that you suddenly realize are familiar.

■ Investigate a local university or college library to see if they have more or better materials for your research. Can you get a community borrowing card or do you need to work on-site?

■ Find out about your state, provincial, or county library and learn how to use Inter-Library Loan to get books from distant collections.

■ Rework your stories to incorporate the new information your research has uncovered about your family or personal history.

■ In a story, incorporate an actual event into a typical day your characters would have had. Your research has probably helped you to be more informed about the sorts of activities your ancestors engaged in. [See Chapter 3, Section A.]

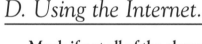

This section shows you how to do "instant" research on the Internet.

D. Using the Internet.

Much if not all of the above can be done on the Internet. Begin with a word search on your favorite search engine. You will be amazed at how much information you can access. Whatever you need, it's likely to be there on the Net. The Internet truly is an information superhighway.

When you find useful info on the Web, you can print it and file it. Your archive will grow quickly. Keep your pages organized by topic or era in a three-ring binder.

Remember: information is only useful if you can retrieve it!

When I am working on certain pieces, I keep the browser window open on my desktop as I write. My story is in the foreground. As I need more information, I simply click on the browser window to bring it forward (while my story goes to the background), type in a keyword and off I go—I'm researching.

As I was doing research for the book of my seventeenth-century Canadian ancestors, I encountered names of "support characters" in my family's history. Though I had already collected much genealogical data on my people, a Web search of a non-relative's name often yielded Web sites where with interesting and useful details. The extra data helped me write a broader, more historically accurate background for my story, and it was immediately accessible! It's a wonderful way to work: a library of the world right there on your desktop!

Exercise your judgement about you find on the Net as you would with any source you use to shape your opinions and your work. Is the site you found professional in its presentation? Is the information (dates, names, historical context) borne out by details you already know or can confirm elsewhere? Is the intent of the organization or individual compromised by an overriding dogma or point to prove? For instance, I have found many factual errors in the Mormon records of my family on their Web site. I conclude that the driving force behind the Latter Day Saints' collection of names and dates is not accuracy. Their data is often based on quickly-gathered census information, not on their own meticulous research.

Census records often contain mistakes. Gathered in haste by temporary workers who may not know the languages or customs of their subjects, it is rife with incorrect "best guesses." It is obvious from the errors in records of my French-speaking ancestors that census info was collected or transcribed by English-speakers. In my case, the parish records in Québec are clearer—and much more reliable. How about your ancestors? Be suspicious! Cross-check your info.

The Internet is an amazing tool—but be wary when facts differ from what you expect or find elsewhere. **You are responsible for making sure your work does not perpetuate false stories or become a source of apocryphal non-history that will be quoted by future generations!**

Beware of the Web. Be skeptical of it. Not all Web sites are equal. Any ill-informed person can throw together a site that spouts his opinions. There are no Internet fact police—other than you!

E. Other kinds of research.

This section validates the time you spend poring over family memorabilia. (Tell your mate it's crucial research— not clutter!)

Library and archival research will create a broad context for your project, but it is not as likely to jog your memory or uncover family details as other more informal sorts of inquiry will.

1) **Examine photos, both those of the family and those of the period you find in library books**. Compare the two. This can provide you with solid clues. Photos of your grandmother with hair coiled tightly around her head when other photos of the period show women with much looser hair styles will tell you something about her character. It may also tell you something about her social class, family background, or about her economic status—all elements that will contribute to understanding your story.

Photos of you and your parents in front of the Statue of Liberty tell you that you did indeed travel with your parents. At some point, they had enough time and disposable income to take a pleasure trip. If that disposable income, and its loss, is something you do not remember about your family—or if it contradicts something you thought true, then explore this discrepancy in an interview with a relative.

Often photos have notes on the back identifying the date and the individuals (the name of that bearded man next to Grandpa who has the same big nose you have). This information can broaden your understanding of family.

Photos can also suggest emotional contexts. A photo of Grandpa and Grandma sitting at opposite ends of the sofa tells you something about them that is very different from a photo of your other grandparents holding hands. This is especially true when you can back up what you find in one photo with many others providing similar clues.

■ **Photos can reveal details that help explain unusual facts or support your intuition.** Look at the background of the image. Does it reveal material poverty or opulence? And the clothing: is it obviously home-made or does it have a tailored

look? Is it new-looking or worn-out? What is the nature of the background? Is it filled with religious artifacts? family photos? starkly bare? What is the function of the background objects: leisure-oriented, work-oriented, religion-oriented?

Be a sleuth. Probe the possible meaning of the details in the photos you have on hand. **Inspect and conclude but take care not to invent.**

2) **Other memorabilia, besides photos, will give you precious information about your family.** Furniture that has been handed down through the generations, for instance, will tell you a lot about your people—especially when you look at a number of pieces and compare these with furniture you see in the library books or Web sites you are studying. Furniture can reveal information about social status, taste, and personality traits, especially when paired with other sources of information. Also, don't forget to scrutinize what it might mean that this *particular* piece of furniture has made it down across the years: it reveals something about another person who saved *this* piece rather than *another* for posterity, about that person's tastes, social status, self-image, etc.

The same is true of objects you yourself acquired 20 or 40 years ago. What do they tell you about yourself at an earlier stage in your life? How have your tastes changed in the intervening years? What symbolic or emotional meaning did the purchase of that teapot or kitchen table have for you at the time?

3) **Clothing and jewelry can also reveal information as can books, diplomas, awards, tools, and personal effects (letters, diaries, poems).** In fact, anything you have inherited that was bought or made can reveal clues that will help round out your research and make three-dimensional (rather than flat) characters out of the people you are writing about.

"Those societies which cannot combine *reverence to their symbols* with *freedom of revision* must simultaneously decay."

—A. N. Whitehead
philosopher

F. Taking research notes.

As you do any research, it is important to take notes. Written notes will assure that that scoundrel—memory— doesn't alter the facts. Notes will also make it easy to compare information with other material that you come across later. Of course, any research is valuable only to the degree that your notes are accurate and accessible.

1) **As you take notes, write meaningfully and legibly and avoid too much spontaneous shorthand!** Haven't you had the experience of creating spontaneous "shorthand" only to discover that somehow what seemed so clear in the reference section of the library seems absolutely cryptic now that you are at your writing desk? You scratch your head, but the information is as unavailable as if you had never taken those undecipherable notes.

2) **Transcribe accurately** and, if you are undertaking oral research (interviewing), ask for spellings of *all* names, or for sources that would provide the correct spellings. Accuracy extends to *all* dates, figures, and pertinent details.

Don't forget: whenever precise information is crucial to interpreting a story, verify it with additional relatives, at newspaper archives, libraries and Internet searches. If something occurred "the year of the flood" in your town, you can check the date by going to your newspaper archives, etc.

"When I asked Dad who the woman in this photo was, he said it was his first wife. I was flabbergasted! He had a wife before Mother!"

—Workshop writer

3) **Resolve discrepancies in information.** Sometimes dates or other information given to you informally will conflict with what you gather from written sources. This may be due to a simple lapse of memory on the part of your informant. If altering information does not change the story, you can simply do a correction and let it go at that—otherwise, you'll need to go back to the person and work through the discrepancy. Trust the written sources of the period over the oral ones that depend on memory and are recalled many years afterwards.

Discrepancies in information can reveal a family's (or an

individual's) need to rewrite history. This will occur often in the context of **inherited theme** and **personal mythology**. (Chapter 5, Sections D and E)

Both time and ego alter memory. The changes that time brings to memory are perhaps unavoidable, but the need of a personality to affirm itself is not. A person may "forget" that she was chosen to play violin in the youth orchestra at eighteen rather than at thirteen. At eighteen, this is an achievement but it is not precocious—while playing with the orchestra at thirteen is. This "lapse" of memory *alters* the personal story of the individual and transforms her from a talented person into a prodigy. In writing about this person, you will need to ask yourself *why* she restructured her experience. You cannot seriously continue your writing without answering that question. It is a key to understanding your story and will reveal much about this person's past and his view of life.

4) **Make notes of the sources of your information in case you need to go back to them.** When you find information, you may not understand its importance or its future role in your stories. Later, while writing, you may become aware that a date, a place name, or the nature of a relationship is more important than you had supposed. You may need to return to your sources to gather the additional detail that will create the context to understand the information.

There may also be discrepancies in your notes. Did you simply copy the information incorrectly or was there an error in one of your sources? But it is more likely you just didn't understand the meaning or significance of your information and inadvertently altered it in the transcription.

If this happens, you'll need to know where you got the data. Was it from an encyclopedia, a biography, an interview, or over the Internet? Did you gather the notes from the newspaper you read at the city library, the book at the university or the town history you found at the historical society? **Always note your sources of information—it could save you hours of trying to**

retrace those sources!

Providing your readers with access to additional information for their own research into an era, a place, or an ethnic group is easy if you have kept careful notes. You will have already compiled a bibliography for them to begin their own research. In this way, your important lifewriting project can be continued and expanded. Others will be able to pick up where you left off.

G. *Accessing your research information.*

This section shares a few tips to ensure that you get the most out of your research.

You must have access to your information when you need it. The most useful and significant information buried in a smudged scrawl in the midst of a sheaf of notes (all of which have been lost somewhere!) is of no use at all to you!

1) My favorite place to gather information is in my three-ring binder. Use headers—or topic titles—on the top of each page, and keep similar headers within a section set off by tab separators. All information, such as "interesting things happening in the world when I was child," ought to be kept together for you to access easily when you are writing. Be as specific as you can with your headers so it will be easy to find what you're looking for. A recipe might get lost under the header, "kitchen"—just as information on cookstoves under the header "recipes." Always change sheets of paper and headings when you move on to new information. Otherwise, it is complicated to retrieve information because you can't remember on which page you jotted down the detail you now need.

Always print or write down the Web page address where you found your information and place it directly on the information page. This makes it easy to look up again.

2) Alternatively, use 3" x 5" cards or half sheets so that each paper can clearly contain a separate bit of information. If you are a penny-pincher, using large sheets may induce you to include disparate facts on the same page—"just so as not to waste the space." Don't. Always use a different sheet when you jot new information.

3) Allow for space on every page or card to jot down

additional information. This can be done by leaving wide margins or by double spacing. Sometimes additional research or reading can uncover new facts you'll want to juxtapose with what you have already collected. Cramming information on a sheet does not give you room to expand. Give yourself a lot of space.

4) **Use ink if you are handwriting.** Pencil marks have a way of fading and smudging. If you use felt-tip markers, be wary of any water—raindrops, tea, tears. Water in any form smears water-based inks in no time!

5) **Write legibly.** This suggestion cannot be taken too seriously! Time you save writing quickly (and most likely illegibly!) will be spent over and over again in deciphering—or having to repeat your research.

And don't forget to avoid spontaneous shorthand writing that may be gibberish later!

6) **If you are using a computer, be sure to save your information on a back-up disk or CD.** Sooner or later, your hard drive will give you trouble and you may lose precious information. At that moment, you will not think it a waste of time to have backed up your information on a separate disk.

Remember—in every phase of lifestory writing— *enjoy yourself!*

LIFESTORIES FROM THE WORKSHOPS

Searching for Poppa's Song
by Marilyn Geary

In this story, the author is stumped about the origins of a song she recalls her grandfather singing. Intrigued enough to dig for what she wants to be ethnic treasure, she finds an unexpected answer to her puzzle. *In the photo (page 109): the author and Poppa.*

I remember only a few of my grandfather's words, but they echo loudly in my memory. He never made a speech, gave a toast, or lectured on the values he held true. Yet I'll never forget a song he used to sing to me after dinner when I was quite young. That song has haunted me throughout the years, as the only words from my grandfather I can recall.

Head of a family that grew as strong and as vital as the trees in his orchard, Poppa, as we called him, spoke little and did much. Domenico Luigi Longinotti was born in the *Provincia di Parma* in Italy in the late 1800s. His village, Bedonia, perched high in the lush forests of the Apennine Mountains, supported no industry and very little farming. To make a decent living, many men from the region went abroad to England or to America.

In 1906, at the age of seventeen, Domenico left his native village in the mountains for Le Havre, France. At the port, he boarded the vessel *La Savoie*, which took him in steerage to Ellis Island. From New York, he found his way to California and the lush, fertile Santa Clara Valley, then known as the "Valley of the Heart's Delight." His older brother Luigi had already settled on a ranch there. To earn his living, Domenico took a job hauling manure by horse cart to some of the many vegetable fields that carpeted the valley. By working in the orchards for Italian friends and relatives, Domenico scraped together money for his future.

Through mutual friends, Domenico met my grandmother, Clara Peirano. After a suitably long courtship, Domenico and Clara married and settled down to create a family. Their first child, my Auntie Maria, was born in East San Jose in the house (and not in the cabbage patch, as she so liked to tell us) on my great-uncle's fruit ranch. Domenico and Clara managed to gather together enough savings to purchase an orchard of fifteen acres located in the Willow Glen district of San Jose. The orchard was stocked with peach, bing cherry, sugar prune, walnut and apricot trees planted in straight rows lined neatly across the acreage. A white Victorian house stood surrounded by green foliage. Two barns on the property housed chickens, geese, a horse and various farm equipment. Clara gave birth in this house to three sons: Eugenio, Giovianni and Carlo, my father.

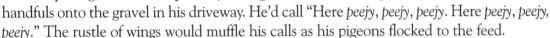

Poppa was a big, burly man with hands like tree stumps, gnarly and stained from the tannin in his walnuts. He dressed in Big Ben overalls, a long sleeved checkered cotton shirt and a crumpled hat that he never removed as he trudged beneath the valley sun through the rows of fruit trees. On Sundays and holidays, Poppa would dress for church in a brown suit with very thin yellow stripes, a crisp white shirt, suspenders, and a brown felt hat that covered his balding crown.

Although he had never farmed before, Poppa loved working the ranch. Most of all he loved his pigeons. He built roosts high up the side of the barn to house them. Each evening Poppa would dip a big hand into a pail of yellow grain and throw huge handfuls onto the gravel in his driveway. He'd call "Here *peejy, peejy, peejy*. Here *peejy, peejy, peejy*." The rustle of wings would muffle his calls as his pigeons flocked to the feed.

At dusk when Poppa could no longer see to work outside, he came into the big kitchen for the evening meal. Auntie Maria made the most delicious squab with risotto, and she simmered her ravioli in olive oil and basil. Her meals filled the kitchen with the exquisite aromas, but no matter the fare, Poppa always reached behind the big round oak table into the large tin drawer for his bread and cheese. He took large chunks of cheese and carved thick slices of bread with a huge knife he kept for this purpose. The bread was tough and crusty, the cheese rock-hard, yet the knife in Poppa's massive hands dug in and sliced these staples into slabs, crumbs falling to the table. And while the rest of the family savored minestrone or veal, tender squab or spaghetti, Poppa chomped on his meal of choice: dry bread and Parmesan cheese.

We never could understand why Poppa preferred these simple foods. It's just one of many questions we had about the man. He was a mystery to his grandchildren. He never did learn to speak much English, but Poppa never spoke much Italian either. Conversations with Poppa kept to the basics.

"How's it going, Poppa?" one of his children would ask in a very loud, clear voice.

He'd shrug his shoulders good naturedly, shake his head and say, *"Va be', va bene."* ("A' right, things are going all right.") That would be it. End of conversation. He'd then sit back in his chair and survey his rich harvest, his children and grandchildren, who led lives so vastly different from his simple life in the Old Country. We got the sense from the twinkle in his eyes that he was very proud of his sons and his daughter, and their children, as they became accomplished professionals, successful in the ways of his adopted country.

Sometimes after dinner, Poppa would take me on his knee and bounce me up and down as he sang in pigeon English: *"Ta da da da dada, my little red veen, my little red veen, ta da da da dada."* I loved hearing his song as I rode on his knee. This great big burl of a man seemed to be having as much fun as I was.

Yet, with each bounce, I wondered, "What is he singing about?" I could not make out the words. I wanted desperately to recognize them, as they were clues to understanding this strange and mostly distant grandpa. Back then, I thought maybe he was singing a traditional Italian song about a tiny bird with red wings that he fondly recalled from back home in Italy. Later, I thought he was probably singing about another love, the red *vino* that wetted his evening meal of dry bread and cheese.

But it was neither of these.

Lately, I learned that the song was a popular tune of the 1920's called "Little Red Wing, the Indian Maiden." I was stunned at this discovery. Where did Poppa learn this popular tune? How could he be singing of Indians, while I was dreaming of Italy?

I have so many questions I'll never resolve about my Italian grandfather now long gone. Yet even though my search for this song ended far from the Italian roots I had expected, it has brought me closer to Poppa and to my memories of a giggling little girl bouncing on Poppa's knee as he sang its sweet melody.

Chapter 5—The Truth

A.   What is the truth?

B.   Make "guess-timates" of the truth.

C.   Use your intuition.

D.   How much truth should you tell?

E.   How do you tell the truth?

LIFESTORIES FROM THE WORKSHOPS:
    The Last Word by Robin L. Waldron

A. *What is the truth?*

Telling the truth in a lifestory may seem simple, but "it ain't necessarily so!"

■ **To begin with, the truth may not be evident.** Was mother nurturing? Your brother says, "yes" and you say, "not really!" Who is telling the truth? It often comes as a surprise to lifewriters to learn that the truth they believe inherent in a story is a personal interpretation, one of many versions of the truth.

■ **How much truth should you tell?** When I don't mention that mother spent hours on the phone every afternoon and hardly greeted us when we returned from school, have I crossed over into creating a lie about the truth of her relationship to her children?

■ **How should you tell the truth?** Gingerly? Brashly? So vaguely that no one will grasp what you are writing about?

It's easy to see that in writing your lifestories, you will not be able to bypass problems about truth. In the end, the way you think about truth and how to tell it will influence the *what*, the *how*, and the *why* of your story.

Here are some guidelines to help you write the truth in your memoirs.

1) **Facts are the baseline of truth.** As the temperature on a cold day can be verified by reading a thermometer, facts can also be verified by referring to authenticating sources (people, documents, records). Sometimes issues that families debate are really a matter of public record.

Did Mother graduate from high school in 1939 or 1940? Arguing the date is a waste of time: it can be authenticated by a visit—or a phone call—to her high school.

In this chapter, you will learn how to identify and to write about the various versions of truth in your lifestories.

One of the rewards of lifewriting is setting the record straight.

Reminiscing with a parent or a sibling about family history may be an opportunity for you to deepen your relationship. When your versions of the past differ, you have a chance to discuss the "why."

Did your family live at 27 Shawmut Street starting in January 1945 or January 1946? The research needed to determine the true date might be as easy as bringing forward a letter dated March 1945: your mother writes about getting the last of the moving boxes unpacked! Or, you ask an elderly aunt and she says, "Your cousin Bob was born prematurely after I helped your mother and father move boxes. He was born on January 25, 1945." Or, if your parents owned the house, you can find out when they bought it from the municipal registry of deeds. In fact, you can learn the entire history of some houses—when the additions were built, when the plumbing was put in, etc.

■ **All stories, even those you presume true beyond doubt, must be cross-checked if the "facts" run counter to another person's memory.** Verification is all the more necessary if you are basing an *interpretation* of your story on these facts. Go to relatives, documents (letters, diaries, newspaper accounts, etc.), public records (birth, census, death, tax), library, etc., in order to double check your facts.

■ **Authenticate your information beyond reasonable doubt.** In the end, as a lifewriter, you are a historian who must verify facts to build a solid case for your version of history. Even one piece of dubious information can cause your readers to lose faith in all your stories.

■ **Attribute your version of the truth to yourself when you cannot find documentation to back uncertain "facts."** An honest, workable solution is simply to write "I believe my grandparents lost their house in 1953 because..."

An older child may remember poor, but youthful, parents full of energy for playing with them. A younger child may remember financially secure, but older, parents who did not tussle on the living room rug.

2) **Other "facts" in your lifestories may be easy to evaluate as improbable or impossible because logical sequencing of events contradicts them.** For instance, your daughter was born in 1968; she cannot possibly remember how she loved to sleep over at your parents' apartment on Lincoln Avenue because they moved away from there in 1967. Your cousin Fred, who was killed in Normandy on D-Day, 1944, could not possibly have swindled your grandparents out of their savings

when they were persuaded to invest in phony stocks in 1945!

Undocumented stories like the cousin Fred one can survive in a family and become the "documentation" people use when they talk about Fred's character. After all, didn't he swindle your grandparents in 1945!

3) **Learn to distinguish the difference between truth that is relevant and truth that is irrelevant.** In some matters, digging too deeply can sometimes be a waste of time.

For example, do you really need to authenticate whether it was John or James who pushed you off the swing when you were four and you broke your collar bone? John says it was James; James says it was John. After fifty years, a fog has rolled over your family's collective memory. You have no wish to carry out a vendetta. Beyond idle curiosity, who pushed you is irrelevant. More interesting is your learning experience and how your family members reacted. You need to write about your visit to the doctor, the tender care you got at home, the status you had in the neighborhood as a result—not about who was guilty. In this instance, you might write: "According to John, James did it and, according to James, John was the culprit. At any rate, I had an exciting trip to Dr. Muzzey and got to watch cartoons for a week…." More truth than that is simply immaterial and nit-picky. It is not worth pursuing.

4) **Attribute to someone's opinion what cannot be authenticated.** Whenever you decide that pursuing the truth is irrelevant or impossible (e.g., events occurred a long time ago and everyone involved is now gone), you can embed the opinion in a phrase that makes it clear whose it is. Use phrases like "My brother Francis believes that…," "My mother always said that…," "According to me…."

Do take that step of challenging your memory by checking the facts to the fullest extent possible and practicable. If no clear, verifiable truth emerges as unrefutable, **remember that your ultimate goal is to record *your* version of the truth—not someone else's.** (Writing their version is their job!)

As lifewriters, we take one element here and another there to build a case for a version of a story that is, in its whole, likely to be the most true.

exercise

Honor the truth of your stories.

■ Practice distinguishing between relevant and irrelevant truths in a story.

■ Have you verified the accuracy of the information you believe to be relevant? Would everyone in your family, for instance, agree to your "facts" (vs. inferences or intuitions, which we'll discuss in the next section)?

■ List available resources (specific relatives, letters, newspaper archives, etc.) to authenticate the points you question. If you cannot, acknowledge that the version you have included is unproven by introducing it with a phrase like "It would seem to me that..." or "My guess is..."

■ If, while you are cross-checking your information, you uncover discrepancies or differing versions of the truth, do your best to arrive at a version that makes sense to you, one that is plausible given all the info you have. This is a "guess-timate" that is covered in the following section.

B. Make "guess-timates" of the truth.

This section will help you make some "guess-timates" (educated guesses) in order to tell as much of the truth of your stories as possible.

Once you have verified all the facts that can or need to be checked, other truths may become evident. But these truths may not be of the sort that anyone can authenticate.

For instance, your parents were married in 1930. Most young couples are without solid financial backing when they start out. Your parents, as much as you (and anyone else) knows, didn't have any "rich uncle" to ease them through these first years. Are you justified in concluding they must have felt the effects of the Depression during their first days together?

"The artist 'lies' in order to achieve another kind of truth."

—Pablo Picasso
artist

You can't "prove" this, of course. If, as scientists do with their theories, you proceed as if your hypothesis were true—that your parents must have had a lean time of it then—what insight does this assumption give you about decisions they made during those years, or about attitudes they held in their later life together? Interpretations like these, based on ***reasonable inferences***, can make another person's life more understandable and your portrait more full.

As you include your interpretations, always attribute them to yourself by attaching phrases like "If that were true, it seems to me that…" Your interpretation or inference will take its place as a possible truth in the story you are writing. **Although it is essentially different from verifiable truth, the inferred truth has a rightful place in your writing.** Without it, your story will be more slight.

As you allow yourself to arrive at conclusions in this way, be sure to recognize clichés. These are the ill-fitting shortcuts that actually obscure the individuality of your characters. If you find yourself writing, "Everyone in those days was like that," let the alarm bells go off! You have left the firm ground of inference behind and are tromping into the sloppy swampland of cliché!

exercise

Look at the interview and research notes you have gathered or at the stories you have written.

■ What guess-timates can you make from this material? How might these inferences deepen characterization? (Important: introduce your "guess-timates" in a way that allows the reader to grasp both that you are inferring and what it is that you are inferring. There are many ways of doing this, one of which is to write something like, "I would think that…"

■ Have you made all the inferences you can? Are you holding back, not because you feel your inferences are wrong but because you fear someone's reaction? How can you resolve your hesitation to voice your inferred truth?

■ If telling the truth hurts you or someone else, and you are not sure how to proceed, reread Chapter 2, Section E, about dealing with pain.

■ Go back to your source material to see if you can make more inferences! Return to the stories—have you included inferences where appropriate?

C. *Use your intuition.*

This section will help you trust what you know but don't realize you know about the people and events that fill your stories.

"I wasn't inside my parents' heads! How do I know what they felt?" writers ask. True. But if you lived with them for years, observed their reactions and witnessed their shifting moods, you can use your intuition to arrive at a sense of what they were feeling.

There is another sort of truth that is neither verifiable, nor an educated guess. This truth is entirely intuitive.

"Mother never liked living at 27 Shawmut Street" is an example of intuitive truth. No matter what others may say, and your sister Edna is convinced of the opposite, you have a "gut" feeling that your perception of your mother's unhappiness is correct.

If your mother is no longer alive, authenticating your gut feeling may be impossible—and even if she is, your mother may be unable, for many reasons, to admit to the truth. (See the following section of this chapter: "How much truth should you tell?")

As in the earlier example where I urged you to proceed like a scientist with a hypothesis, ask yourself if your gut feeling helps to explain other things. Does it, for instance, account for behavior or attitudes otherwise attributable only to a failing in your mother's character?

As you apply this test, it may become obvious that your gut feeling explains a lot of things that happened in your family. How will you write about these intuitive truths? Not only are they not provable, they may also be the subject of disagreement or conflict within your family.

My suggestion is to state your intuition and say why it seems right to you. Then give other points of view equal space. (A footnote is a good place for alternative opinions.) Your family readers need and deserve to have the different interpretations—especially when there is no way to authenticate which is correct or nearer to being correct.

At the Workshops

After Helen finished reading her story of going to a lakeside camp for part of the summer when she was ten, she closed her notebook and looked around the room, waiting for our response.

Like others around the long table, I said nothing. Something was missing from her story—or had something false been added? It simply didn't feel right. My intuition was that Helen was not telling the truth. Had she somehow reconstituted events to hide the truth about someone or something? Did she even know that she had altered the story?

"Who wants to share what you liked about this piece?" I asked, but no one answered. On both sides of the table, the men and women of the class seemed as reluctant as I was to open the discussion.

People often have a sense about when they're being told a "tall tale." That day was no exception. I waited. Helen waited. The workshoppers waited.

Then, across the table, Linette, a small woman in her mid-sixties, shook her head and said, "I don't think that's the way it happened."

We gasped. Linette had expressed what we were all thinking! How would Helen react to the challenge?

Helen looked up. "As a matter of fact, it didn't happen that way! I didn't want to say the way it happened."

Around the table, a few heads nodded, "I thought so!" and the group seemed even more uneasy at this development. No one spoke.

"You don't have to tell us what happened," I said. "You have a right to your privacy, always. But you need to know you can't not tell the truth and expect us not to notice."

Softly a woman beside Helen added, "You can keep the truth from us, but you haven't fooled us. What's important is that you don't keep the truth from yourself. I hope you can be honest with yourself about what happened."

Then, as the mood in the room relaxed and expanded to support the courage it took for her to speak up, Helen volunteered why she had changed her story. She spoke about the pain and the fear she had that summer when she was a little girl of ten.

She seemed relieved that our intuition had uncovered that the story she had written wasn't true.

exercise

Allow your intuition to develop.

■ Write about an incident in your life in a way your intuition tells you is true. Be sure you include many facts to serve as a baseline for the story.

■ Whenever possible, include intuitive interpretations in your stories , even if they vary from each other or from versions you held before. Now your story will have greater depth and you will have established yourself as a reliable storyteller. (But don't be surprised if those who maintain different versions find fault with you! Remember: this is your memoir.)

D. How much truth should you tell?

This section may seem contradictory: it will urge you to tell all at the same time as it counsels you to hold back!

There is another dilemma to face when you are dealing with the truth. How much of it do you have to tell in order to tell the truth? At what point does *withholding* the truth become a lie? For instance, in all her famous diaries, as Anaïs Nin celebrated the freedoms of her life as an artist, she never once mentioned that she was bankrolled by a husband. True, she could not mention his name or details of his life because he had refused her legal permission to do so in print. But wouldn't the truth have been better served if she had mentioned the working husband who paid her bills and made her financial freedom possible? In that sense, her diaries have always seemed to me to contain a fundamental lie. Nin clearly wanted her readers to believe that she lived independently as a woman and a writer. The fact of her husband's support makes it evident that the self-sufficient persona she projected was wishful thinking.

Don't worry about making your prose beautiful. Instead reach for truth. "Tell it like it was!" Hemingway wrote about writing "true sentences." Truth is perhaps all you can aspire to. And it's not too little. With truth, as Keats would have it, comes beauty.

How much truth to tell is always a subjective decision that can be made only in the context of the writer's life and family. The following are considerations to keep in mind as you decide how to solve your "truth problems."

1) **Withholding information can significantly alter your reader's interpretation of a story.** Sometimes, telling a story

without all the information is really telling a lie. Aren't you lying whenever you choose to hide a part of the truth that alters how a story can be interpreted? (Remember Anaïs Nin.)

2) **Conversely, writing memoirs is not the opportunity to tell everything!** Nor is it the time to impose your version of an ugly scene and get your revenge on the people who are not available to defend themselves.

In a conversation, when someone tries to get you on his side, don't you feel that your good will is being abused? Your readers will feel abused, too, if your goal is to enlist them against someone else. Your readers are looking for understanding—not for partisanship! You may unwittingly force them to stop reading in order to protect their own integrity.

3) **You do not have to tell something you do not feel comfortable telling.** You have the right to your privacy and do not have to divulge details that you do not want to share.

This is different from withholding information to affect the reader's understanding (see #1 above). A case can easily be built around your need to protect yourself! You are neither an exhibitionist nor a masochist. **Relationships, and your dignity as a person, are sometimes more important than the truth.** This is your decision. Unlike Helen (whose story appeared in the previous *At the Workshops*), be aware that **you have the choice—and don't ever hide the truth from yourself even if you choose not to share it with others.**

4) **Be wary of recording someone else's views of your life or of the lives of other family members.** For example, within a family, stories sometimes acquire the status of the "official" version. Writers will assume these stories are true and opt to record them one more time.

These "official" stories are often initiated by the *dominant* parent (the one who makes the rules or sets standards in the family). These stories serve as "propaganda" for that parent's point of view (See *At the Workshops* below.) In many settings (family, work, politics) non-dominant individuals and groups

---

If you experience a delicious feeling of revengeful righteousness as you tell all in your memoir, it may be the better part of wisdom to exercise some restraint in sharing your work with others. Set it aside to review and rewrite once you have had your say on the page.

"I want to keep some things private. My children don't have to know everything about me!"

—Workshop writer

You have the right to maintain comfortable boundaries, but you do not have the right to tell lies in your memoirs.

are evaluated on the criteria set by the dominant one. Writing family stories that step outside the established doctrine can be one of the major challenges lifewriters face in truth-telling. Don't underrate the difficulty of this; choose to deal with this challenge courageously, and perhaps repeatedly.

Be a sleuth. Go beyond (or beneath) the *apparent* story to get at the *real* story. Be honest with yourself—and write the story your intuition tells you is true.

At the Workshops

Nancy wrote about her father. In her family, it was always said that he was a bit shiftless and that he had no ambition. As Nancy delved into her father's life however, "walking a while in his shoes," she grew to have a different interpretation of his life's journey—but it was *not* easy for her to give up the "official family version" that had been created and sustained by her mother.

The facts did bear out that her father had gone from one job to another, but she uncovered a reason for this she had hidden from herself all her life. Her father had shown a dedication to music through his longstanding participation in church and community music groups, advocacy of music education in the schools and the patient collection of a large music library. Nancy had never seen a relationship between his love for music and his lack of career ambition, but now it began to make sense.

Her father had passed up a promotion at work in 1947. This had been an important piece of evidence in the family's (i.e., her mother's) documentation of the father's shiftlessness. But Nancy now realized that the promotion would have required her father to work evenings and to travel. He would have had to forfeit directing the choral group he had been working with since 1946 (This is an example of how accurate dating can be crucial to interpreting family history!).

As Nancy continued examining her father's life, she realized that other allegations of shiftlessness and lack of steadfastness were not necessarily true. To the contrary, her father had shown an admirable ability to meet fundamental family responsibilities while nurturing his gift for music, the primary passion of his life. The emotional reinforcement that his work provided was secondary to him.

Blind to the emotional rewards music brought to her husband's life, Nancy's mother had not prized his dedication to something she did not value; she decried the loss of higher pay and social status in her life and blamed him for it. In her version of the truth, she had suffered much due to her husband's "character flaw." She sustained her portrait of him as a shiftless head of the household, demanding praise for her endurance. Poor Mother!

Nancy, as she wrote the story, realized she had been taught to view her father's life through a wife's eyes, not a daughter's! Now she began to wonder what might have happened if her mother had been able to support his efforts to develop his talents rather than urge him to drive them under. Might her father have found a way to support the family with work as a musician?

Determined now to write as a daughter, Nancy nonetheless felt herself pitted against her mother and her mother's long-standing interpretation of the man on whom she had so bitterly depended for status.

Initially, despite what she felt to be the truth, Nancy's conditioning was still strong, and she could not easily reveal what she now saw as the truth. Ignoring it was what she had done all her life, just as her mother expected. She felt telling a different truth would be disloyal to her mother and her pain.

In the end, however, Nancy, having had the insight, had to accept that the view she had once held was not her own. As an adult now, she was free to see her father as he might have been, without the bitter disappointment voiced so strongly by her mother. She was also free to say to her mother, "I love you. I acknowledge your pain. And I do not see my father as you saw him."

exercise

Become aware of "official" versions of family stories.

■ Identify an "official" version of a family story that makes you uncomfortable.

■ Write your own version of this story. Don't forget to make "guess-timates." (Remember: you do not have to share your writing with anyone! You can even throw your story away once you have written it!)

■ How does it feel now to have told a truth that you were uncomfortable about? Can you include this story in the final version of your lifestory? What will you do about the other version of the truth—the one that may have been propaganda for someone else's point of view?

■ Who might be responsible for this version and why? What's your feeling for, and your evaluation of, that person? It's important to understand why he came to create and circulate it. (This understanding will illuminate some facet of that person's character and its role in family dynamics and values.)

E. *How do you tell the truth?*

Other issues arise, not around *what* the truth is, but *how* it is told.

We all love well-told stories. We love the entertainment, the sound effects, the punchy plot built around solid characterization. As we share stories in our everyday conversations, we inevitably use fiction techniques to keep our listeners' attention and interest. When we say "And then she said…," we are using dialogue—that's a fiction technique.

In our memoir writing, we will often veer toward the same techniques fiction writers use. In fact, we don't seem to need urging at all to adapt our stories to make them more compelling or to ensure that they drive our point home. We do this spontaneously.

Many lifewriters ask, "But, am I twisting things when I use fiction techniques? Is it really okay?"

■ **Should a writer invent dialogue between his characters?** He does not, after all, have a tape recording of the conversations of the people he is writing about.

■ **Can the writer ascribe articles of clothing to an individual?** He can't really be sure that that individual wore that article on a particular day.

■ **How does a writer share with his reader the thoughts that he *suspects* an individual might have had?** After all, he was not in that person's head!

Different individuals come to different solutions to the

problems posed in these questions. Here are three possibilities available to lifewriters who feel a conflict in ascribing dialogue or other details to their stories.

1) **Write an introduction or preface to your lifestory.** In this piece, mention that you are using fiction techniques when you ascribe specific conversations and reactions to an individual. You attest that each of these elements are, to the best of your knowledge, typical of what the character might have said or worn or done. You might write that the tone and choice of words ascribed to a person is in keeping with how the person might have spoken and in a tone the person would have been comfortable with. As to clothing, you might write that you wish to give a sense of the total person and are sharing information about the character and inserting this information in such a way as to be unobtrusive, but the reader should not infer that all the pairings of clothing and times are factual.

2) **Use indirect dialogue.** Indirect dialogue is speech that is introduced by "that" whether used or implied. "My grandmother said [that] she would not leave her house" is an example of indirect dialogue. ("My grandmother said, 'I will not leave my house'" is direct dialogue.)

Indirect dialogue is often used when you don't have exact quotes, when you are reluctant to attribute specific words to an individual, or when you want to soften the impact of a piece of dialogue.

With indirect dialogue, you will sacrifice immediacy and impact. Because of this, indirect dialogue is often less attractive to writers than direct dialogue. But it is a useful tool when you don't want to, or can't honestly, place specific words directly in someone's "mouth." Indirect dialogue permits the writer to manipulate the presentation of a story.

3) **Never use dialogue or make any reference to action or setting that is not authenticated.** This choice can be very limiting in terms of storytelling. In this instance, your char-

Fiction techniques need to be used to *enhance* a story, not to avoid getting at its truth.

Indirect dialogue permits the writer to put the *illusion* of words in a character's mouth without ever mentioning exactly what was said.

acters never actually say anything in their own voices. They never appear on the page with particular pieces of clothing. They probably don't ever look out of windows or eat a meal—all fiction-based details that will make your characters come alive.

Without fiction techniques, your story will have a certain flatness rather than the you-are-there immediacy of storytelling at its best. But, if your choice is to eschew fiction techniques altogether, you will have told your story in the way you want to tell it, with utmost truth.

exercise

Introduce fiction techniques in your writing.

■ If you have not already used dialogue to portray truth, introducing some into one of your stories. Keep the dialogue to no more than two or three exchanges. (Long dialogue is more difficult to write.)

■ A good spot for dialogue is as a replacement for an adjective. An adjective such as angry ("I will never, never allow you to do that—not ever!") or generous ("Take these seedlings, and if you need more, just come back.") can easily be translated into dialogue.

■ Introduce descriptions of clothing, gestures, and thoughts into your writing.

LIFESTORIES FROM THE WORKSHOPS

The Last Word
by Robin L. Waldron

The Saturday morning sun came up too early that day in 1957, at the end of the first week back to school, and I was mentally spent from it all. I knew right away the sixth grade wasn't going to be an easy ride.

I had forgotten to turn off the alarm the night before, and it had rudely awakened me. My eyelids cracked open to no more than slits, allowing in the minimum of daylight. Then it dawned on me—it was Saturday, and I didn't have to go to school.

I quickly snuggled deep into the comfort of my bed and closed my eyes to go back to sleep. No sooner had I closed my eyes than I heard the door at the bottom of the stairs open.

"Robin, are you going to sleep all day?" Grandma called up to me. "Better get up. You know you have to do all your chores on Saturday, now that school has started. Can't drag them out all week. Come on!"

Grandma's thick German accent and sing-song rhythm invaded the privacy of my inner sanctum.

"Robin! Are you awake, Robin?"

"Okay, Grandma. I'll be down in a few minutes."

"See that you are, young lady. Don't be makin' me come up there!"

"Yeah, yeah, yeah," I mumbled under my breath.

In this story, Robin Waldron effectively portrays a hard truth about the grandmother who raised her. She does so in an unflattering yet not vengeful manner. Robin is a certified Soleil Lifestory Network teacher who lives and teaches in Franklin, Indiana.

Now I was fully awake but still reluctant to move too fast. As I lay in my bed thinking, I had to remind myself how lucky I was to have Grandma and Grandpa. After all, I could have ended up in foster care like my brother and sister.

My folks divorced when I was 14 months old, and my father took the three of us home to his parents. When I was seven, we moved into the house on Tekoppel Avenue. My brother and sister lived with us for a short while before the decision was made that Dad and I would continue to live with my grandparents and my brother and my sister would be placed in foster care together. Since they had left, I had had my own bedroom, a real luxury. Not many of my friends enjoyed such a comfort, but the room couldn't make up for my loss.

Rolling over, I put my bare feet on the cool linoleum, telling myself that even though I had to get up, life was good. There were two unusual pets in the backyard, and since it was Saturday, I would be able to spend some time with them later.

The aroma of bacon frying and coffee brewing wafted up the stairs to my room, adding to my growing enthusiasm for the day ahead. Anticipating the good breakfast I would have, I dressed and went downstairs before Grandma could get back to the door with her resounding "last chance" orders. But when I reached the bottom of the stairs, a stern look from Grandma's steel gray eyes altered my mood and set the tone for the day.

"You have to burn the trash today," she said sternly. "Don't forget! The trash is running over in the kitchen, and you know we can not burn after 4 o'clock."

Something in her demeanor presented itself as a challenge to me. As I stared back, I felt an overwhelming sense of defiance. I'll empty the trash when I get good and ready, I thought to myself, and not a minute sooner!

Outside, the sky was heavy and gray, a gloomy fall day in Indiana. It was my job to burn the trash, but I just didn't feel like doing it right away. I chose to ignore Grandma's request. I told myself that maybe it would rain all day, and I wouldn't have to do the chore after all.

The day wore on. As lunch approached, Grandma reminded me a second time to burn the trash. "It's going to be 4 o'clock before ya know it, girl, and ya still won't have da trash burned."

The battle of wills was now at full hurricane force. I knew I was getting on her nerves, because her German accent always grew thicker as she became more agitated. But she always knew how to get to me.

"If I have to burn da trash, you will go to bed right after supper, and for sure ya won't be a watchin' *Boston Blackie* on da TV tonight."

Saturday night was the only time I was allowed to stay up until 10 o'clock, and *Boston Blackie* was my favorite detective story.

Well, with that news, I knew I would have to burn the trash, but I vowed to myself it wouldn't happen until 3:30. That way, it would be me who'd have the last word.

The back yard had already become a risky place for Grandma, and I knew she didn't really want to burn the trash herself. The problem in the yard had started one day when she came home from one of her frequent doctor's visits and said to Grandpa, "Well, Everett, the doctor says I have stomach ulcers and the only way to heal them is to drink goat's milk."

Grandpa began checking around Evansville to find out where he could buy goat's milk, but it just wasn't to be found. The nearest goat farm was 40 miles away in McCutchenville. Grandpa reasoned it just wouldn't be practical to travel that far regularly for milk. One day, he journeyed to the goat farm. When he returned, he announced that he had bought two goats and would pick them up in two weeks. In the meantime, he had to decide where he would keep them.

Grandpa researched his property survey information and found what he thought he had remembered. Part of the property was in the city and part was in the county. The house and a small portion of the backyard were bound by city limits and rules, while a parcel in the back lot was within county limits and under county rules.

Further research at the courthouse revealed that the city would not allow goats inside the city limits, because they weren't considered domestic pets. At the county offices, however, Grandpa found no such ruling. In fact, he was told that as long as the neighbors didn't complain, there was no reason he couldn't have goats on his county parcel.

Being a law-abiding citizen and, of course, not wanting to pay hefty fines for harboring illegal animals within the city limits, Grandpa measured off exactly where the city-county line was located on his property. There he stretched a fence that essentially divided the property into two sections, each governed by a different set of rules.

Two weeks later, as Grandpa promised, we had two nanny goats living in the far back lot. We named them Nanny and Judy.

Typically, only billy goats have horns, but I soon learned that Nanny was not a typical goat. Yep, her pointed horns curved back over the top of her head at about a 30-degree angle. At will and with amazing accuracy, she could pick just about anything off the ground and send it sailing into the air. She never missed her target.

Grandpa played rough with the goats, and they loved him. I watched how he handled them and learned to play with them, as well as to respect them. Soon, with Grandpa's guidance, I was able to control them as skillfully as he did. Grandma, on the other hand, didn't like the goats and had no control over them. In fact, truth be known, she was a little afraid of Nanny.

Grandma was not known for her patience. (Later in life, I learned that some of that impatience was caused by poor health and had nothing to do with me or what I did. But as a child under her stern rule, I only understood that she was continually peeved with me.) When she asked me to do something, she didn't intend to have to ask twice.

Clearly, that Saturday, I had already crossed that line. At 3 o'clock that afternoon, without issuing any further orders, Grandma marched to the back door, where her old brown sweater hung on the coat rack. Removing the sweater from its place without saying a word, she put it on, picked up the wastebasket in the kitchen, and continued to march her five-foot, two-inch, square-framed body, clad in a brightly colored paisley print house dress and brown sweater, out the door and down the sidewalk toward the goat yard, where the burning barrel was located.

I knew instantly I had lost this battle of the wills. Quickly guilt swept through me and my mind raced as I considered all the potential outcomes of this scene that would pit Grandma against Nanny. I was right on Grandma's heels, fearing Nanny's inevitable victory if Grandma entered the goat yard.

"Grandma," I begged. "Don't go in there. I'll burn the trash. I was getting to it, you know."

"No, I'm goin' to burn da trash, and you're going' ta stay out of da goat yard!"

"But Grandma! You know how Nanny is. She's going to think you're coming into the yard to play. Don't go, Grandma. Let me go."

Knowing there was no reasoning with her now, I stood on the city side of the fence, as I was told to do, to watch the most incredible scene unfold right before my eyes.

Grandma was about to dump the wastebasket of trash into the burner when a gust of wind rose, carrying the trash across the goat yard. In the meantime, Nanny, as I suspected, seeing all the action at the burning barrel, thought Grandma had come to play. As Grandma bent over to catch a piece of trash, I caught sight of Nanny preparing to charge her target.

"Nanny! No, Nanny!" I yelled as I climbed the fence and landed in the goat yard. Nanny, with her head down at full charge, reached Grandma with lightning speed. She hooked her horns under the hem of Grandma's dress and was about to raise her off the ground when I reached them. I wrestled Nanny to the ground and somehow freed Grandma's dress from Nanny's horns.

Grandma righted herself, and as if nothing had happened, and glared at me. "I thought I told you to stay out of da goat yard!" she said. "But since you're here, pick up the trash and burn it." She turned and marched out of the goat yard and up the sidewalk to the house, her silver gray hair ruffling in the wind. She never looked back.

Nanny and I sat there staring at each other, as if asking, "What just happened here?" I let go of her and she ran to the goat house. I began picking up the trash that was now strewn all over the goat yard.

Shaking my head, I knew in my heart that Grandma had just had the last word again.

Chapter 6—More than *"Just the facts, Ma'am"*

A. Getting it right: the basic *what*.

B. Going beyond *what* to *why* and *how*.

C. Theme: it's the life of your lifestories.

D. Inherited themes.

E. Personal myths.

F. Don't preach to me!

G. The glazed-over-eyes test.

LIFESTORIES FROM THE WORKSHOPS:
   Hardball with George by Jan McLean

A. *Getting it right: the basic* what.

Dates and facts are necessary to lifewriting in the same way route numbers are necessary to maps. It's not only that dates and facts provide interesting information but that they keep your readers on the right track as they make their way through your lifestory.

The dates and facts you include in your lifestories can be written up in a variety of ways.

1) **You can write a *chronology*.** A chronology is a narrative of dates and facts. As entry level lifewriting, a chronology is important in conserving family history because it records data for your readers."Grandma and Grandpa bought a farm in Washington, Missouri, in the spring of 1932. They planted a large market garden; in June of the same year, they added three cows and two pigs to their venture."

■ **A chronology leaves out big pieces of information that are neither dates nor facts.** It does not tell your readers *why* your grandparents moved to the farm and *how* they felt about being there. Your readers will wonder whether your grandparents had an easy or a difficult time of farming. Did the experience help them to grow personally? Was it a good decision on their part?

Remember: guidance and reassurance are important functions of storytelling. To provide answers to these questions, you must write more than a chronology.

2) **You can add *action* to your chronology.** Action will make your stories easier to understand and more interesting to read. You are introducing action when you place events (and the dates and facts that surround them) into a cause-and-

> This chapter will help you to write both the upfront story and the deeper, bigger one that lurks within it, the story that gives uniqueness to your *what*.

effect relationship. "Because the drought grew worse week by week that summer (cause), Grandpa and Grandma hauled water every evening to the gardens (effect)." Another word for the action of a story is *plot*.

3) **You can heighten the impact of your action-enhanced chronology with** *suspense*. Suspense emphasizes the effects which the causes you write about are likely to have on your characters. It suggests the *consequences* they do not yet foresee but which will, as you know, play a role in their lives.

With the addition of action, especially of suspenseful action, what might have started out as a chronology is now fleshed out and your readers are more likely to be intrigued and concerned as they read your story. "Day after day, the sky was clear without any clouds. The gardens were very dry. Grandpa and Grandma wondered about what they would do if the crops failed. All over the United States, jobs were being eliminated as the Depression deepened. Would there be any job for Grandpa away from the farm to help tide them over—or would they simply have to forfeit their land and join the ranks of the urban poor?"

Generally speaking, the action, or plot, of a story will provide the interest to keep your audience reading—especially if it contains suspense. **Action is the framework on which characterization, setting (Chapter 3) and theme (see Section C below) are built.**

Enhanced by action and suspense, your story is now more entertaining than if it was as a simple chronology. There is still an element missing however. Without telling the **why** of your story, you will fail to satisfy your readers' curiosity about the characters you present.

B. Go *beyond* what *to* why *and* how.

Why do basic facts in one person's life sometimes resemble those in another's and yet produce such different effects? Frequently, it is not so much *what* we do that touches and changes our lives as *why* and *how* we do it. The intentions behind our actions, as well as the manner in which we act, have often more impact than the actions themselves. To be successful in conveying the essence of your subject, write about the *why* and the *how* as well as the *what*.

1) **Add interpretation to your chronology and plot.** Tell why and how your grandparents persevered in this difficult work (perhaps something about their belief in working for themselves and in how working together would deepen their relationship, or perhaps about their certainty that life was meant to be hard in this way.)

Consider the following: "Because the drought grew worse week by week that summer of 1932, Grandpa and Grandma hauled water every evening to the gardens. They had invested all they owned in that farm, which they had dreamed of buying for years. If it failed, they would be forced to go back to the city to live on the dole. Both Grandma and Grandpa were go-getters. Losing not only their livelihood but also a source of meaningful activity was unthinkable for them."

In the example above, the necessary facts and dates as well as plot (even if only a slight one) are joined by something more: insight into *why* and *how* of your grandparents' lives. Your readers will know your grandparents better than they would by reading a mere chronology or a simple action story. You have added motivation, the *why* that lends meaning to your story, and the *how* that shows us your grandparents' unique style.

2) **Look inside and around you to uncover the *why* and the *how* of your stories.** To write the previous example, you might have recalled statements your grandparents themselves made in their conversations, statements in which the *why* and the *how* may be very clear. Your parents knew things about your grandparents that you don't. Look for answers for your *why* and *how* questions in the stories they shared with you when you were a child. If your parents are still alive, interview them about your grandparents. You might ask other relatives, too, for their

"Some of these things happened fifty years ago! Interpret them?! How do you expect me to remember the *why* and *how*!"

—Workshop writer

versions of the "bigger picture." In looking for insights, do not overlook your intuition: do visualization or use a combination of all the above. (see Chapter 2, Section D on Memory Jogs.)

3) **Avoid writing without insight into the *why* or the *how*.** Without these, your writing will not be satisfying for you to do or your readers to read. Most stories on TV are proof of this. They are well-plotted, but they offer no insight into the motivations of their characters other than what is necessary to wrap up the plot within its half-hour slot. Because these TV stories depend entirely on action rather than on well-rounded characters with internal motivation, TV characters can be called "stick" characters—portraits about as interesting as the one dimensional "stick" figures drawn by children and adults without much drawing ability.

These well-plotted TV stories leave thoughtful viewers unsatisfied, feeling they have wasted their time. How long can stick characters hold anyone's interest? Such vacuous stories demonstrate, once again, the importance of writing in not only the *what* but the *why* and the *how* of an action.

"I had no idea I was revealing so much about myself through my writing."

—Workshop writer

exercise

Analyzing a TV program can help your writing.

■ Record the plots of several TV shows.

■ Which were stuck at the chronology stage?

■ How did they make use of suspense? Was suspense enough? How so?

■ To what degree did each program depend on action that did not require the inner motivation of the character: the blond fluffhead was similar to the dark-haired fluffhead on another program; the dark, strong-but-silent type of one show could have been substituted for the blond, strong-but-silent type from another?

■ To what degree did each program attempt to show a character that was truly individualized (that could not be substituted for any other)?

■ Do you find the "fleshed out" characters more satisfying? Why?

C. Theme: it's the life of your lifestories.

Underlying all of your stories is its **theme**. The theme is really a message, the global way in which you understand your story—either in its entirety or in its parts. The theme conveys the essence of the *you* (or the *them*) that you want the reader, and history, to know and understand. The theme provides spirit to your piece, the breath of life that individualizes your lifestory.

All writing has a theme or a message. Theme can be superficial or deep. Sometimes you can recapitulate it in one word (e.g., perseverance). At other times, you need a phrase or a sentence (e.g., what happens to us in our lives is always part of our journey and not separate from it). Even the superficial, all-plot TV program has a theme, but it is likely to be something as shallow as "we're the 'good' guys and they're the "bad' guys" or as insidious (and hidden) as "materialism brings happiness."

1) **The theme is dependent on your *insights*.** Insights, as I mentioned in the previous section, are glimpses of understanding. ("Oh, that's *why*—or *how*—she did that!") When insights accumulate, as you view your stories over time, and bring them into ever sharper focus, you begin to see larger, broader conclusions about your subject's life—and even the meaning of life itself. The themes of your stories evolve from, and are synonymous with, these conclusions.

■ **Self-serving excuses should not be confused with insight.** For instance, we might write in our lifestories that it was because of our parents' style of raising children or of the strictures of our ethnic group or of the limitations imposed by our socio-economic class that we have not achieved certain goals. Of course, this "insight" fails to account for our failure as adults to create our own opportunities to overcome these very real shortcomings or to turn them into advantages in a creative way. This so-called "insight" then is really a self-serving excuse to avoid doing work on how we live our lives.

In this section, you will examine the message you impart to your reader through your lifestories.

"Desire is where perseverance comes from, where a certain necessary stubbornness comes from, and finally, it should be what makes people try to become better in the absolute sense."

—Madison Smartt Bell
writer

Our choice of theme tells us a lot about how we view life.

"Why *didn't* I hide Jews from the Nazis?" one man asked incredulously. "You have to understand—I had children. How could I risk their lives?!"

"Why *did* I hide Jews from the Nazis? another responded. "I had children! How could I *not* hide Jews? How could I risk leaving them a world like that, a world without Jews?"

—Dutch interview subjects in a TV documentary

2) **Theme influences choices for every element in the story: plot development, characterization, and setting.** Let's look at these elements. Here's the shell of the plot: your father was laid off; a difficult time followed for the family; your father received additional training and obtained a different job.

Your treatment of this plot will vary according to your theme. Let's suppose the following is your theme: "events whose consequences we can't understand happen gratuitously to us in our lives, but we can always make the best of things." In the elaboration of this particular theme (message), you will find it natural to set your father's being laid off not only with his reaction at the time but also with its consequences. Because of your positive theme, you will write about the new circumstances that developed for your father and about his psychological growth (character). To develop your theme, you will show how important it was for him to "roll with the punches," to allow himself to experience being without the identity his job and his role as family provider had furnished, and ultimately to exercise choices that led to new, satisfying pursuits.

So much for one plot development. Now imagine that your theme (obviously based on different insights) had been: "life deals each of us gratuitous, unwarranted dirty tricks and my father was no exception." In this story you would emphasize the role other people played in your father's being laid off and how no one helped him. You would dwell on the negative elements—how the economic demands made on him by his children left him with few choices, how his insufficient education (due in turn to his parents, his ethnic group, etc.) limited his job options. You would probably undervalue the training that led to a different job and fail to acknowledge the psychological growth that he experienced as a result of training and his new job challenges.

Both of these plot developments would be based on the same facts, but the stories themselves would be very different because they are inspired by very different themes. As a writer, you must be aware that your theme (the message you seek to impart) affects the interpretation of every fact in your story. By conscious use of theme, you can make a story into your own distinct and unique account.

3) **Discover the theme of your story** *as you proceed.* It is all right to begin writing without a specific theme in mind. As you write, and re-write (rewriting is crucial in deepening your sense of the story's meaning), be attentive to the theme which may gradually reveal itself to you. This process can be an intriguing one if you are open to it. Theme is revealed as you find yourself using certain words and phrases or expressing certain ideas over and over again. Discovering your theme in this way is not only important but it can catch your interest and make your lifewriting compelling. It will keep you coming back to your writing.

"A writer is not so much someone who has something to say as he is someone who has found a process that will bring about new things he would not have thought of if he had not started to say them."

—William Stafford
poet

e x e r c i s e

Look at the stories you have written so far and examine them for theme.

■ What are your stories saying beyond the facts? To find your theme, finish this sentence for each of several of your stories: "This story shows how it is important for people to..."

■ Are you gearing your theme to an intended audience (i.e., children or grandchildren)? How has this influenced the plot development, the characterization and your use of setting?

■ What have you discovered about your theme while writing? Has the theme changed? How has this affected your interest?

D. Inherited themes.

As you articulate your theme (whether you set out with a sense of it or "discover" it as you proceed), ask yourself if this theme is really yours—does it reflect your present understanding of your story and of life itself? Or is it is a residue of the accepted "wisdom" of someone else: a parent, another adult figure, society at large?

1) **A theme that is authentically yours makes for better writing.** Writers who recognize, acknowledge, and explore their own themes in their writing are more apt to present us with clear, to-the-point stories than those who repeat inherited themes or who think they can ignore the issue of theme.

Early in our lives, you and I were naturally and rightfully the recipients of someone else's—a parent's or grandparent's—understanding and interpretation of life. As long as these interpretations correspond to our own adult views, we can write easily within their context. What often happens, however, is that we continue to espouse a point of view inherited from another without realizing that it has ceased to correspond to our own. When challenged, we will say "Well, I guess I really don't believe that anymore. Isn't it something how I wrote (or said) that!"

■ **Inauthenticity in your theme will show up as a muddled point of view and mixed messages.** When you write—consciously or unconsciously—from someone else's perspective, and there is conflict between your view and theirs, your writing will show it. Your readers will sense that you're voicing someone else's themes, not your own. They will be uncomfortable with your story and may tend to dismiss it.

If you want to be taken seriously as a lifewriter by others, as well as by yourself, you have to accept that you are in charge. *This is your story.* You don't have to let someone else's perception dictate what you write—although it is often useful and honest to tell the reader how another person understood an experience or relationship differently. Elsewhere in this book, I have suggested that you include varying and even opposing accounts in your lifestories and that you attribute these accounts to the people who expressed them. You can do so by using phrases like "this is Irving's version of what happened…" Doing this will make it clear that you are not writing from anyone's point of view but your own.

■ **Championing someone else's themes is a major source of *writer's block*.** The natural way to see things is through your own point of view. The unconscious quickly refuses to provide "inspiration" to writers who subvert this natural relationship to life when they uphold someone else's point of view rather than their own. The result of this boycott by the unconscious is the dreaded writer's block. Sometimes writer's block is a way the unconscious has of telling us that we are not paying enough attention to our own insights. Next time you are stumped in your writing, ask yourself if you are being entirely authentic and personal in your choice of lifestory themes.

2) **When you distort your insights in order not to contradict other people's themes, your readers will tend to dismiss what you write.** They will know that your interpretation is not the product of insight but another instance of family white-washing. For instance, if you are driven (by your loyalty to a family theme) to depict a character as always fighting for good and justice, a true heroine, but in your heart you experience her as overbearing and rigid, your readers will intuit this conflict. Distorting your point of view to support a version you do not hold will lead your readers to distrust your writing both here and elsewhere (and possibly everywhere).

At the Workshops

Ursula wrote about her brother who was nine years older. Her story, an oft-told family tale, featured her brother as a cute prankster—at her expense. While babysitting, he had snuck castor oil into a drink he then offered her as a reward. Her miserable night of diarrhea as a result became a family joke, repeated over the years when relatives got together.

As she read, Ursula laughed about running to the toilet sixty years ago. "What a joker he was!" she said, as if it had happened to someone else. Her piece was well-written technically, but it lacked authenticity. The story was off balance.

When Ursula asked for our response, participants were restrained. Was it politeness because the group was new, I wondered, or had they not picked up that something was amiss in this story?

As leader, I wanted to assure the success of future discussions by making sure that we addressed story problems tactfully—and honestly.

"I need to know why your brother had permission to play such a trick," I ventured.

Ursula was surprised. He certainly didn't have permission to give her diarrhea!

In both my birth family and my present family, I went on, a child would have been prohibited from such behavior by his "inner censor." Such an abusive prank would not have been acceptable, to the child or anyone else because its "humor" depended on another's suffering. A discussion of family cultures ensued and broadened as others shared examples of values fostered and permissions tacitly understood within their childhood homes.

Ursula's mother, we learned, was a widow who indulged rather than disciplined her fifteen-year-old son. Her mother often gave in to him, Ursula admitted, though he repeatedly tormented younger siblings. Was this behavior a test of limits by a teenager seeking the security of an active parent in his life?

He was certainly right that he could get away with the castor oil prank. Even sixty years later, Ursula herself laughed as she told the story—she shared in giving him permission! Gently in the group we asked the questions Ursula had kept herself from asking all these years. Was it ok to deliberately make a six-year-old ill? Was it acceptable to hurt anyone else or just her? What other tricks were okay?

Her brother, she told us, left home early and had had little contact with the family since.

Several sessions later, I gave the assignment to re-write an earlier story using all the techniques we had since discussed to produce a more polished version. Ursula brought in her castor-oil story. Eyes glued to her paper, she took a deep breath and began to read. This time, she did not laugh. The story was no longer funny to her. In fact, she was angry—but not at her brother. He had acted out of immaturity. Rather, she was angry with her mother. Why had she not set limits as a parent should? How could she have allowed such behavior to pass as a joke? What were the costs to the family? Was she the only victim of her mother's diffidence?

Ursula understood that she had experienced her mother's attitude as abandonment. In her re-write it was obvious at once that she had produced a larger, better story because what she wrote was now her own authentic version. She had freed herself from repeating the family tale that cast her as the fall guy for a brother's abuse in order to mask a mother's neglect. In that official family version, her mother was absent. In Ursula's story, the mother was responsible for her out-of-bounds son, and more.

The group, now in its final weeks of meeting, told Ursula that they had been uncomfortable with her first draft and that they found this one more real. Ursula smiled with relief. She was a woman in her late sixties, but the abandoned child in her had been afraid of being chastised for airing what she had come to see as true.

Ursula referred to this story several times in remaining sessions. Re-working it from an inherited family tale to an authentic story of her life gave her valuable insight into her family culture and her life.

E x e r c i s e

Write about a theme in your life you've had a difficulty accepting as your own.

■ First, write the story from the point of view that was imposed on you. This is often a view, an attitude or a "truth" held by a parent (or teacher or clergyman). It's a story told about you that restricted your growth or that simply wasn't true for you. Typically, this parallel reality was confusing. Unable to contradict an authority figure, a child accepts misinterpretations as "truth." In this way, we can come to believe ourselves to be stupid, incapable, ugly, untalented (or worse) when, in fact, we are not. Sometimes children come to believe the opposite—that they are smarter, handsomer, more special than others than they really are.

■ Write about believing this false message and its effect on you and life choices you've made.

■ Now, write about the experience that altered your understanding. Did a new school or job or love affair contradict the negative messages you once accepted? How did you grow to know who you were and to look at life from your own point of view? ("I'm actually quite musical!")

■ What purpose did the untruth serve in your family or other contexts? Whose agenda or doctrine did it support?

■ In what ways, or in what parts of your life, do you remain loyal to this untruth that is an inherited theme? How can you remind yourself of the truth you now know is valid from your point of view?

E. Personal myths.

© 2005 M. Blowen

Myths **are the story forms of how we perceive the world and life.** How we live our lives is determined by our myths, but our lives also reveal our myths to ourselves and to the world.

■ **No life can be understood separately from its myths.** A myth is not a fantastical made-up story nor, as the word is commonly used, is it a synonym for "lie" or erroneous belief ("three myths about losing weight!").

■ **Dominant psychic forces, according to the Swiss psychoanalyst Carl Jung, play a powerful role in our lives.** He called these strong instincts (or patterns of thought) *archetypes.* Just as migratory birds have an instinct to fly north and south at appropriate times, we also are said to have a form of character instinct—archetype—that governs many of our actions and reactions. **These archetypes determine the contents of the *personal myths* by which we live our lives.**

■ **Throughout our lives, these archetypes have an influence on us—positive, negative and sometimes alternately one and then the other.** As we write lifestories about ourselves or other people, we need to assess their archetypes and how individuals were able to capitalize on or compensate for them.

The following archetypes—the *martyr, orphan*, and *prince-left-at-the-pauper's-door*—are only a few examples to help you to understand the role of personal myths. There are many more archetypes and, if you find you are interested in learning more about this topic, read some of the many books available on the subject. (See Appendix B.)

1) **People who are "giving" types can be said to be "martyrs."** They are the ones who always volunteer to take on extra tasks. As such, they are instrumental in the life of a community or organization and get much of its work done. Martin Luther King, Salvador Allende, and Mother Theresa are well-known and praiseworthy examples of the martyr archetype.

Society often clearly benefits from the sacrifices of martyrs who, pushed to their limits, are moved to give even their own lives for the higher good of the community at large.

On the negative side of this archetype is the martyr's need to be rewarded for his sacrifices by either gratitude or dependency. If others do not appreciate their devotion, some martyrs grow resentful or hurt. Martyrs don't always understand that their giving may be crippling or intrusive to others who may need to experience life's trials themselves in order to experience and attain their autonomy.

The martyr may use giving as an evasion of personal growth in other areas (e.g., "I'd love to take the Turning Memories Into Memoirs® workshop but my wife needs me at home. I can't possibly impose on someone to stay with her while I'm gone").

The life challenge of martyrs may be to find alternatives to giving to achieve personal fulfillment. Sometimes it is as hard for martyrs *not to give* as it is for selfish people to give!

For the lifewriter, the challenge is to differentiate between the positive and negative aspects of this archetype when it is encountered in a memoir character. The writer needs to explore how successful his subject was in combining the need to give with the need to pursue other areas of self-growth and with others' needs to be autonomous.

2) **People who do not develop or maintain personal ties can be said to be pursuing the orphan archetype.** Artists are an example of the positive side of this archetype. Because they feel detached from roots, family, etc., they are free to tell the truth as they see it, to risk much in the pursuit of their art. On the negative side, the orphan throws everything out too easily and starts again from scratch time after time—that start-up phase is exhilarating but the long term effect is exhausting. While orphan artists make use of their rootlessness to create, other orphans may be oppressed by their tendency to abandon what they have accomplished before they can benefit from the results.

The person who says she wants to write her lifestories but always allows herself to be interrupted by her family's demands is an example of the martyr. She uses giving to others as a way of avoiding doing her own important personal work.

© 2005 M. Blouin

The person who always tells you how he did everything for himself in life, how no one ever gave him anything, is an example of the *orphan.*

The *Cinderella* waits for Prince Charming to save her from the unpleasant drudgeries and responsibilities of her life.

Orphans often feel besieged by life, alone against the superior forces of the universe. In retaliation, they may react to life with cynicism and bitterness. Orphans love to tell you they are self-made—and will neglect to mention any help they received along the way.

When writing about a person who fits the orphan archetype, the lifewriter should certainly appreciate the struggle this person has waged. But she must also assess whether the orphan has been blind to the support available to him or the gifts life has offered him. Would a more objective account of his lifestory give credit elsewhere for his success or identify his cynical doomed-to-failure attitude as key to another one of his failures? The lifewriter should ask where the memoir subject found or made community and how he overcame the orphan's pervasive sense of alone-ness and abandonment. Since orphans often remake the facts to support their *self-made* views of themselves, writers must verify from other sources the hardship stories orphans tell.

3) **The prince-left-at-the-pauper's-door is imbued with a sense of his innate worth.** They may happen to be poor at the moment but they are "princes" (or "princesses") and have a right to special ("royal") status in life. Princes-left-at-the-pauper's-door aspire to be more and to have more than might seem reasonable to others and they often have the strength and courage to match their struggle to achieve. An example is the poor immigrant who arrives in a new country penniless and sees no reason why he should not rise "from rags to riches." Another example is a poor child who aspires to a fine education despite inferior local schools and lack of family support.

Of course, there is a negative side to the prince-left-at-the-pauper's-door archetype, too. These people may look disdainfully on the other "paupers" among whom they live ("I'm too good for these peons!") and so cut themselves off from participation in the community available to them. The prince-left-at-the-pauper's-door may be as lonely as the orphan. Inevitably, too, the high achievers, whether disdainful of others or not, will attract the resentment of the many they leave behind.

The lifewriter must look carefully at these princes-left-at-the-pauper's-door to distinguish which parts of their struggle were necessary and inevitable to attain their goals and which were needlessly injurious to them and others (forsaking relationships as not good enough, for instance).

■ **Writing from the perspective of personal myth can explain a lot about the stories you are recording.** In addition, consciously living archetypes in your own life and turning them into positive forces is a rewarding path for self-growth.

■ **Although archetypes can be compared to animal instincts, they are not as fixed.** They are inclinations that we are both born with *and* molded into, and they are strengthened by many factors.

Birth order is one of these factors. Older children, for instance, tend to be rewarded for being martyrs. Parents need their help to manage the younger ones. Encouraging an oldest child to be a wanderer or a dreamer would get in the way of the routine tasks of maintaining a large family. (An older child whose dominant archetype is the wanderer or dreamer may compromise and assume the role of victim. This fits the parents' goal but exacts its revenge by casting guilt on them.)

A youngest child sometimes has older parents who are financially at ease They may be ready to have more fun as parents than they could with the older children. They encourage "the baby" to take on the archetype of magician or clown. The baby can then be a playful person who is both more fun to be with and less likely to grow up too fast and move away from the parents.

■ **Our archetypes are not the only elements that create our personal myths.** Other's responses and the characteristics of the culture we live in play significant, complex roles.

■ **Lifewriting, because it enables us to become aware of various elements that create our personal myths, empowers**

People who have risen out of modest backgrounds and achieved much are often rejected by their siblings and former friends who have not achieved as much.

The *warrior* is the person who is always fighting city hall. He says, "I won't take any of that guff!"

> "People must not dissolve into a whirl of warring possibilities and tendencies imposed upon them by the unconscious, but must become the unity that embraces all possibilities and tendencies."
>
> —C.G. Jung

us to *choose the stories we will live out in our lives.* As you write about yourself or other people, be attentive to your active personal myths and interpret your stories in light of them. Know, too, that some of your lifestories are not yet finished! Insights you gain from exploring the past can be put to good use in your present and your future.

exercise

Fantasy can reveal what myths are operative for us.

■ Finish the following sentence as though you are telling a fairy tale: *"Once there was a (man or boy) (woman or girl) who——."* (Use your own gender for the fantasy character.) Make up a story, even a far out one, that comes readily to mind about him or her. Give your imagination free rein! Write for as long as you want. <u>Do not read the rest of this exercise until you have done this.</u>

■ Examples of fantasy starts:

"Once there was a man who did his best in his life. He wasn't the smartest or richest guy in the world, but he met each challenge as best he could."

"Once there was a little girl who loved to curl up in Mommy's lap. She was so cozy there she wanted never to get up. One day, Mommy's lap was smaller. It got smaller and smaller every day!"

■ Reread your story. In the place of "man" or "girl," insert your own name. What does this story now say about you? (Yes, it really is about some part of you!) In what sense does the story reveal a myth in your life? How does acknowledging this myth help you to understand what you have lived and how you feel about it? How can you use this understanding to achieve more depth in your lifestories? more awareness in your life?

F. *Don't preach to me!*

This section conveys how the misuse of theme can backfire.

The negative underside of theme is *preachiness.* You are preaching when you insist that your reader endorse your theme, message or point of view.

■ **Here's a way to distinguish between preachiness and the right use of theme.** Read your text out loud to yourself. If you have been preachy, your grand, all-inclusive phrases will jump out at you. Sometimes, in Turning Memories Into Memoirs® workshops, people laugh aloud with awareness as they read aloud such phrases as:

> "I'd like to see how many kids today would…"
> "In those days, we weren't afraid to…"
> "If you're going to do it right, you have to…"
> "The evil we see today is all due to…"

"Teenagers today don't realize how important little things in life are" is the beginning of a sermon. It is not the start of an insight.

On the other hand, "It was all I had for Christmas and it didn't matter to me then. We were all together and for that I was grateful" is not at all preachy. It states your reaction and the reader is free to accept or reject it.

Now let's alter this last example: "It was all I had for Christmas. Kids today wouldn't have been satisfied, but it didn't matter to me then." That little phrase, "kids today wouldn't have been satisfied," as innocuous or even true as it may seem, is preachy. As a grand, all-inclusive statement, it is likely to cost you your reader's attention. You lose credibility when you promote your *particular* experience as a *universal* truth.

In writing your story, you are sharing your experience and perhaps that of your generation, or ethnic group, or religious/philosophical community. Tell your story. Period. Don't thrust it on the reader as an example of the life-well-lived or of the superiority of a bygone era.

exercise

Successful lifestories stay clear of "preachiness."

■ Examine your stories for the kind of preachy phrases listed above.

■ Reread your stories to detect whether you are guilty of *pushing* your theme rather than *showing* it through the use of specific and striking details, character-based action and dialogue.

■ Now rewrite passages or stories without that preachy tone; allow your theme to unfold as an inevitable result of the plot you unfold.

G. *The glazed-over-eyes test*

> This section will help you save yourself from sliding into righteousness—and losing your reader!

1) **Submit your writing to a righteousness test.** Sixteen-year-olds have a built in preachiness detector. Recall one of your children or grandchildren at sixteen (or for that matter: remember yourself at that age!). Recall a time when she had a problem or unhappy situation.

Suppose an adult said the following to her, "Here's what you have to do!" Would those teenaged eyes glaze over? Would she get angry, change the subject, grow distant, leave the room? Or would she thank the adult profusely for setting him straight?

When you were preached at when you were sixteen, did you go out and alter your life to the advice? Fat chance!

Now imagine a slightly different exchange. Instead of saying "Here's what you have to do," the adult says, "I once had a similar situation. This is what I did."

Doesn't the prospect of a child or a grandchild asking, "How did it turn out? Is there anything you wish you'd done differently?" seem more likely now that the adult is not preaching?

Remember: a way to avoid preachiness is to focus on the individual and to *show* rather than *tell*. The next time you question whether or not your writing is getting preachy, try applying this litmus test: read your story to a sixteen-year-old!

2) **Be subtle rather than heavy-handed.** Literature (as is

true for any art form) works best on a subconscious level. Art can change lives—but not by hitting people over the head. Your story is more likely to uplift and inform if its theme is subtly presented. In fact, the reader will resist your preachiness and stop reading (just as the sixteen-year-old stops listening) if you use too heavy a hand.

The guidance your stories can provide is a major function of the tale well told. **Stories prepare us for living the future; they reassure us that we are not alone in our struggles and that we all share common problems.** Don't let the valuable lessons you have to share be dismissed because of preachiness.

LIFESTORIES FROM THE WORKSHOPS

Hardball with George
by Jan McLean

My oldest sister, Tinker, and her new husband, George, are living with us until they find an apartment. George is 23, Tinker's 22. I'm 10 years old, but people guess me to be around six 'cause I'm only 47 inches tall and weigh about 50 pounds. My nickname is Birdie.

My brothers and the neighborhood kids often play ball, "up the field," after supper. This night, George decides he'll play, too. When Ronny and Charlie divide up the teams, George asks, "Birdie's not playin', is she?"

"Ya, she's playing," says Ronny, who is 13. "We need her to even up the sides."

Which is the only time I get to play, I think to myself.

"We don't need her," George argues, looking at me. "She's too little, what can she do? I'd rather have less players than have her screw us up. We'll be sure to lose with her on our team."

"No suh," I yell at him. "Whadda' you know? You've never seen me play." I was not afraid to speak up when my brothers were around.

"Shuddup, Birdie," says Ronny. "I'll decide who's playin' and who's not."

"Well, I don't wan' 'er on my team," George says.

Jan McLean elicits our sympathy for one character by showing us another's meanness through the eyes of a child. Note that she uses active showing, not passive telling, and

avoids preaching
altogether.
Jan is a certified
Soleil Lifestory
Network teacher.
She lives in Exeter,
New Hampshire.

"She's already on your team. You can take it or leave it."

Wow! Ronny's sticking up for me? That's a switch.

"Is that right?" George says, stepping forward.

Paulie, who's 12, and Jerry, my twin, say, "Yeah, that's right," pushing out their chests, pulling themselves to their full height.

George looks at them for a few seconds, turns and says, "Okay, we'll see." He punches his hand into his glove as he walks onto the field.

My hands are sweaty, my heart's pounding. I take a deep breath. *Oh brother, I'm really gonna have to show 'em. God, please help me.*

The game starts. George is covering first base. Paulie's covering shortstop and second. I'm third baseman. Ronny is pitching. Jerry and Jimmy are playing right and left field. I don't have a glove. There aren't enough to go around.

Ronny tells me, "You won't need a glove. You won't be doing that much."

Wanna' bet? We'll see.

George catches a fly ball between first and second base. It's an out. Suddenly, a ball is flying fast and hard at my head. I duck.

"See, see, I told cha'," shouts George, running and pointing his finger at me. "I told cha' she couldn't do it. Look at ha', she ducks when I throw it to ha', for god's sakes. She's a real plus to this team, isn't she?"

I slam my hands on my hips. "Why did cha' even throw the ball to me?" I yell. "There was no one on base. I didn't expect ya to throw it."

Ronny yells from the pitcher's mound, "What the hell are ya doin', George? Why did cha' throw the ball to her?"

"I was testing ha'," he says in his New Jersey accent. "And she flunked. She ducks, for cripes sake."

"Ya' threw it right at my head. You'd duck, too."

"Oh, sure, right, ya, right," he says. "Ya' always have to be ready. That's the name of the game."

"He's right, Birdie," says Ronny. Ya' do that again and you're out."

I'm out? What about him? I twist up my face in disgust, roll my eyes, and shake my head. "Jerk," I mumble to myself.

"And George, you didn't need to wing the ball at her like that," Ronny adds.

"Is that right?" George asks.

Paulie, Jerry, Jimmy, and Charlie MacLeod on the other team yell back, "Yeah, George, that's right!"

Wow, everyone's stickin' up for me. This is great. I feel strong and powerful.

The game goes on. Charlie's on first. George runs for a fly ball to right field and catches it. He throws it to me. I catch it and tag Charlie out. My brothers are yelling and jumping up and down, throwing their fists into the air. "Way da' go, Birdie, way da' go. Great play! Yahoo!"

George shakes his head. "Aww, she was lucky. I threw the ball right to her. How could she miss it? Wait'll she gets up at bat. We'll see."

When I'm at bat, I bend over the plate like I see the boys doing, making it difficult for the pitcher to throw the ball between my shoulders and knees for a strike.

Ronny yells to me, "Remember, Birdie, keep your eye on the ball. Let 'em walk ya."

I want so much to hit that ball, but I'm scared. If I miss, they'll kill me. Ronny'll yell, "I told cha' not to swing at the ball. Now look at what cha' did."

As always, I get walked. "Way da' go, Birdie, that's watching it." My team yells and hoots as I walk to first base. *Big deal,* I wanna say.

When the game is over, George, who is standing about 10 feet away, yells, "Quick, Birdie, catch this one."

He throws the ball straight at me, like a jet plane at full speed. With no time to think, I catch it with my bare hands. It pushes me back a few feet. My right hand burns and hurts like a big iron door's been slammed on it. Within seconds, it puffs up to twice its size. I walk across the field and and back to my house. My hand has now turned black and blue. I rest it against my right shoulder. It pains, throbs.

But I say nothing to George. I don't want him to know he got me.

I sneak some ice from the refrigerator, go to my room, wrap the ice in a face cloth, lie on my bed, and carefully hold my hand over the ice 'til the throbbing lessens.

George seemed so nice at the wedding, I think. I wonder if all men turn out mean after they get married.

Chapter 7—I Need to Know

A.   Writers must be readers, too!

B.   Take time out from writing.

C.   Let's get personal.

D.   Lifewriting as therapy.

E.   Journal keeping.

F.   Men and lifewriting.

G.   Be a "real" writer.

H.   *Vive la différence*—using foreign words.

I.   Buying a computer.

J.   Learning more than word processing.

K.   Tape recording your stories.

L.   Writing when you have young children.

LIFESTORIES FROM THE WORKSHOPS:
    Grandma's Last Laugh by Libby J. Atwater

Writing your lifestory is a highly personal process. *Turning Memories Into Memoirs* offers guidelines to maximize your experience but it shies away from presenting fixed procedures because what will seem immediately compelling for one lifewriter may not interest another for a long time. The questions answered in this chapter sometimes get asked early in one workshop while in another they might not come up at all until I bring them up.

> This chapter answers the questions that come up frequently during lifestory writing workshops.

A. Writers must be readers, too.

Q. Will reading make me a better lifewriter?

A. Absolutely! Familiarity with other writers can teach you a lot about effective writing techniques as you develop your own style. *Reading* good memoirs will help you to *write* a good memoir. As children, we learned by imitation—it's still a key strategy for adults as we practice the skills we need to master. Reading others' memoirs is an essential first step in writing your own.

In general, read widely and voluminously. In particular, read memoirs, autobiographies, and biographies. (See Appendix B for a reading list.) Read not just books but periodicals. Read as a writer—i.e., study how others have handled their stories. What can you repeat—or use as inspiration? How do the writers introduce their characters and their action? How do they develop the conflicts that make up the action of their stories? Have they used the technique of suspense? Have they started close enough to the final crisis or climax? What are the

> It makes as much sense for a writer not to read other writers as it does for a composer not to go to concerts, an athlete not to attend sports events or a gardener not to visit other people's gardens.

Reading as a writer will teach you effective writing techniques. A good writer is necessarily a good reader.

turning points of their stories and how are the conflicts resolved? Have they used specific and striking details in describing characters, actions and settings? Is point of view used effectively? Is the tone in each story appropriate for its theme? Is the theme presented without preachiness? How are unpleasant truths handled? How have the authors ended their stories? How do these writers handle transitions from one segment (or one story) to another?

Reading beyond technical matters, study how others have dealt with stories whose topics or themes are similar to yours. Which effective elements in these stories can you include in your own? What fresh perspectives does this create for you?

Certainly, at the very least, reading memoirs will jog your memory and give you an expanded sense of possibilities. Don't forget: the more you know, the more detailed the background of your writing will be and the fuller your stories.

B. Take time out from writing.

"As for my next book, I am going to hold myself back from writing it until I have it impending in me: grown heavy in my mind like a ripe pear; pendant, gravid, asking to be cut or it will fall."

—Virginia Woolf
novelist

Q. *How will I know the difference between avoiding writing and taking time to let an idea mature?*

A. Writing is hard work, and there will be many times when it seems too difficult. You'll sit at your desk and not much will come. Your impulse will be to get up to do something—anything—else, as long as it's not writing! You'll think of the lawn that needs mowing, the closet that needs cleaning, etc.

In order to distinguish between avoiding writing and letting an idea mature, think for a moment about exercising. You may not always enjoy exercising but you know the difference between avoiding it and having a legitimate reason to skip it this time—a reason such as being sick or having a temporary crunch in your schedule. After you avoid exercise, you feel guilty; after putting it off for a valid reason, you feel disappointed.

Even if you have avoided writing in the past, you can

decide not to do so in the future. Remind yourself of your writing objectives: reread your mission statement. Instead of wasting energy on self-recriminations, rededicate yourself to the task and its rewards—and get writing!

There will be times, however, when writing is blocked. Rather than forcing yourself to continue, you feel compelled to put your work aside and go out for a walk. You may feel a bit jumbled at first, but, as you do something else—clean house or make a cup of tea—you'll become aware that you are still grappling with your story, not avoiding it at all. Suddenly an idea arises "out of nowhere" and, *voilà*, you understand your story. Sometimes the breakthrough presents itself later that day or the next over a stack of dishes, or in the quiet of a walk in the woods, or as you look out the window watching the snow.

As you write many stories, it is likely the process will call for this kind of time out. Don't be afraid to let it happen. Don't force your writing. Give yourself permission to step back and reflect on your experience—then get back to writing.

C. Let's get personal.

Q. *Isn't it self-important to record my inner life?*

A. Not at all! *Our lives are composed not only of facts and dates but also of dreams, expectations—realized or denied—and hopes.* Since you are not alone in having lived an inner life, you are more likely to attract praise rather than scorn for sharing it.

If there is a place where you can say "This is who I really was and who I really am," where you can share with others who'll understand the hero's journey you have undertaken, it is in your lifestories. Here, you can document the inner changes, the emotional turmoil, the psychological victories, defeats and challenges that have made you the person you are today.

You'll derive several benefits from being personal.

■ **You will gain respect for the inner journey you have**

> "If there is a secret to writing, I haven't found it yet. All I know is you need to sit down, clear your mind, and hang in there."
>
> —Mary McGrory
> columnist

> "Why is it that I get my very best ideas in the morning while shaving?"
>
> —Alfred Einstein
> scientist

"The soul becomes dyed with the color of its thoughts."

—Marcus Aurelius
Roman emperor

"I wrote the most angry letter I have ever written. It felt good. After I read it over, several times, I tore it up and threw it away. I didn't need it any more."

—Workshop writer

taken in your life; you will appreciate the uniqueness of your responses to people, events and developments.

If you have not always lived your life wisely, what better time than now to come to terms with that? Lifewriting offers you the chance to examine without judgement patterns of behavior and attitudes from the past and to explore new ways of how you go about being yourself. Fresh insights gained from lifewriting will infuse your awareness. Your writing—the act itself and the resulting stories—will allow you to see and utilize new ways of being that serve not just survival but positive personal growth.

■ **Your readers will be comforted.** By not holding back, you offer reassurance and guidance that others may need, and even crave, as they make their own ways through life.

■ **You will create access to your family history's inner story—a benefit future generations can use and enjoy.** Understanding the inner life of your family can help you and your descendants to appreciate your cultural inheritance. (And those who ignore family history are destined to repeat it!) Don't shortchange yourself and your family with a memoir that is just a chronology of dates and facts. There is so much more that posterity deserves to know!

Remember: it's okay to write something you do not reveal to anyone! You don't have to share every scrap you write. Once you have benefited from the insights you gain, you can destroy that piece or store it where only you will see it.

Interestingly, even insights you don't share will become part of your legacy. Shifts in your understanding will influence your theme; your understanding will have an impact on the on-going inner life of your family and its awareness of its past.

The journey of self-exploration is as old as the human race. Writing it down it is not vulgar or self-important and it certainly is not always easy. Rather, it is a commitment you make to your true self and a gift of understanding, guidance and reassurance you give to those who come after you.

D. Lifewriting as Therapy.

Q. *I still don't understand: why does lifewriting sometimes feel so much like therapy ?*

A. We all have facades, views of ourselves that we are willing to make public. When you meet someone at a party, it's his public self you see. Later, should you become friends, you may have access to his private self—if he is willing.

It's natural to maintain privacy boundaries. Unfortunately, living with a facade can make us strangers even to ourselves. Lifewriting gives us both permission and a process for going beyond the public facade in the stories we and our families have told about ourselves.

Witnessing one's true self is a healing experience, so the more objective and truthful you are, the more integrating and healing is the result.

Our lives fall out of balance as we live out the dichotomy between others' versions of who we were, are, or should be, and our own. Lifestory writing helps us to accept our versions and to discard the ones others impose so that, ultimately, we can become ourselves.

Psychological therapy, at its best, integrates how we view our lives with how we live them. It also provides us with the strength to stop living as if our facades and other people's views of us were our true selves. That's why lifewriting and therapy resemble each other in so many ways.

> "Writing has helped me heal. Writing has changed my life. Writing has saved my life."
>
> —Louise DeSalvo
> writer/teacher

> "Writing is a form of therapy; how do all those who do *not* write, compose, or paint manage to escape the madness, the melancholia, the panic and fear which is inherent in the human condition?"
>
> —Graham Greene
> novelist

E. Journal Keeping.

Q. *What tool or technique can you suggest to overcome writer's block—and lack of fluency?*

A. When keeping a regular (even daily) journal, some people feel a release of energy they don't have in other writing forms. Because of that, journal keeping can be an important develop-

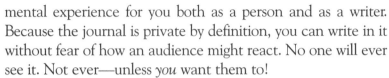

"Is Turning Memories Into Memoirs® a consciousness-raising group, a psychological exercise or a literary workshop? —I found that it's all of these; the different threads of awareness weave in and out and together they make the fabric of a written lifestory."

—Workshop writer

mental experience for you both as a person and as a writer. Because the journal is private by definition, you can write in it without fear of how an audience might react. No one will ever see it. Not ever—unless *you* want them to!

1) **Your journal is a kind of writing laboratory.** Scientists use a laboratory to conduct experiments. They check what results from adding this to that, from changing relationships and quantities and sequences. Sometimes when the results are interesting and prove worth pursuing, they continue conducting experiments in similar areas, pairing these findings with those from other experiments.

The journal can be this sort of laboratory for your writing. What if you record your dreams? What if you make lists? What if you do free associations of ideas? What if you recreate the past as you wish it had been? (Give yourself a commanding role! Have everything turn out "the way it was supposed to!")

You can also experiment with various styles and techniques to record your feelings and perceptions. What if you write only in long sentences? or only in short ones? Or never use the word *I*? Or use stream of consciousness (thoughts just as they come without any editing)?

Perhaps your writer's block is due to being cramped by the emotional limits you have imposed on yourself. Use your journal as a place to break free to a more authentic you.

2) **Your journal will help you to be fluent in your writing even if you do not experiment.** As in anything, the more you do it, the better you are likely to become at it. Swim every day and, after a month, you'll find yourself having become much better—and, after six months, a whole lot better. Writing in your journal regularly, you will get practice time that will serve you well. Your writing will grow to be a more familiar and comfortable experience and you will be more fluent and accomplished with it.

3) **Writing in your journal before starting your lifewriting sessions can be an effective warm-up.** Athletes don't start

their sport immediately without warming up. Why shouldn't a writer warm up, too? Limber up your writing muscles with a page or two of journal writing.

4) **Journal writing will provide you with memories and perceptions that will inform your lifestories.** If you assure yourself of the journal's absolute inviolability, the inner censor who insists "You can't write that!" will grow less demanding. You will feel freer to write your own feelings and thoughts. Later many of your entries or parts of them can be transcribed into your lifestories as you give yourself permission to tell a different version of your life. In the privacy of the journal, you will grow comfortable with your new "heretical" versions.

Remember: there are few rules in journal-writing (honesty, however, is one of them). You can include journal entries in your lifestories (where there are some rules).

exercise

Try these journal stretches. You don't have to share them—unless you want to.

■ Make a character profile of a person from your past. Can you include this profile in your lifestories?

■ Make a "word portrait" of an animal you loved dearly as a child or an adolescent. Transcribe it from your journal into one of your stories.

■ In your journal, as free association, write ten words that describe your mother. Include the words in your lifestory. You can also use each of the words as a jumping off point to create scenes.

F. Men and lifewriting.

Q. Why do fewer men than women undertake lifewriting?

A. I don't know why it is that fewer men write their lifestories.

Perhaps the reason is one of these:

■ **Men often feel they lack permission to express their feelings.**

■ **Men often feel that introspection is not in keeping with being masculine (whatever that may be).**

■ **Men often accept that family affairs are under women's jurisdiction and that passing on family culture and history is therefore women's responsibility.**

In the Turning Memories Into Memoirs® workshops I have presented over the years, there have always been many fewer men than women. Men are also more likely to drop their memoir projects. Why this should be so is all the more difficult to understand since history has given us many artists and philosophers—explorers of both the feeling life and of the depths of the psyche—who are men. This is the very domain in which lifewriting excels.

Assigning exercises in workshops, I have seen men turn to their wives and ask, "Now why did I do that?" One man even asked his wife, "What were the important events in my life?"

At least since the advent of the Industrial Revolution, society has had a vested interest in keeping men far from their feelings. How else could men have accepted to spend their lives at dreary, repetitive jobs that held no intrinsic meaning for them! Even today, our society would collapse if men refused to do the work they are conditioned from boyhood to do—conditioned both by their fathers and their mothers.

Although some men break through stereotypes—some at the price of being seen as less "masculine"—to become artists, visionaries and philosophers, many reject the idea of engaging in what they perceive as a "feminine" domain like lifewriting.

Undertaking the challenges of lifewriting can go against a lifetime of masculine indoctrination. Contacting one's feelings is a powerful—and therefore frightening—experience! In the end, it's the healthiest challenge a person can accept, regardless of gender.

"You need only to claim the events of your life to make yourself yours."

—Florida Scott Maxwell
writer

"I felt that if I told my story, I would be struck by lightning."

—Workshop writer

So, women—liberate a man in your life—your mate, your father, your son, your friend—so that he can connect with his feelings. Buy him a copy of *Turning Memories Into Memoirs*, and support his lifewriting in every way you can.

G. Be a "real" writer.

Q. *Will lifewriting make me a "real" writer?*

A. Have you approached lifewriting with a hidden agenda? Have you wanted to be "a writer"—even "a Writer"—for a long time but aren't sure how to do it? As a reader all your life, you may feel you have a book or two of your own in you—a memoir or a novel? Or are magazines and newspapers where you long to see your own stories in print?

Have you undertaken lifewriting with the hope that it will lead you into being "a writer" (or was that "a Writer")?

In workshops, participants ask me, "Do you think I'm good enough to be a 'real' writer?" It's impossible to answer this question directly. In a now often-quoted letter, the poet Rainer Maria Rilke answered a young writer who posed this very question: you must ask yourself if you *need* to be a writer.

Writing is not easy. Most writers don't write for money—it just doesn't work that way in our society. They don't write for fame—it evades most who seek it. Most writers write because they must—the process itself is soul-nourishing for them in a way that nothing else is.

If this is true for you, then you are a *real* writer. Real writers whose voices are mostly heard regionally and locally tap the same internal source as nationally and internationally known writers do—the inner need to engage in the process.

Writing, if you do it intently and regularly, every day, must be impelled by that inner force. It's one thing to write now and then as you feel moved—early in the morning over coffee or on a rainy, moody day, or to write short pieces to enter-

Don't let "success" at writing be defined by someone else! Determine for yourself what your criteria for success will be.

"Ask yourself in the stillest hour of the night: must I write?"

—Rainer Maria Rilke
poet

"...the arranging of artists in a hierarchy of merit is an idle and essentially dilettante process. What matters are the needs which art answers."

—John Berger
art critic

"Writing is easy: all you do is sit staring at a blank sheet of paper until drops of blood form on your forehead."

—Gene Fowler
writer

Emily Dickinson is a well-known, major American writer. She published seven of her 1800 poems during her lifetime!

tain your friends on special occasions. It's quite another to plan and execute a book project of several hundred pages, to achieve unified tone, sustained imagery, and consistent development of thought, character and theme. Writing then is a job and it calls for discipline and commitment.

Unlike many other jobs, writing is speculative. Very few writers are paid before they produce a piece. When most people have a bad day at work, they still collect their paychecks. When a writer has a bad day, he has a full wastebasket (or these days, an empty computer disk)—and no paycheck at all. **So if you are going to keep writing, there must be something internal driving you!**

Your writing may well command a larger audience, and it may interest regional and national publishers. Your ambition to reach out, however, ought not to cloud your need to first write the best book you are capable of.

Remember: selling your work doesn't come first. Writing comes first. Strive to be *real* (authentic) in your inspiration, your commitment, your practice; money and fame have nothing to do with these. It is the *process* of writing itself that can make you a real writer. The *product* is the end result, not the starting point. That product can be real in many forms. Many writers I have worked with have seen their stories published in periodicals and newspapers and in self-produced collections. These writers have the rewards of reaching and coming into contact with their audiences directly—something many authors published by a mega-publisher seldom experience.

The life experience you share in your writing may fit the niche of regional or local publications that regularly seek seasonal and historical stories—holiday customs, gardening tips of yesteryear, reminiscences of extreme weather. Collections of such stories with a theme or setting to link them make a book of local interest. Make a research project of educating yourself about the publishing opportunities in your area; adapt your pieces to fit the bill, and you may find a natural vehicle for your work.

Remember: you can be a "real" writer wherever, however you publish and even if you do not publish.

H. Vive la différence—*using foreign words.*

Q. *My grandchildren don't speak our language. Should I eliminate all non-English words and phrases from my text?*

A. My preference is to use foreign words in lifestories because it recreates a world that was once yours. That's what we are all doing with our writing: celebrating a world that no longer exists. Yvette Audet's story in Appendix A would be impoverished had she eliminated *Mémère* for *Grandmother*. These and many other "foreign" (to some but not to her) words in her text give us the flavor of the home and community she grew up in.

One way to make sure that these words are understood is to do any of the following:

■ **include a translation** in parenthesis immediately after you have used the word—e.g. "*placek* (a sweet Polish bread)."

■ **paraphrase the word or phrase right away**—e.g. "'*Arrête!*" she said. "Stop!'"

■ **provide a translation in a note** at the end of your book or at the bottom of the page.

Remember: italicize all **non-English words** (except place names, personal names, or foreign words that are now accepted terms in English, such as "matinee," "facade" or "pizza").

I. *Buying a computer.*

Q. *Should I buy a computer if I don't have one?*

A. Most people who do lifewriting do so on computers. Unfortunately, there are still some diehard technophobes out

Why should society be a melting pot? Think of it as a tossed salad of different flavors and textures, each ready to be experienced. A bowl of plain iceberg lettuce?—not for me, thanks!

"You mean I won't have to sit down every night and force myself to type three pages until I catch up with my stories?"

—Workshop writer

there who have resisted purchasing a computer. If this is you, don't let your uneasiness keep you from learning to make use of this valuable tool.

I encounter two types of *technophobes*. (See if you recognize yourself here. If so, there's hope! You can become a *technophile*, if you choose to!)

1) **First are those who absolutely refuse to use a computer.** I urge you—if you intend to write more than a handful of stories—certainly if you intend to write more than fifty pages—buy a computer. The difference between typewriting and writing on a computer is the difference between a washboard and an automatic washing machine.

For many lifewriters, a second-hand computer is just fine. Most people don't need the latest gadgets. A system that's a few years old will cost much less than a new one and, for all practical purposes, will serve your needs quite well. Perhaps your child or grandchild has a used machine to pass on to you?

Writing your stories requires significant emotional and artistic commitment. Why add the drudgery of typing page after page multiple times?

Using a computer makes every mechanical step of preserving your story easier. For instance, adding a sentence at the beginning of a story involves typing just that new sentence, not retyping the entire story or trying to eliminate another sentence with the same number of words so your page break will still fall in the same place. For those who long ago made the switch to computers (or who have never used a typewriter!) time and effort spent on retyping is a senseless waste of valuable writing time.

Today's word processing programs have a **spell-check** function and can even check your grammar and sentence structure. These are helpful guides as you work towards a clean, professional manuscript.

Other benefits of computers include the ease of incorporating photographs into your text and of producing quick, easy and inexpensive duplicate copies of your document. It's also simple to share your stories with others via e-mail.

2) **Then there are the people who own computers but can't access the benefits because they haven't committed to learning how they work.** These computerphobes do a little word processing but don't know how to format text, organize their files, send e-mail attachments, or use basic photo-editing programs. Whether they feel bad about this or not, they are missing out!

What can you do if you're a computerphobe?

■ **The first step is simple: fully appreciate the advantages** of using a computer, as I've described above (and your kids have been telling you for years!).

■ **The second step is to make the transition** by overcoming your fear, reluctance, impatience, or discouragement. (Recall other complex things you have mastered in your life. Think of yourself as someone who *can*, not as someone who *can't*.)

You can make this transition in a number of ways.

■ **First, accept that there is a learning curve.** The first month of concerted effort is likely to be awkward; you'll be tempted to give up. Don't! Learning to use a computer takes time: its logic may be unfamiliar to you—or you may discover that you are a computer natural! In any case, be easy on yourself. **Don't expect too much too soon.** Do simple things first; find the Help program, get familiar with the manual. Once you get used to your computer, you'll wonder why you ever waited!

■ **Use your manuals again and again; follow suggested steps.** Computer programs come with tutorials that lead you step-by-step through learning the basics. These are well worth your time. Or you may want to stop by your local library or bookstore to pick up an expanded instruction manual. Choose one that uses easy-to-understand language.

■ **Take computer literacy classes.** Your community adult education program is a great resource. It puts you in touch with others who are at your level (no need to feel self-conscious) and gives you access to a teacher who is an experienced com-

"I thought everyone in the class would be way ahead of me and I'd be embarrassed to be so ignorant. The first night, I stood
in the door and watched the class for a minute—and suddenly it occurred to me—the reason they're here is the same reason I am—they don't know anything either!"

—Adult ed learner

puter user and whose job it is to help you understand.

Please note: I don't recommend that you turn to computer companies or expect more than troubleshooting from phoneline help. Their interest is in selling computers, after all, and while simple mistakes can be unravelled by the young fellow you talk with (if that particular problem is on his list), you'll do better with a relative or friend who can advise you. (Don't forget that your adult ed teacher is familiar with the kinds of problems new users have and can help you.) Computer literacy is now so widespread that it's highly unlikely that you don't know someone who can help. An experienced user may also be able advise you before you purchase to clarify your needs and then be available to facilitate your learning.

Here's a final encouragement. Despite the fact that computers seem intimidating, they're actually quite simple. Designers have gone to great lengths to develop programs that are user-friendly. Their success depends on yours!

Remember: the more effort you put into learning, the more you'll get out of your training. With a little patience and a positive attitude, you'll learn to use this valuable writing tool successfully. Good luck—and go for it!

εxεrcisε

Start today to make your transition from technophobe to technophile.

■ Identify a person you know who is knowledgeable about computers. Ask that person to help you. Make a first date for a specific, limited time. (Remember: you'll get overwhelmed fast!)

■ Read through the index of the Help program that is part of your word processing program.

■ Read the program's manual. Don't try to memorize details; instead look for how info is organized. This will tell you where to look for categories of functions when you need help.

■ Challenge yourself to do one computer function you've been afraid of before. Use your Help program when you get stuck.

■ Remember: you have already done many hard things in your life. You can do this, too!

J. Learning more than word processing.

Q. *I know how to get words on my computer screen. Should I learn more complicated functions?*

A. Today's computers are very sophisticated. Most of us won't ever learn to use everything they offer. But it is useful to master many of the functions that will facilitate not only writing your lifestory but also making the page layout for a book or booklet and publishing your memoir in multiple copies. Page layout can be as simple or as advanced as you choose.

At the very least, you will want to use the most basic word processing functions—adding and deleting copy, moving paragraphs, cutting and pasting, saving files under various names, spell-checking, and printing. But if you want to individualize the look of your manuscript, you'll need to know how to change the fonts and font sizes, add bold or italic text, alter the page size and margins, make headers and footers. and insert page numbers.

Perhaps you'll want to add photographs—you'll need to know how to scan images, import them, and wrap text around them. You may want to insert large sections of text from another file, or link separate stories together as one document, or e-mail your stories to a friend. All are possible. The people who designed the program you are using knew you'd want to do these things and more.

The great thing about a computer is that you can learn as little or as much as you want. First, ask yourself what you want to do. Then, learn it by reading the Help program, attending classes, asking someone to show you, and then—practice what you've learned. You'll be surprised at what you're capable of doing!

K. *Tape recording your stories.*

Q. *Is tape recording a story okay? It's easier!*

A. Preserving a story in any form is always better than letting it be lost. Audio-taping a story can be a marvelous way to record people's voices and all that reveals about their lives. (You might also think of video-taping.)

Taping can be a creative option, but it is not necessarily easier than writing. If you think so, you are in for a quite surprise!

You can, of course, record stories "off the cuff," but these will have the same rough quality as the first drafts of a written story.

For the best results, that is, to finish your project with a comprehensive, thoughtful, meaningful, entertaining and satisfying life on tape, you will need to:

■ **prepare your recording with the same Memory Lists that a writer makes.** Elements in your Memory List should be grouped together. You will have to decide whether you want to link your stories chronologically, thematically, biographically or by the era.

■ **grapple with the questions of theme** as you try to make meaning out of your life's experience.

■ **deal with truth.** What is it and how much of it should you tell? (Is it really easier to speak the truth aloud on tape than to write it on the page?)

■ **conduct interviews and do research to make sure your facts are correct.** You will also have to make use of memory jogs.

■ **face pain and experience the therapeutic effects of telling your story.**

■ **listen to your story and have others listen to it to help you to edit it.** You will have to re-tell it in the same way that a writer has to re-write.

> "She had that old-time Newfoundland accent. I've got it down on tape. Listening to it really takes me back."
>
> —Workshop writer

Remember: tapes need tape players; books can be opened anytime, anyplace—even years from now. Books are bigger and less likely to be misplaced. And, you can't erase or melt a book in the same way you can destroy a tape!

L. Writing when you have young children.

Q. *I have young children. I don't seem to have the writing time I need.*

A. People with young children *can* find time to write. Here are several options.

■ **Enroll the child(ren) in an occasional pre-school program or arrange for other childcare.**

■ **Parents can negotiate with their child(ren).** Whatever their age and in keeping with that age, children can learn how to respect a parent's commitment.

Whenever I say this to people, there are those who snicker, "Ha, we can tell you don't have kids!" On the contrary, I have two and I often wrote while caring for them. Like everyone else, children learn to meet the expectations that are set for them. Parents whose kids demand constant attention are parents who have trained their children by giving them implicit permission to be tyrants. When kids get the cue that their parents expect—or will tolerate—interruptions, then that's what they do—on cue!

When my own kids were as young as three and four, they were able to respect the occasions when I needed to meet a publication deadline. Alone in the house with them, I would point to the clock and tell them that when the hands were at a certain place, I would stop work to read them a story or go for a walk. Meanwhile, I made sure they had toys available and a snack ready. I put them in charge of having the snack at a certain time. Because I always honored *my* part of the agreement, my children almost always kept *theirs*. There were even days

When you tell your child, "Mama's been working too long and she 's sorry you had to interrupt her again," you're giving him *permission* to interrupt you. Children make their choices based on experience: interrupting Mama when she is writing is okay—Mama will stop so you can get away with interrupting her anytime.

when under pressure of a deadline, I wrote both morning and afternoon. Even then, the children respected my need—but my writing day was always interspersed with meeting theirs, too: snacks, meals, readings and walks as well as interventions—*patient* interventions!—to settle squabbles.

Your children recognize the seriousness of your commitment to many things in your life: your job, your house and yard chores, bill-paying, cooking, keeping dentist appointments. It is because you will not put these tasks off that your children accept your commitment. Why not put lifewriting in this category?

Remember: expectations are often self-fulfilling. When others consistently play the role of obstacle to your writing and you consistently fail to overcome the difficulty, you might ask yourself, "Am I avoiding my commitment to writing? Am I using others as excuses not to write? Am I unconsciously evading this work? Why?"

LIFESTORIES FROM THE WORKSHOPS:

Grandma's Last Laugh
by Libby J. Atwater

Libby Atwater has written a sad story with much laughter in it. Her use of the

As the plane descended through thick cloud cover, sleet falling heavily on its wings, the world outside seemed as cold and gray. The weather in Chicago this first day of spring mirrored our feelings. We were here to attend Grandma's funeral.

When we walked out the gate at O'Hare, I saw the security checkpoint where Grandma had been stopped eight years earlier. She'd led the delegation of aunts, uncles, and cousins who'd come to see us off for Los Angeles. As Grandma walked through the security checkpoint, the alarm sounded. She stopped, emptied her coat pockets, and walked through a second time. The alarm rang again. The guard had asked Grandma to step aside. His colleague ran a detection wand over her body. "Beep, beep,

beep," had gone the wand. The guard asked Grandma to hold her arms out, and he frisked this 85-year-old woman in an old wool coat and a *babushka*.

Although she usually liked being the center of attention, that day, Grandma laughed nervously. Aunt Ella and I stood nearby, so convulsed with laughter that tears ran down our cheeks. The guard finally discovered that the wand only beeped around Grandma's head: her hearing aid had set it off.

flashback technique allows for a breadth of emotion. As a Soleil Lifestory Network teacher, Libby offers workshops and writing services in the Ventura, California, area.

As I passed this checkpoint, I smiled even as I thought, *She was gone from us now.*

The sleet turned to snow during the 40-minute ride from the airport to our cousins' home. Two days before, on the Feast of St. Joseph, Grandma had eaten her breakfast and died. St. Joseph is the patron saint of a happy death, and Grandma had been praying to him for a long time. After 93 years on earth, she was ready to go on to the next world and join the rest of her generation. Born on All Saints' Day, dead on the Feast of St. Joseph: the two most significant events of her life occurred on holy days. In the eyes of our family, she was special—even holy.

Images of Grandma flashed through my mind as the car slowed on the slippery streets. I pictured the Halloween that she had answered the door in a Star Wars' Yoda mask, startling the young children at the door. Her short, white hair stood up in wisps around the green rubber mask. We laughed, and she insisted we take her picture.

I didn't feel sad—she had died as she had wished—but I was sorry that she could no longer be around to laugh her infectious laugh as she told one of her stories. Grandma's eyes lit up each time she recalled the winter night when she and two girlfriends had walked home from ice skating. A man approached them. Grandma noticed that his pants were unzipped, exposing his private parts. She made the sign of the cross and yelled, "Jesus, Joseph, and Mary." Then she slammed him with her ice skates. The man howled and limped away as Grandma and her friends ran the rest of the way home.

Grandma managed to find the humor in every situation, even the Great Depression. During this period, Grandma's family of five shared their three-bedroom flat with her sister's family of four. One day, her sister announced that she was pregnant. "Can you imagine?" Grandma giggled. "There was no privacy in that apartment, yet they managed to conceive and now that child is a nun!"

Although I'd heard her stories many times, I knew I'd miss them. I'd also miss putting my arms around her, kissing her soft skin, so supple for someone her age, and burying my

 face in her cotton-like white hair as I bent to hug her shrinking frame. Although she'd been a good eater and had had a full figure most of her life, thanks to strudel, ham, sugar, and cream, her body shrunk as she aged and her appetite waned.

There would be no more pale blue eyes to look into as she told the story of how she left Austria. "I grew up in a village along the Austro-Hungarian border, and my family had a farm. My job was to collect the eggs from the hens each day before I left for school. One morning, I went to my father and said, 'I hate collecting eggs. I don't want to do it any more.' My father glared at me and said, 'Everyone in this family has a job. Yours is to collect eggs, and that is what you'll do!' I stared back and said, 'I will not! I am going to America.' I left the next day."

The village repeated this story for the next 50 years, especially when Grandma returned for a visit. Today, when people heard the bells of the village church announcing her death, perhaps the egg story would be repeated one last time.

Grandma was a better participant than a listener. If you told a story, she'd wait for you to finish, then try to top it.

Once when our two sons were younger and frequently ill, I sat down with Grandma for a cup of tea. "Grandma, it's not fair," I whined. "Poor Ross has had two ear surgeries and he's only two. Now he and Darryl have had tonsillitis continually for seven months. They keep passing it back and forth. I'm so tired of this."

She calmly replied, "When my children were small, we were quarantined in our house for three Christmases in a row. One year, it was scarlet fever, the next measles, and the third whooping cough. Don't ever think that life is fair."

Grandma had endured many rough times, yet she kept going thanks to her sense of humor. With her stories, she taught me to find the humorous side of even the least funny of situations.

I was remembering those stories as we arrived at our cousins' house to drop off our bags. Then we were whisked away to Grandma's rosary service to visit with family and friends. Sadly, only one of Grandma's children could attend. Her daughter was home in Los Angeles recovering from surgery to remove a brain tumor, and her younger son was convalescing from the strain of his mother's death in a nearby hospital's cardiac care facility. It was up to her grandchildren and great-grandchildren to carry on with her arrangements.

Grandma looked beautiful lying in the open, ornate casket, her beauty frozen in death for all to admire. *Good old Grandma*, I thought. *She'd be pleased with how well she looks.* Just then, our Austrian cousin, Paul, came up and insisted that all the cousins line up in front of the coffin for one last photo with Grandma so that he could show it to the family back home. As he snapped the photo. I remembered, *She always liked to dress up, especially for a camera!*

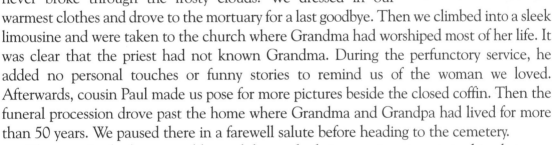

While the adults stood grim-faced, 3-year-old Patrick, her youngest great-grandchild, made us smile. He knelt beside her and said, "Grandma, eat your soup. You'll feel better."

My husband, our sons and I slept soundly that night after the long trip and the emotional rosary. Snow fell silently while we slept, its white powder covering the roads, trees, homes and street signs. It covered the ground where Grandma would soon be interred.

The day of her funeral dawned cold and clear, but the sun never broke through the frosty clouds. We dressed in our warmest clothes and drove to the mortuary for a last goodbye. Then we climbed into a sleek limousine and were taken to the church where Grandma had worshiped most of her life. It was clear that the priest had not known Grandma. During the perfunctory service, he added no personal touches or funny stories to remind us of the woman we loved. Afterwards, cousin Paul made us pose for more pictures beside the closed coffin. Then the funeral procession drove past the home where Grandma and Grandpa had lived for more than 50 years. We paused there in a farewell salute before heading to the cemetery.

The morning had grown colder, and the sun had given up its attempts to shine between the clouds. We shivered as we headed for the shelter of the mausoleum to listen to a few final words. As I stood in the snow with my teeth chattering, I realized that Grandma had played one last joke on me. A year earlier, when she was staying with my in-laws in Los Angeles, she and I visited in the living room on an especially cold day. I shivered and searched for a sweater. Grandma said, "If you think this is cold, you should be in Chicago. If I died today, you would have to fly back there to bury me in real cold "

"Oh, Grandma, don't be so morbid," I replied. Yet here I was, shivering in a cold, snow-covered cemetery this second day of spring, realizing that Grandma had had the last laugh.

Chapter 8—Success is in the Details

A.   Use a notebook.

B.   What about writing order?

C.   The active vs. the passive voice.

D.   The third person.

E.   Is good grammar important?

F.   Say it once. Period.

G.   What's verisimilitude?

H.   Avoid clichés and stereotypes.

I.   Be complete. Be concise.

J.   Use precise language.

K.   The 10% rule: be even *more* concise!

LIFESTORIES FROM THE WORKSHOPS:
    Herb by Pam Bell

"What should I do with a memory that pops up suddenly as I'm going through my day?" someone asks in a workshop.

Another wants to know, "Is it okay that I wrote a story about myself using the third person?

"Should I be worried using about using proper grammar?"

This chapter provides answers to these questions and to others like them.

> This chapter offers workable answers to questions workshop writers often ask about the day-to-day aspects of lifewriting.

A. Use a notebook.

Q. *How do I keep from losing ideas that come to me "out of the blue?"*

A. After they commit themselves to writing, lifewriters notice that scenes, conversations, and images from the past come quickly and unexpectedly. The same writers who wondered if they'd ever have enough memories to write about ask themselves if now they have too many to handle!

If memories and ideas come to you unexpectedly—at the grocery store, in your car as you wait for a light to change, in front of the TV at your sister's, try keeping a pocket-size notebook handy to record them. Your notes can be mere jottings ("Aunt Elsie wore a fur coat made of skins caught by Uncle Fred") or they can be whole stories that pour out on the spur of the moment. Essentially, these are items for your Memory List.

At your writing desk, later, you can incorporate your jottings into a story or use the details in a longer piece. You can also file the material under an appropriate heading in your three-ring binder to retrieve later ("clothing," or "aunts/uncles").

■ **Keep a notebook next to your bed to record your**

> "Make notes—I've lost more material than I've ever written. Contrary to popular opinion, it's not still up there in one's brain. It's in outer space and it ain't coming back."
>
> —Judith Guest
> novelist

Use a tape player to record a story (or fragment) you suddenly recall as you are riding in the car or doing housework or chores.

dreams, those wonderful out-pourings of the unconscious. If you pay regular attention to your dreams, they will provide clues to understanding your past. They will reveal something meaningful about even those events and relationships which may not have made sense to you before.

■ **A notebook will preserve you from the fear of losing good scenes, conversations, or images as you move through your day.** With ideas safely noted, instead of feeling anxious, you'll feel eager to get back to your writing! Here's a tip: buy several small spiral notebooks, one for each spot—the car, the bedroom, the kitchen. Always write a new thought in the next blank space, and establish the habit of crossing out each entry as soon as it has been transferred to your memory list or file. Then return the notebook to its place.

B. What about writing order?

Q. *Is there a correct sequence in which I should write my stories?*

A. No. People sometimes think they should write according to the order on their Memory List. They feel compelled to begin with the first item and proceed systematically to the last (often somewhere near the present) or they think they ought to write stories in the order they want the reader to read them.

If it feels good to proceed in a 1-2-3 order (only moving on to the second story when you have completed the first), go ahead. But if it doesn't feel good to do that, don't! **You don't have to write according to any order.** Here's another way:

■ **Start wherever you feel like starting**—in the middle or at the end, anywhere. The third piece you write may ultimately be the first piece in your story sequence, while what you wrote first may fit better toward the end.

■ **Don't feel compelled to write entire stories at once.** It's not only acceptable but potentially more creative to write fragments (scenes, conversations, images) on separate pages. Write as inspiration moves you; that is, at random, in snippets. A benefit of proceeding this way is that your stories get composed bit by bit—which, for many lifewriters, is easier than writing many pages at one sitting!

Once you have written a number of fragments or completed stories, arrange them in a chronological or narrative order appropriate to telling the larger story you are writing.

■ **Don't think in terms of *the* order but *an* order.** There may be several appropriate orders to organizing your fragments or stories (see Chapter 3)—each order is dependent on the themes that guide you. (See Chapter 6, Section C.) For instance, if you want to convey that you worked hard and rose out of nothing to achieve success, you might set a story about being poor next to one about having achieved financial success. This will highlight the relationship and the disparity between these two times in your life. If, however, rags-to-riches is not a theme that particularly interests you, it will seem normal to insert many stories between those of your "poor" period and your "rich" times. By distancing these two periods within your manuscript, you will downplay the link between the two.

■ **Transitions will help link your narratives (whether jottings or polished stories) into an appropriate order for your memoir.** Generally speaking, a transition is necessary every time a jump in thought or in the sequence of events may not be evident to your reader.

Transitions can be as simple as a linking word like *next*, *however*, or *lastly* in front of a paragraph or group of paragraphs, or a phrase like *as a result of this* or *in consequence*.

Other transitions, however, will require additional writing. For instance, your story about yearning to get an education that seemed beyond your reach is not logically followed by another about the fine professional-level job you obtained. These two stories benefit from transitional material to show how you overcame difficulties and received the education that prepared you for the fine job.

"The last thing that we find in making a book is to know what we must put first."

—Blaise Pascal, philosopher

"I'm taking a real risk! What if no one likes what I write?"

—Workshop Writer

As part of your editing process, give your writing to someone to read. If your reader has to re-read your manuscript to understand how the parts of the stories fit together (as opposed to re-reading because it provided so much pleasure the first time!), then what you need may be better transitions.

Think of your writing as a chain. All of your stories must have a connection to those before and after them or else the chain will not be whole and strong.

C. *The active vs. the passive voice.*

Q. Is there something wrong with using the passive voice?

A. Generally speaking, the passive voice of the verb (the subject has the action done to it) is weaker than the active voice (the subject does the action).

"Mary baked a cake" is active. *Mary*, the subject of the verb *baked*, is doing the action of baking. On the other hand, "A cake was baked by Mary" is passive. Here *Mary* is not the subject. The *cake*, which is *being baked* by Mary, is the subject. The action is being done to it.

■ **The passive voice has less impact than the active voice.** The reader will experience it as an evasive attempt on your part to not "own" the action of the verb.

■ **Dependence on the passive voice may reveal the writer's own passivity.** The writer is perhaps having difficulty coming to "ownership" of the topic.

"The requirement to wear long sleeves was rejected by the women" evinces less ownership than "The women rejected the requirement to wear long sleeves." In the passive, the writer does not own refusing to wear long sleeves. One feels the writer seeks distance (even if unconsciously) from the action.

If you use many passive constructions, ask yourself why. Would using the active voice help you come to ownership of your stories—and perhaps of your life?

exercise

Become more aware of the passive voice.

■ Look through your stories for the passive voice. Rewrite the stories so that every passive construction is changed to an active one.
■ How does the change to the active voice affect how you feel about the story? Does it give new muscle to your writing—and your life?

D. The third person.

Q. *Is it permissible to write about myself in the third person, to say "John did this" instead of "I did this?"*

A. Using the third person (he/she) is like using the passive voice. It evades "owning" a story.

It *is* a useful tool for a person who is working his way through a difficult situation that cannot yet be faced head on: the death of a mate or having been abused or feeling extreme guilt. Using the third person can be a way of beginning to accept what may hitherto have been too difficult to incorporate into one's life. Frequently a Turning Memories Into Memoirs® workshopper who writes in the third person is rehearsing living with the truth. The third person gives him something to hide behind if the pain begins to assault him.

Ultimately, as lifewriters, we all need to write our stories in the first person so that the "I" can "own" the life. Our task (at least in terms of self-growth) will not be completed until we have done so.

"Writing in the third person gave me a place to start dealing with my pain. I couldn't have written about that experience in the first person right away."

—Coaching client

ᴇxᴇʀcɪsᴇ

This exercise will sensitize you to some of the possibilities of the third person!

■ Write your obituary as if you were a reporter. Tell the world about the person who was yourself. Write in the third person, saying "she" or "he," not "I." What animated her life? What are the qualities of mind and spirit (vs. what she did) that she should be remembered for?

■ Look at your lifestories. Have you incorporated in them the essential qualities you have described in your obituary?

E. Is good grammar important?

Q. *Is good grammar essential in lifewriting?*

A. Yes and no. To anyone beginning to write lifestories, I would caution, "Get your story down on paper and don't worry about "good grammar"—at least, not at first."

Composing a fluent first draft that tells the story line is more important than producing a grammatically-correct one. Forget the curmudgeonly high-school English teacher who used to peer over your shoulders; forget your inner censor. The correct placement of a comma is not the most important issue in the world, nor is it proof of your worth as a human being. Your first task is to flow with the prose and get your ideas and feelings written down.

■ **Grammar plays an important role in writing.** What may sound fine when spoken can become merely dull, repetitive, and inexpressive in writing. In conversation, we have recourse to facial expressions, voice inflections, pauses, hand gestures, etc., to complete our spoken words. On the page, however, all we have is the writing itself—and commas, dashes, periods, paragraph breaks. That's why grammar, and the conventions we call correct usage, are ultimately important to you as a lifewriter.

Think of grammar as a code that we agree on to make communications clearer. Periods, commas, capital letters, past tenses, the spelling of words—all of this is meant to communicate the meaning of a text to a reader who is unfamiliar with you and with your story. Good grammar helps us to avoid such foolishness as "I threw the hat over the fence that I was wearing." (How did the fence fit around your ears?) **Good grammar is not a matter of "putting on airs" or being a snob. It's a matter of effective communication.**

Our language experience (especially in its written form) is codified so that both writer and reader can (as much as possible) mean the same thing by the use of the same symbols. You can understand the writing on this page because we both agree on the grammar that is in use here—I, the writer in my office in Maine, and you, the reader wherever you are.

Within the range of "good grammar," there are many perfectly acceptable—and different—decisions. That's a wonderful thing about grammar that your curmudgeonly high-school teacher probably didn't tell you. Where to start or end a paragraph is subject to choice—yours. The same is true for commas and periods and dashes, and the correspondence of tenses.

Buy yourself a contemporary grammar book to refer to whenever necessary. They are available in many bookstores. (I recommend that you avoid your old high school grammar text. Its rules are probably outdated now. Language is not static; it is always in process.) Confidence will open you up to the flow of language, and you'll notice that your writing will become more fluent and fun to do.

When you want to ask, "Do I need to use good grammar (or correct spelling)?" try reformulating your question. Ask instead, "Do I need to be understood?"

The rule against splitting infinitives is an example of meaningless "good grammar."

The rule originated in the days when Latin was still dominant in British academic circles. Since Latin infinitives consist of just one word, it was considered more faithful to the original to translate infinitives into unbroken English units—hence no splitting.

This is a "good grammar" rule that has nothing to do with good usage of present-day North American English—and everything to do with an out-dated-standard from another language.

F. Say it once. Period.

Q. *Should I try to recapitulate my story at the end of it, in order to wrap it up?*

A. No! Do not repeat the theme or any part of your story in a tag-on summary sentence or paragraph at the end of your piece—just in case no one got the point! Not only is this unnecessary but it is also an insult to your readers' intelligence and to your writing ability!

Here is an example. In a piece about a death in the family, the writer shows the members of a family mourning together and supporting one another through difficult days. The writer carefully chooses dialogue, image and detail to reinforce the fact of family solidarity and its benefits. Great stuff! So far so good! Not a dry eye left in the reading audience. The story line has achieved its purpose.

Then, having effectively shown this family successfully dealing with its grief, having up to then resisted the impulse to "tell" the reader what to think and feel, the lifewriter concludes: "And so if members of a family support one another in times of adversity, they too can find themselves reinforced, uplifted, blah, blah, blah…"

Well, besides being objectionably preachy, and telling rather than showing, the interpretive tag-on is redundant. The writer has already made her point through effective writing. There is nothing recapitulating can tell that her story hasn't already shown dramatically. (See Section I below for conciseness.)

■ **Your last paragraph (or two) may be unnecessary.** Reread your ending with an eye to eliminating some of it. Very likely, your conclusion is repetitive and dull writing and your story will almost always be improved by cutting all or some of it out. Always let the story speak for itself!

■ **The first paragraphs in a story may be only a warm up.**

> "Shouldn't I be sure the reader gets what I am trying to say?"
>
> —Workshop writer

> Good lead paragraphs thrust the reader into the story immediately.

The real beginning of your story can sometimes occur in a later paragraph. Move the paragraph that ought to serve as your lead to the beginning of your story and consign your warm-up paragraphs where they belong—in the waste basket! You'll be glad you didn't hide your true lead under unnecessary false starts.

G. *What's verisimilitude?*

Q. *Do my stories really need to seem real?*

A. Verisimilitude is that quality in a piece of writing that makes it seem "like the real thing" (*verum* means *true* in Latin and *similis* means *like*). Every story needs a good dose of verisimilitude if it is to be accepted by the reader.

If a movie is allegedly set in France, verisimilitude can be established by showing a *café-terrasse* scene. There will be French spoken in the background. The viewer then accepts the fiction that the story "really" takes place in France. If the scene is shot in an apartment with English music on the stereo and an American newspaper on the coffee table, it is much harder for the viewer to accept the fiction that the story takes place in Paris. Verisimilitude will be harder to attain (and maintain) not only because the necessary props are missing but also because the cues furnished contradict the fiction of the stated locale.

Your reader willingly makes a compact—implicit, of course—with you, the writer. As long as you provide enough clues to make the story seem real, the reader will *suspend his disbelief*. In other words, he'll go along with the idea that the story really is happening *when*, *where*, and *how* you say it happens.

In practice, this means that the writer must select appropriate details to reinforce and corroborate the story. If the story is set in 1935, the people must be doing things people did in 1935—listening to news on the radio, for instance. Conversely they cannot be doing things people were not doing in 1935—

"Mais oui—certaine-ment, monsieur," said the Montréal waiter.

"En verdad, señor—si si," said the Mexico City parking attendant.

watching the news on TV.

■ **Establishing verisimilitude in your story does not mean including every detail of a certain time and place.** There are far too many details in your life for you to do that. Were you to include all the false starts and the dead ends—not to mention all the delicious dinners!—experienced in life, your story would soon be overcrowded, like a room so stuffed with furniture that people cannot get around easily within it. No, you will need to select carefully what you will include. A few judicious details here and others there will do quite nicely— and will be quite enough if you have chosen well. (Think of the Paris *café-terrasse* and of the waiters speaking a few well-placed French words overheard in the background.)

The analogy of the tip of the iceberg is *à propos* here. Only ten percent of the iceberg sticks out of the water while ninety percent is submerged. Seeing just that exposed ten percent of the iceberg, a ship's navigator knows what to expect of the floating mountain of ice.

That's the effect you want to achieve in your writing: by including only the most effective and revealing details of your past, you suggest the entire story. If you want to show your family's poverty, describe the worn, faded linoleum in the living room. Going on, however, to describe the mismatched chairs in the kitchen, the frayed towels and the chipped dishes, blah-blah-blah, begins to seem like you are creating a catalogue of facts rather than a story. (Suddenly the whole iceberg looms out of the water and the reader is overwhelmed!)

Remember: verisimilitude requires that you steer a clear course between boring your reader with too many details (that may only have meaning for you) and leaving your reader up in the air because you have not made the story seem real to others by including just enough specific and striking details.

H. Avoid clichés and stereotypes.

Q. *Why are clichés and stereotypes ineffective?*

A. Clichés and stereotypes place people in categories. They are short-hand ways of writing and speaking that reflect ready-made thoughts. They adversely affect the ways we relate to our families and friends as unique individuals.

> "She was a mother-hen—you know how mothers are!"
> "My father had a heart of gold."
> "Those were beautiful days when we were happy."

These examples of clichés and stereotypes reflect ways of thinking that get in the way of seeing people as individuals and events as unique. If you think of your mother in generic terms as "a mother," you will be weighed down with all the sentimental good and bad that second-rate movies, novels and songs sell us. Instead, strive see her as a unique person, a woman who met the challenges of mothering as successfully as she did or could. Do the same with your father—and everyone.

And that goes for "youth" and "love" and "family" and everything else that can get sentimental really fast.

■ **Beware of words and phrases that have the ring of having been heard elsewhere.** If you sense that a phrase you use is not your own original pairing of two or more words and that you may have "borrowed" it, chances are you have a cliché or a stereotype dripping off the end of your pen—or popping up on the computer screen—to embarrass you later!

■ **Create a language that is as fresh as you are.** The challenge of writing is to have your words reflect you and your story, not someone else's version of you and your story. By using clichés and stereotypes, you slip into someone else's version and away from your truth.

"Sentimentality is the failure of true emotion."

—Wallace Stevens
poet

To write well—honestly, deeply, connectedly—about someone, you must write from a place of affection or respect influenced by clear vision. Otherwise, you will record "stick figures" who have little to share with your readers.

"Simplify, simplify, simplify!" said Henry David Thoreau. (But didn't he mean to say, "Simplify!"?)

"I was having a hard time throwing anything away. So I highlighted all my repetitive, summarizing last paragraphs and copied them into my journal. I didn't seem to be done with some of the issues but I could see it wasn't improving the story.*"*

—Workshop writer

I. Be complete. Be concise.

Q. *When have I said enough and when too much?*

A. This is one way to write: You write everything you need to write on a topic (completeness) and then eliminate all that you can without changing the meaning of the story (conciseness). What's left is your story. It's really that simple.

As you write, keep looking at your prose as a stranger would. Is there enough information to understand all you are trying to communicate? If not, keep adding details. Unless you are very good, very experienced, don't edit at this point. Just let your text grow.

Yes, you are likely to repeat yourself and to include irrelevant information. You might even babble on. But don't hold yourself back. Your writing needs to flow in order to be as complete as it can be. To every thing there is a season… Once you feel you've said everything you have to say, then you need to undertake two tasks:

1) **Eliminate everything that is redundant.** Examine your text. Have you said exactly the same thing before (or something very similar)? Choose the most effective version and delete the rest. Saying it once is usually enough.

■ **Don't forget the redundancy that creeps in when you have your narrative repeat the dialogue.** Put meaning into the dialogue, not into a narrative. "She was very hungry. 'After not having eaten for days, I am starved,' she said." Have the dialogue carry the meaning here and eliminate the narrative sentence *She was very hungry.*

■ **Linking phrases can also be redundant.** "Our house in Des Moines was a two story brick building. In comparison, our house in Cincinnati had only one story and was built of wood." Here the two sentences are obviously a comparison, and you do not need the words *in comparison.*

■ **A third form of redundancy occurs when an adjective**

attempts to act as a superlative to a word that is already itself a superlative. Examples of this are: *complete silence* is not more silent than *silence*; a *dead corpse* is not more dead than a *corpse*; *very sincere* is not more sincere than *sincere*; *true facts* are not more true than *facts*.

2) **Eliminate material (even if interesting) that does not contribute to the overall impact you are aiming for within a story.** Writers can find themselves with interesting, well-written material that belongs elsewhere. Sometimes this material can be an excess of description—remember the tip of the iceberg. Other times, you may have written a story within a story, a separate tale with its own beginning, middle, and end, its own set of images and characters. It may even be a lovely tale that will move the reader. Nonetheless, take it out. File the story-within-a-story away for future use. It won't go away—it'll be waiting for you later. Perhaps it can fit into the flow of your lifestories— but at a different spot. Or, perhaps you have a lovely description that you need to expand and make into a story of its own.

Michelangelo, when sculpting his statue David, is said to have remarked that he chipped away at the block of stone until the statue emerged. He eliminated all he could and what was left could not bear any more elimination: at last, Michelangelo had the statue that had been waiting for him.

Within the many pages you have written may be your much smaller—and better—memoir. Is the story you want to end up with encrusted in excess prose? Keep chipping away at your text until you can't chip any more without detracting from your story. That will be your "David" of a memoir.

J. Use precise language.

Q. *Can you write well without an extensive vocabulary?*

A. An extensive vocabulary can only help you—if by "extensive" you mean many precise words, not just big ones.

> "The difference between the right word and the nearly right word is the same as that between lightning and the lightning bug."
>
> —Mark Twain
> writer

Precise words are specific and not vague and ineffective like *nice, awful, big,* OK. "She was nice" is vague. "She understands different points of view" is specific.

"He was awfully big" is vague. You might write instead: "My father measured six foot three and weighed 225 pounds."

Don't write: "The job was OK." Write: "The job was in my field of competence, but its salary was inadequate and its requirements did not challenge me."

In each of these examples, I have added meaning where I replaced vague words with precise language, but I did not use big words. "She was nice" does not qualify how she was *nice* or what I understand *nice* to mean as opposed to what the reader might understand *nice* to mean.

Go over your text. Look at individual words. Does each of your words carry full weight or do you have flabby words like *nice* and *awful.* If you do, replace them with specific (not necessarily big) words and phrases that contribute precisely to your meaning.

When writers make use of vague or flabby words and phrases, they have not taken the time to explore the depth and breadth of what they are writing about. Like clichés and stereotypes, flabby words and phrases are lazy forms of writing. They say very little—when you need so very much to communicate all you have lived!

■ **Remember:** replace all flabby words or phrases with others that convey precise and full meaning. You will not be there to notice the confusion appear on your reader's face as she struggles to understand your text. You will not be there to say, "What I really mean is…"

Make each word work for you!

K. *The 10% rule: be even more concise!*

Q. *Do you have a favorite rule to keep in mind?*

A. One rule I often practice in my own writing—and always to my great benefit—is to eliminate 10% of my text.

Even when I think there's nothing left to cut, I find something I can eliminate to make my prose both more concise and more precise. Always.

More words simply don't add up to more meaning. Don't be one of those writers who leads a reader up hill and down while he works out what he wants to say!

Think of yourself as a publisher who has space for only 90% of your current text. What can you eliminate *without changing the meaning*? If you have five pages, cut half a page. If you have ten, cut one full page.

Many writers who published their own work in the days before computers and desktop publishing have written about how typesetting—placing each lead character by hand in a frame and then handling hundreds of heavy frames—taught them to value conciseness. Diarist and novelist Anaïs Nin wrote about learning to ask herself whether this or that word or phrase was essential enough to warrant the extra work she would have to do to typeset and print it.

Although publication is not such a physical experience today as it was, it can be costly. Play the editor who's trying to meet a budget: eliminate 10% of your text!

LIFESTORIES FROM THE WORKSHOPS:

Herb
by Pam Bell

"From away" as we say in Maine, Pam Bell attended several Turning Memories Into Memoirs® workshops. After more than three decades in Maine and having raised two natives, we can now safely say that she is "from here." This is a tribute story that tells how she got "here."

It was the middle of April 1972, past the peak of mud season but not yet spring, when we first drove up Libby Road. The fields were mostly bare, though we could see patches of snow in places, and there were still snow banks that had been piled up by plow trucks during the winter months.

We were on our way to look at a house advertised in *The Maine Times*, a 100-year-old Cape on a dead-end dirt road. About halfway up the road, we passed an elderly man in green rubber boots, blue pants, a short green winter jacket, and a green cap. Standing off to the side on a snow bank, he held on to the collar of a shaggy, black-and-tan dog.

This was our first glimpse of Herb Libby, the man from whom we would buy our farm—and the man who would become one of the most important people in our lives.

Herb Libby, who was 82 when we moved to Leeds, was the quintessential good neighbor. Up until that time, he had been driving one of his son Raymond's dump trucks 50 hours a week, hauling-in at Blue Rock. But when we moved in, Raymond hired Bruce, my husband, to drive the truck, and Herb took on the job of introducing me to Leeds and the surrounding area.

We covered a lot of miles that first summer. We drove to Hartford and Sumner, Turner, and Greene, stopping here and there for a lunch. Herb told me that just about every culvert we crossed over during our journeys had been his responsibility when he worked as a patrolman for the state. Herb got a kick out of squiring around a young woman, and I'll never forget the expression on his face when he introduced me to Carl Geores, our minister, at Rose and Pratt's store in North Leeds. Herb was sure that Carl noticed he was riding with another man's wife!

That was the way our life in Leeds started, with our neighbor offering a job and his friendship. Over the years that followed, there was a steady stream of companionship and help from Herb. Those first years, the stream ran pretty much one way, east from the Libbys' across the road to the Bells'. Herb and I walked our road every day. His old dog Fred and my puppy Eben kept us company as Herb pointed out the sights. He showed me where the mayflowers grew and told me of picking them when he was a boy. We spent long hours picking blueberries and raspberries. Standing among the prickers, he told me of hitching up the horse and wagon on a summer's day and going with his mother and his wife Sadie and  the children to pick blueberries in the bog by the old Will Libby place. He told me about his youth, and he taught me the history of Leeds as it used to be.

And what did we do for the Libbys? I think we mostly provided amusement for them in those early years. I know Herb had a good laugh when, all excited, I announced that my peas were up, just days after I had planted them in my first vegetable garden. Herb dutifully climbed the hill to look at them and pointed out to me that what was popping up all over the garden was pigweed and mustard, not peas!

He shook his head in disbelief when we brought home our first workhorse, Becky, especially since she had never been worked. But he agreed to help us train her. After experiencing a few flying trips around our garden, hanging on to the handles of the plow while Bruce tried to hold the horse, and watching Bruce and the horse race across the fields and down the road, bits and pieces of harness flying off with every step, Herb pronounced her "a good-looking mare, but notional." And notional she was; her notion of working in harness was to do it at a run, and if the going got tough, to sit down.

Good-naturedly, Herb helped us teach her a thing or two, and undoubtedly went home knowing just why he had traded in his last team of horses for a tractor back in 1952. The mare, sadly, is long gone, but the tractor is still on the farm. We bought it from Herb.

When we had children, a new dimension was added to our relationship with Herb. Bruce's and my parents lived too far away for the boys to see much of them, so Herb became the perfect substitute grandparent. When Nat was two, I'd walk him to the edge of the road, help him across, and watch him go up to Herb's door. When Herb answered it, Nat would shout, "Herb, cookie!" Herb always had a supply of oyster crackers on hand and would pass Nat the box.

Herb took the boys on outings to McDonald's and Cote's Ice Cream. He babysat them, and he watched their baseball games. When they went to school, Nat and Ben would wait for the bus each morning over at Herb's, discussing how the Red Sox were doing and help-ing themselves to candy from the bowl on his counter. Herb was unceasingly tolerant, and his house was a refuge for the boys when Bruce and I got too picky at home. He gave them loyal support and a lot of love.

It's been over 30 years now since we moved to the town of Leeds. We have never doubted it was the best move we could have made. Living across the road from the Libbys has made our lives much richer than it could possibly have been if we had chosen a different road.

Herb Libby died in 1991 at the age of 100, ever the gentleman, ever the friend, ever the very best of neighbors. We miss him terribly—even now, many years later.

Chapter 9—Keep It Going, Wrap It Up

A.   Stay with the process.

B.   Your writing time.

C.   Lifewriting groups.

D.   The finished product: "do-it-yourself."

E.   The finished product: a "real" book.

F.   Good luck!

A. *Stay with the process.*

You may already be looking forward to the moment when you hand over an attractive collection of stories to your children, your grandchildren, your relatives and your friends!

It's understandable that you are impatient to reach this stage—understandable yet dangerous. Rushing your lifewriting may subvert your effort. You may end up with a memoir that is only a portion (in quantity and/or quality) of what you wanted.

Too early in the process of discovering their stories, some lifewriters yearn for a finished product—often something that is recognizably a book. They begin preparing a final version or have a manuscript bound.

Later, they think of something they forgot to include—something interesting and very important, perhaps even something that may force them to rethink their story! Because of the amount of "finish" work they have already invested in their manuscript, these writers may be reluctant, or even refuse, to do the rewriting needed to insert new material in their lifestories. They settle for what they have—a finished product that is not the story they and their families deserve.

Don't let this happen to you! Slow down! Linger over your stories: let lifewriting be a process of discovery for as long as possible. Allow yourself to add a little or a lot, to delete a word, a paragraph or a whole section, to change the placement of events and ideas so that emphases change and interpretations become more clear. (Think of lifewriting as a soup that is simmering. Long, slow cooking will produce a tastier meal!)

When you approach writing as a process, you are likely to ask yourself, "What will I learn today!" Your writing sessions

This chapter will help you bring your writing to its successful completion.

Sometimes a writer's idea of producing a "real book" is based on a standard of perfection beyond her current ability.

When you think of writing a book, does the task seem to be a challenge beyond your reach?

If so, I urge you to stay with the process and commit to writing with the skills you now have. With time, your writing will only get better— and so will your book!

Thoughtful people don't make decisions in haste. Thoughtful writers don't write in haste.

will be times of discovery, times of learning, always fresh and tantalizing as your sensibility, intelligence, and imagination reveal the workings of your life to you.

Learn to enjoy the process of inquiring into your past and getting your memories and insights into the appropriate written form. You will work with considerably more pleasure and freedom than if you rush your lifewriting into a final version.

єхєrсisе

Evaluate whether your stories are finished.

■ Have you written as much about the characters, the plot, the setting as necessary to enable the reader to understand them as you understand them?

■ Have you developed your theme, your tone, and your point of view so they convey what you wanted them to in your story?

■ Are your stories supported by all the information available through interviews or research?

■ Make the necessary changes. It may seem difficult now to do, but it will be even more in a year or two when you are very sorry that you have failed to do justice to your story.

B. Your writing time.

This section reviews the importance of where you write and what conditions facilitate your success.

You will maximize both the quantity and the quality of your output if you make a habit of your work time. **Nothing gets words on the page like habit.**

■ **Set up writing times you can meet consistently**. Especially at the beginning of your effort, your writing schedule should be blocked out on a calendar so you can be consistently reminded of it. After a while, when you block out regular times, you will know when your next writing session is without having to look it up.

A predictable commitment also frees the writer from the nagging burden of "I ought to be writing!" No, you ought not to be writing if it's not your scheduled time! When your writing is well contained in a predictable schedule, you can relax.

■ **Create rituals around your writing.** In addition to regularity, writing ritual are very important. Rituals may include playing a certain sort of music, having a cup of coffee, or using certain props (like lighting a candle).

■ **Negotiate for writing time** with your housemate(s). Do so clearly on as regular a basis as you need to. Depending on the scope of your memoir project, they will have to accept your shorter or longer commitment. This open communication can foster the success of your project by keeping time available for regular serious work, time that housemates will not impinge upon.

Duplicate the conditions of successful writing experiences— at first—whenever you write. A cup of coffee and classical music, a certain table or time of day— arrange for these props to support you as you establish the habits of being a writer.

The unconscious is powerful—and it can be unleashed by the most trivial stimuli.

εxεrcise

Re-examine the schedule you created in Chapter 1.

■ Has it proven appropriate? What specific changes would make this schedule a more effective tool? Decide on the necessary changes and enter them on your calendar, inform your housemates, and stick to your schedule.

■ If the schedule you created earlier remains appropriate, have you been able to stick to it? If not, why not? Have others respected your commitment to your schedule? If not, what do you need to do to get them to respect your writing time?

■ What do you need to change in your environment to maximize your writing schedule? These might include: noise, telephones, not enough heat, too much heat, a computer that doesn't function well, too small a work area, etc.

C. *Lifewriting groups.*

This section looks at the benefits of being part of a lifewriting group.

A good writers' group can give you invaluable support and see you through to the end of your project. Regular meetings essentially become writing deadlines to complete portions of your project.

Group deadlines can be very stimulating (after all, who wants to show up at a meeting and be the deadbeat who hasn't brought any writing to share!)

An established end date is a benefit to almost every writing project.

A group is especially important if your mate or others in your life do not understand what you are doing and are disparaging of your efforts. ("Why don't you just enjoy yourself at your age! Why do you want to write instead of going to the Tupperware party!")

■ **In forming a lifewriting group, the first people to look to are your friends, your relatives, or your mate.** If you don't know anyone who is interested in lifestories, advertise or otherwise "go public" (church bulletin, poster at a book store or library, etc.).

"Sometimes I just had no idea how to be more clear and more detailed. Good thing I had my writing group. They always came up with suggestions."

—Workshop writer

If you specifically need the support of people similar to yourself, advertise in a newspaper of your ethnic group, of your vocational background, or of your religion.

If you do advertise in a general circulation magazine, be sure to identify those features that will be important to you in fellow writers (e.g., women in their 60s).

(The first few times you meet with a group of strangers, consider getting together in a safe, public place like a senior center or a library rather than in a private home.)

■ **A functioning group may consist of only one other person or of many others.** Establish ground rules (meeting time and place, length of meeting, regular operating procedures) and reassess these rules periodically to ascertain that they continue meeting your needs. Having a structure for your get-togethers will also encourage you to take the group seriously—even if there are just two or three of you.

■ **After a few meetings, it will be obvious whether you can or cannot work with a particular group.**

Remember: you want to learn to write better; you have not come to learn group dynamics or to create long-term strategies to get people involved. Resist the urge to be a missionary, a counselor or a change agent. (Review the concept of archetypes discussed in Chapter 6, Section E.) After a reasonable time, if the group is not helping you to meet your writing goals, assess whether you can change it to meet your needs. If you feel you cannot—or don't want to, quit that group. It's not the group for you. It's that simple.

■ **There are many reasons for a group not working.** Some of these are: lack of chemistry between participants; too great a difference in education or experience; dependency or other emotional shortcomings on the part of members; discrepancies in members' commitments to writing and to improving themselves as writers.

If the group is not working for you and you are convinced that it is not likely to meet your needs in the future, let the members know that you will not be continuing to meet with them. It's not easy. I know, I've had to go through that process myself. It's common courtesy, of course, to let people know you are leaving. It is also good practice in openness (a quality essential in the writer). Once you have made your decision to leave, look for or create another group.

■ **When a successful group has done its work, let it end.** Often, you will know the time has come to disband when usually-regular members begin to miss meetings or keep showing up late. Make a clean finish of it and let the members go off on their own—or, of course, you can continue contact (a social or writing connection) on some basis with whichever members you want!

"The Soleil tele-group turned out to be just the right thing for me. I don't know how I could have found such a stimulating group of fellow writers to meet with locally."

—Tele-group writer

Being part of a writing group is still a good idea even if your first attempt to get one going isn't successful. Don't throw the baby out with the bath water! Try again.

Exercise

If starting a writing group appeals to you, take the time right now to assess your needs and goals.

■ Note how many and what kind of people would be ideal, how frequently you would like to meet and for how long. What public spaces in your community are available?

■ Reach out to potential group members. Devise a list of people, including librarians and writing teachers, who can connect you with other beginning writers to call or write. Post an announcement, or buy advertising space in an appropriate publication.

D. The finished product: "do-it-yourself."

This section explores how to "publish" your book in small numbers, doing all the work yourself. The next section looks at options for a professional product.

At last, it's time to consider some options for packaging your lifestories. Since you have been printing copies of your lifestories all along for your three-ring binder, you already have one complete version of your memoir. While it is very satisfying to hold this basic presentation of your stories in your hands, you still need to produce additional copies for others. How will you package these copies if your goal is to share your stories with only a few friends and family members?

1) **Your do-it-yourself lifestory "book" for family and friends can be bound or collated in various ways** using widely available low-cost services.

"I wrote an inscription and autographed every copy I gave away. It made me feel like a real writer."

—Tele-group writer

■ **A three-ring binder is inexpensive and easy.** Use the kind with a transparent pocket cover so you can make a title page that includes an illustration or photo. A binder permits you to include sheet protectors and photo sleeves in which you place copies of pictures and documents you want to include. You can produce a clean copy of the text from your computer and go to a quick copy printer to duplicate your "book."

■ **Copy centers also offer simple options that use plastic or cardstock covers with comb or "velo" bindings.** These produce a business-like presentation and are more book-like than a binder. Again, formatting a clean copy on your computer is the first step. Visit your copy center to check options, colors, styles and costs.

■ **You or a craft-y friend can make unique covers** using some of the many interesting papers and materials now available for scrapbooking. (Check your library for how-to info on handmade books.) You may want to decorate your covers with art work: drawings, photos of people and places, color images of family heirlooms, or paintings.

■ **Buy a ready-made binding** that uses elastics, clasps or pegs to hold the manuscript. It's a step up from the three-ring binder or the comb binding, and comes in various sizes and colors.

■ **You can have each copy of your book bound as a hard cover book.** Local or Internet-based printers can give you a price for binding ten or more of your photocopied manuscripts. The price tends to be high per copy and would be prohibitive if you were doing a thousand but it's affordable when you produce just a few for family and friends. Such books will look official—but plain, with few or no artistic choices.

2) **Your lifestory presentation can contain many things besides your stories.** It will feature the narratives this book has helped you to write, but other personal history materials will substantially enhance your written accounts.

■ **Include photos and documents.** Photocopy these and insert them into each copy. Documents (*always make them copies, not the originals, which you should store archivally in acid-free folders*) such as birth and marriage certificates, obituary notices, letters, diplomas, children's drawings, etc., can be included in sections, or if you have mastered the scanning and text-wrap functions, these can be set right near the text they illustrate.

Photocopiers will reproduce your photographs with remarkable fidelity to the original at a reasonable cost.

We recommend photocopying multiple copies of your

Leave blank pages at the end of your book—a reminder to your children to take up the writing of family stories for their generation.

memoir from the master "hard copy" you print from your computer rather than printing out many copies yourself on a desktop printer. Inkjet ink is not cheap and it is both subject to fading and vulnerable to moisture. A photocopy, black or color, adheres the toner to the page permanently and may even be less expensive in the long run.

Scanning your photos and archival materials and incorporating them into your text document is the best way to go in terms of the ease with which you can then produce more copies. Look for friends and relatives with the equipment and know-how, or take the plunge yourself. You'll need a desktop scanner, time and patience.

■ **Include the extra items that don't fit directly into the narratives.** For example, lists of favorite foods (with recipes, of course!), songs or hymns (with words and music and even audiotapes or CDs), novenas, devotions, and colloquial expressions. Set this material aside from the text in a sidebar (easy to do with a computer) or at the end of a chapter, or make an appendix.

List places significant to your characters and story. Add a description, drawing, map or photo of each place then and now. These help your reader picture the settings of your stories.

A genealogy chart is a precious addition to any memoir. But, creating one is a different activity altogether from lifewriting. Genealogical research is a demanding enterprise and merits that you learn its methodology. Before you do, be sure to inquire if a relative has done the work already.

A simple family chart of the last generation or two is a useful reference. Your kids may not remember the names of Aunt Olga's six children. A chart can spare you the need to place explanatory tags in the text ("my cousin Rita who was Aunt Olga's third daughter and fifth child…"). These tags get awkward fast! Genealogy charts can go either at the beginning of a story ("Cast of Characters") or at the end (in an appendix).

E. The finished product: a "real" book.

Today, technological advances, centralized distribution systems and a growing interest in reclaiming regional identity makes self-publishing a viable option for many authors who want their books to reach a wider circle than their immediate family and friends. It is not true that your book is not worthy to be read unless it has been purchased by a New York corporate publishing house. Self-publishing has many benefits, not the least of which are that you can control production decisions and can recoup your expenses. Of course, learning how to control the production and having a viable "marketing strategy" are important.

You can opt for a professionally prepared book that will be sold in on-line and area bookstores. (In general, local bookstores will shelve memoir titles in their regional section.) But, the bookstore will not be your memoir's real home. The discount that stores demand and the paperwork required to chase payment isn't worth it to most one-time authors. We find that most self-published memoir writers find their natural "customers" through personal networks of friends, associations and local organizations, clubs, schools, and at library readings, conventions, fairs and festivals. In short—in their own backyards.

Authors who choose this route often do so because they feel deeply that there is an audience beyond their home crowd that will be receptive to their work. Connecting with that audience is part of the pleasure of writing a memoir. Your story will touch many people who will recognize in it their own histories, families, experiences and yearnings. If you agree, don't forfeit the rewarding experience of taking your book public! Many authors we have worked with have been amazed (and revitalized) by the response from strangers who have been moved by reading their books.

If you choose to publish your memoir in hundreds or even a thousand copies or more, doing it yourself using the quick

If you think you can succeed, you most likely will!

Green Rider
Thinking Horse
My Journey with a Standardbred

Karen Douglass

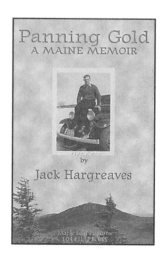

copy options suggested above is expensive and impractical.

You'll do better to hire professional book design and production services that will turn your manuscript into an attractive trade paperback that has all the hallmarks of a "real" book. You can act as your own publisher and broker all the services yourself (like being your own contractor when you build a house), but if you do not plan to do this sort of project again, you may find the learning curve pretty steep. Having an experienced advocate see your book through every stage from first design to final proofs to books in hand ensures that you are protected from glaring first-timer gaffs.

■ **Know the difference between between a publisher and a printer.** A publisher (whether that's you or Random House) assumes responsibility for all the tasks to get your book designed, printed and marketed. A printer puts ink on paper according your specifications (it's all computerized now!) and binds the books.

Printers can be like lawyers—if you want it done, they'll do it—no questions. Their job is to do whatever the customer says he wants. (You want to leave your fortune to your dog instead of your children?—just sign here!)

■ **Convert your manuscript into the form the printer requires.** Designing and formatting to create electronic files according to printer specifications is called **pre-press production.** This is aesthetic as well as technical work that involves many steps and skills. While anything can be printed as a book cover, professionally-produced designs have certain features. It's unlikely that your-niece-the arty-one knows the standards unless she is a professional graphic designer. Use her drawing or painting—but hire a designer to prepare the book cover design. People really do judge a book by its cover!

■ **Broker your own printing and binding—using your electronic files.** Do a cost comparison, however, before settling on a print house. (In fact, you should do this first because details of the pre-press work should be informed by the particular printer's specifications.) Prices can vary a lot! So request estimates. Large plants that specialize in books offer lower rates than smaller firms—but long distance communication and shipping costs are a disadvantage! Your local printer is not a good choice because, like doctors, printers have specialties. Someone who's the best at letterheads and business cards doesn't necessarily have a handle on book design standards or even have the best equipment to print and bind books. *You must educate yourself about the process in order to make informed choices—and get the end result you want.*

Self-Publishing the First Time—but with Experience!

■ Soleil Lifestory Network has assisted many writers to produce lovely books which are printed in runs of 500-1,000 or more. These authors identify their target markets and sell their books through personal and regional networks. Most recoup their production investment when they have sold 400 to 600 copies. We are repeatedly impressed with how do-able (and enjoyable) it is for first- and one-time authors to sell this number of books within six months to a year.

When you ask a company like ours to act as contractor (publisher) for your book production project, you are purchasing our design expertise, our long-standing relationships with print houses and our track record for customer service. We can translate your ideas for the look and the feel of your book into a professional design and save you time, money and mistakes. (The anguish of a nearly-nice book—perhaps 800 copies of it in your garage—is not to be underestimated as a depressing end to all your hard work! You can avoid first-timer errors by using experienced help.)

Note that vanity presses offer a different product altogether and rightly bear a stigma for taking advantage of their customers. These companies pretend they are selective, prestigious publishers when, in fact, the customer pays (sometimes exorbitantly) all costs for a final product about which he has little choice.

A book production service company, on the other hand, is upfront about offering professional technical services for hire. Editing, design, pre-press and production decisions will be executed with expertise, but you will have as much choice in the details as you want. The result is a real book that looks like you want it to and represents you well as it carries your lifestory to its appreciative audience.

exercise

Make plans for how you will package your lifestory for your readers.

■ Do you want to reach a larger audience than family and friends? A "real book" will be necessary.

■ Who should read your lifestory? Every story has a natural audience just waiting to know it exists. Who is yours?

■ Make a list of every individual you know who should buy your book. (That's your pre-publication mailing list!)

■ What community groups will celebrate your accomplishment (perhaps even want to plan a publication party!) and be thrilled to make your book known and available to their members?

■ Establish a preliminary timeline. Is there an anniversary, family reunion, convention or holiday in the next three to five months that is your obvious publication date? (Of course, you may need to readjust as you go.)

■ Make a preliminary budget (both time and money) you can/want to invest in this project.

■ Read several books on self-publishing to familiarize yourself with the work that goes into preparing and printing a book. Whether you act as your own publishing contractor or hire a professional, knowledge is power!

■ Have your manuscript edited and proofread so that it is truly as good as it can be. Many new authors are so eager to finish their projects that they short-sightedly omit working with an editor—a final chance to be sure that the text conveys all the meaning you intend. A good editor will not alter your voice. Rather, he will ensure that you communicate clearly in that voice and will find discrepancies you can't see any more.

■ How will you package or present your finished memoir? Visit bookstores to examine examples of what is currently being published. Generally, you want your self-published book to have the same look as that of one from the big houses.

■ Inquire locally about printing, photocopy and binding options. Request estimates from large book printing firms.

■ Explore having your book designed and produced by a company such as Soleil Lifestory Network. Visit www.turningmemories.com/bookproduction.html or call today to talk over the possibilities!

F. Good luck!

We've come to the end of our work together in this book. I hope I have launched you on a marvelous journey of exploration to access the power of lifewriting! Here are a few more suggestions as you continue on your way.

■ **Donate copies of your lifestory, however you publish it, to your local library and historical society.** Your community truly will appreciate your generosity and be interested in your story. More and more, we understand that history does not consist of big events alone but includes the daily lives of people like you and me. Perhaps your efforts will inspire others to write their stories!

■ **Send a copy to Soleil Lifestory Network** so that workshoppers and lifewriters from around the country can celebrate your success. We'll feature your book in our e-mail newsletter. Subscribe yourself on our website at **turningmemories.com**.

■ **Re-read and refer to this book often.** It will provide an on-going source of encouragement and motivation to work the magic of storytelling for you and your family.

■ **Make use of the appendices** to inform and inspire you in your writing life.

In Appendix A, I have gathered examples of lifestories to provide reassurance and guidance as you write. In Appendix B you'll find further reading to broaden and deepen your knowledge and appreciation. Since no list can be entirely comprehensive or up-to-date, be sure to use your public library as the marvelous resource it is to widen your horizons on the interesting subject of memoirs.

■ **Write, write, write:** that's the most important thing you can do. And, be patient: your work and your life deserve it.

Good luck and keep writing!

"I think I can, I think I can, I *know* I can!"

—from *The Little Engine That Could* by Watty Piper

Appendix A: Lifestories from the Workshops

The lifestories in this Appendix are just a few of the many memoirs produced in the Turning Memories Into Memoirs® workshops, or by my coaching clients who have worked one-on-one with me, or by people who have read previous editions of this book. Lifestories play many roles in our lives. In this Appendix, I would like to highlight just some of them, necessarily leaving other aspects unexplored.

As I re-read them for this edition of *Turning Memories*, I was again impressed by the breadth and depth of human experience lived, understood and so generously shared in these stories. It is not difficult to identify with the characters these writers capture and present to us. Their challenges remind us of our own moments of decision and awareness.

Entertaining, reassuring, instructive—these stories fulfill their purpose and richly reward their authors with insight and satisfaction.

I hope they will encourage you to follow suit and start writing your stories today!

—Denis Ledoux

Our Origins: The Family

By their very nature, these origin stories are laden with both subtle and overt messages about how we are to live. In this first section, the focus is our family origins.

As our primary social unit, The Family performs an important task: it acculturates each new generation into its methods and styles of survival and growth. For instance, religious families must raise believing children. To teach their kids to be agnostics would make homelife difficult!

Acculturation is a large task. Beyond assuring peaceful daily life, families teach behaviors and attitudes because members sincerely believe that they will help the next generation to be successful, happy or good in life. The family may be wrong in its views—or it may be wrong for a particular child, but this is the fundamental way our family-structured society assimilates and trains its children.

Lifestories are a highly effective vehicle for just this purpose. Our lifestory collections often begin with "founder tales." These center around a notable ancestor whose life experience represents an example of the values and attitudes The Family wishes the next generation to carry on.

The mantle of founder can, of course, fall on the shoulders of a living parent of whom children so frequently ask, "What was it like when *you* were young?" This primal desire to know reaches all the way back to *in the beginning.*

But, more frequently, the role of founder is conferred on a grandparent or a great-grandparent. When we recount, "When Grandmother came to this country, she…," we are participating in "hero-making" of the founder and presenting a model for imitation. We are playing our part, however unconsciously, in the imperative to incorporate and acculturate new family members into an approved range of doing things, a tradition, a value system endorsed by example drawn from family history.

Some people will say, "The stories I tell are just for fun. They aren't as serious as you make them out to be!"

Stories are, and should be, fun to tell and to hear. But they are almost always more. Even when the teller is an entertainer, our family stories often contain basic instructions about how to behave in order to survive and thrive in the world—and to do so consistently with family identity.

In order to meet its evolving needs, each generation reworks the founder tale sometimes updating it to place the founder in a closer generation. These inherited stories—often based on facts of the past but laced with themes most relevant to the present—are adapted to fit the presently-parenting generation's definition of itself and its vision of the future. Few parents want their children to be radically different from themselves—from previous generations, perhaps, but not from themselves!

In this section, you will read about how Yvette Audet recognizes her grandmother's spirit living on in her own daughters and granddaughters—and she seems to be encouraging them to be faithful to her legacy. Lisa Lehr, whose great-grandfather strode out of New England to become a larger-than-life figure in California, knows she must work to measure up to the past. Don Nylin's mother was committed to providing for her family; her work habits strongly influenced his own with the hidden agenda they carried—a deep-rooted belief in religious tolerance. Faye Miller's father wanted his children to carry on his values of industry and adaptability; in her portrait of him, the daughter pays them homage. Moishe Levin ensures his family will carry on the story that proves it is possible to bargain with God—but not without paying a price.

These writers are people whose lives were shaped by the men and the women who went before them. Anyone who undertakes lifestory writing does well to write—and grapple with the meaning of—the stories of The Family and its founders.

I See My Grandmother

BY YVETTE GAGNON AUDET

Yvette Gagnon Audet was born in Northern Maine of Acadian-American descent. She was part of the first Turning Memories Into Memoirs® workshop in 1988. The mother of six and *mémère* of many grandchildren, Yvette went back to school, first to learn to type her stories, and then to earn her high school diploma. She has since acquired computer skills and has written hundreds of pages of her family history and memoirs.

My grandmother, Edithe Beaulieu Lizotte, the daughter of Pierre Beaulieu and Marguerite Lévesque, was born on September 4, 1868, in Sainte-Agathe, Maine. This small town is on the Saint John River across from New Brunswick, Canada.

During the 1890's, while in her mid-twenties, *Mémère* came to Lewiston with some friends to work at the Bates Mill. However, after a time, she returned home to stay with her brother, Damase Beaulieu, who lived in Lille not far from Sainte-Agathe in Aroostook County. After a few years, Edithe met and married Denis Lizotte. They were wed at the church of Notre-Dame-du-Mont-Carmel in Lille on July 31, 1895.

My grandmother was twenty-seven—already old to be a bride, and her husband was twenty years her senior. At the time, this difference in age was not so unusual.

Mémère and *Pépère* had five children: Pierre, Marie, Alfred, Denis, and Marthe, who was my mother.

When her husband died, Edithe found herself a widow at age forty-one. Determined to keep her children together, she began to take in neighbors' laundry, and when this was not enough, she worked as housekeeper for Doctor Hammond. Years later, she remembered this kindly man and his wife who had given her used clothing for her children.

Over the next fifteen years it took to raise her children, she succeeded in keeping her family together.

Mémère moved the short distance from Lille to Keegan shortly after my parents married in 1924. She lived on Hillside Street, close to the church, the grocery store and my parents' home.

As I remember *Mémère* in the 1930s, she wore a long. ankle-length black dress with black stockings and shoes. She had long, white hair which she wore braided into a bun at the back of her head. This bun she fastened with fancy, shiny hair pins.

She often sat in the rocking chair on her porch. Sometimes, in the afternoons, on our way home from school, my brother and I would stop to visit her. It seemed she would always have a treat ready for us—homemade bread with butter or molasses cookies, the best I have ever eaten.

We children used to watch *Mémère* spin yarn on her spindle. I was always amazed at how fast the wool would turn into yarn. *Mémère* would also do fine embroidery, and she knitted and crocheted.

My own mother would often remind us how *Mémère* always did everything to perfection. "If it's worth doing, it's worth doing right," *Maman* would say in French, quoting her own mother.

Mémère was a very religious person. She walked the short distance to the church every day to attend *la messe*. Once a year in late July, she would go with some of her friends on a pilgrimage to the sanctuary of Sainte-Anne-de-Beaupré in Québec. *La Fête de Sainte-Anne* fell on the twenty-sixth. Dressed in a black outfit with her familiar *cloche* hat and a beautiful brooch, she would walk to the train station and wait on the platform bench for the train to take her and her friends to Sainte-Anne-de-Beaupré.

I was nine years old when *Mémère* first became ill and it was decided that she could not live alone any longer. She moved in with her daughter, *ma tante* Marie, and her son-in-law, *mon oncle* Lézime, and their five children.

Mémère's room was at the top of the stairs. I would visit her there often. She slept in a little white iron bed covered with a brightly-colored handmade quilt. There was a small window by her bed. Also in this room was a huge rocking chair.

Mémère chewed Copenhagen tobacco which came in a small round box. Her spittoon sat on the floor by her rocking chair. The tobacco was as much a treat for her as the bubble gum she handed out was for us.

After a time, *Mémère* got so sick that we weren't allowed to visit her as often. When I did see her, she was always wearing a flannel nightgown and a chenille robe. Her blue felt slippers had pompons on top. Her long white hair now flowed down to her waist.

Mémère died on September 11, 1943. Back in those days, we mourned people in their own homes. In *mon oncle* Lézime's parlor, my grandmother lay in her casket and people prayed by candlelight. She wore her familiar black dress and her lovely snow-white hair was neatly braided and fastened with the shiny hair pins. Seeing her lying there, I felt the need to touch her just one more time. Little did I know how cold she would be! To this day, I have not touched another dead body.

My mother made me a black satin dress with a white collar for the funeral. In those days, wearing black at a funeral was *de rigueur*.

Today, I do a lot of sewing and crocheting, and it still makes me think a lot of my *mémère*, of her smile and her long white hair. My handwork, like hers, also has to be done to perfection or I start over, for I remember her saying, "If it's worth doing, it's worth doing right!"

I have seen traits of my grandmother in my own daughters and granddaughters. Her spirit is still alive in us.

Completing the Circle
BY LISA J. LEHR

Lisa J. Lehr has had a passion for writing all her life. She is a Soleil Lifestory Network teacher who lives and teaches in Grass Valley, California. An earlier version of *Completing the Circle* first appeared in The *Maine Times*.

Even now, northern Maine where my maternal great-grandfather A. C. Hardison was born, is known for its harsh climate, characterized by winters that are brutal in their length and severity. To most of us, taming a wilderness like southern Aroostook County was in the nineteenth century to make it suitable for farming would seem unnecessarily self-punishing. Who would undertake such hard, almost unendurable work?

My great-grandfather A. C Hardison's father, Jacob, was such a man. Born in the settled Kennebec County town of Winslow, Maine, Jacob, as a teenager, had gone north with his father to Lyndon to settle there. (Lyndon was later to become Caribou.)

When Jacob grew up, he married and raised a family on the farm that he established there. In the mid-1860s, before A.C. was born, the Jacob Hardison family home burned down when a neighbor's fire blazed out of control. A year's supply of food was lost, as was all of the furniture, clothing, and household goods. With characteristic stoicism, the Hardisons set to work to replace what they had lost.

A little over a year later, their fourth boy, Georgie, aged four and a half, died of accidental poisoning. Family lore has it that a bundle of matches fell into a pan of milk. The family's hired girl removed the matches and later gave Georgie a drink from the pan. Unbeknownst to her, the phosphorus from the matches had tainted the milk, and when Georgie became ill, Great-great-grandmother Hardison had no idea what was wrong. It was January and snow drifts made the roads impassable. The nearest doctor was 11 miles away, and Great-great-grandfather Hardison was away on business. Georgie died the next day. My Great-great-grandmother always kept a pair of his little shoes in her trunk.

In 1869, their son, my great-grandfather, A. C. Hardison, was born on the family farm. Growing up in this household, A. C. worked hard as was expected of him to help the family survive, but he was different from his parents. He determined that when he was grown he would leave the hardscrabble farm and set out to do something different. Whether he wanted to escape the difficulty of

Aroostook farm life or make proud the mother who had never stopped grieving for her little Georgie or whether he felt pulled to seek his own fame and fortune, I can only speculate.

Unlike his father, grandfather and brothers, A. C. Hardison did not like farm work. He determined early on to learn how to make a different living by pursuing an education. He was the first of his family to graduate from high school and then he went on to graduate from the Engineering School at the University of Maine. With this degree in hand, A. C. accepted an uncle's invitation to join him in business in Southern California.

Over time, my great-grandfather succeeded beyond what he must have imagined when he set out from Caribou to seek his future in the wider world. A.C. was involved, often in a leadership position, in an impressive number of organizations. He was co–founder and president of what was at the time the largest lemon enterprise in the world. He managed gold mines both inside and outside of the United States. He was director of the town water works, a bank and a savings and loan institution. He was chairman of the county highway committee and of the state board of agriculture, president of the California Farm Bureau Federation and of the California Taxpayers' Association, director and chairman of the Agricultural Committee of the U.S. Chamber of Commerce and honorary life member of the State Association of County Agricultural Commissioners. He was awarded an honorary LL.D. by his alma mater, recognized at a U.C. Berkeley graduation ceremony and given the Distinguished Service Award by the California Farm Bureau.

Years after the fact, a local minister was astounded to learn that A. C. deserved credit for the church's structure, which had withstood 60 years of southern California earthquakes—a structure he designed at the young age of 23!

I met Great-grandfather Hardison only once. We celebrated Christmas (the year I was four going on five, I think) at his stately stone Craftsman-style home in Santa Paula. By then, he was the august patriarch, surrounded by most of his nine grown children and numerous grandchildren and great-grandchildren. My great-grandmother Cora, petite and prematurely silver-haired, adventurous and energetic—many said she was the ideal partner for him—had preceded her husband in death by nearly two decades. A. C. died when I was seven, at the venerable age of 96.

Over the generations, A.C.'s descendants have spread like wind-borne seeds across the length and breadth of California. I live near Lake Tahoe in a place where people come from all over to see the state's best county fairgrounds, best fall colors, best traditional Christmas celebrations, best spring wildflowers. Arguably, this is as close to being like Maine as any place in California (except, perhaps, the Mendocino coast). And I don't think my choice of geography is a coincidence. Yankee blood flows in my veins, and it makes me restless for the austere beauty, the sense of history and the authenticity that I fancy are Maine.

I have before me two pictures. One is of A. C.'s childhood home in Caribou, Maine; the other is of the home where he raised his family in Santa Paula, California. Side-by-side, the two represent not only a 3,000-mile journey, but the story of one man's determination to create a different life for himself.

I wish I could tell him how his descendants are all in awe of him.

A Jewish Grandmother Gave Us Christmas
BY DON NYLIN

Don Nylin, a retired educator from Illinois, is a lifewriting junkie. This story was written at a Turning Memories® workshop in 1999. Don has since participated in advanced Turning Memories® sessions and now facilitates memoir writing groups in his area. Don is both a father and a doting grandfather and is enthusiastic about life-long learning.

In early October in Augusta, Illinois, in the late 1930s, the leaves were beginning to fall. The nights were cooler, and there would soon be a hint of autumn in the air. Mother sat in her wicker rocker, homemade covers on the arms, in the dining room bay window. Dad's gooseneck lamp was shining brightly into her lap where she held a linen cloth. Her right hand darted quickly but deftly into the linen and out, into the linen and out. Save for that small motion, Mother was almost a seated mannequin.

Hour by hour, Mother sat there. Never rocking, only sewing. Barely moving except perhaps for an occasional glance upward to give her eyes some rest from the intense concentration, or maybe some tightening and loosening of the shoulders to release tension. There was no other movement but the stitches, the stitches, the stitches.

If the fine linen so expertly held was a lady's sheer handkerchief, the initials were small. But always neat and precise; each stitch so closely placed against the prior one that they must be inspected carefully to see that they were not a small mound of silvery white. After about 15 minutes, Mother would carefully fold the hanky and place it aside so that the three initials showed to good advantage. Then Mother would reach for another, and the process was repeated.

Sometimes the pieces to be embroidered were larger men's handkerchiefs. The initials may have been larger, but the stitches were just as precise. Because the initials were larger, they took a wee bit longer. For these initials, a pearl-gray thread was perhaps used. On rare occasions, the thread was a blue.

Over and over, throughout the better part of the day, Mother embroidered linens. She would often continue into the evening as well, especially if she had spent part of the day at the Ladies Aid Society meeting, or maybe at a church bazaar. Or maybe she had gone with Dad, a Methodist minister, to visit some hospitalized parishioner in Macomb or Quincy.

Less often, Mother would be seated with a large, heavy linen tablecloth on her lap. Still the stitch, stitch, stitch. Sometimes she worked on embellishing a single letter on the tablecloth. At other times, she worked on a much larger and more intricate monogram that consisted of a three-letter diamond. A large letter in the center indicated the family name. There were smaller letters on either side: to the left, the initial of the given name and, to the right, that of the middle name. The monogram was often finished off with small triangles placed to the left and the right of the initials. The center letter would be raised over a sixteenth of an inch above the linen fabric of the tablecloth. These center initials took much longer to embroider, but still Mother managed to make the individual stitches imperceptible. And once the tablecloth was finished and laid aside, Mother proceeded to embroider eight napkins with smaller monograms.

And so it went through October and November and into December. Boxes arrived from the Lace Shop in Evanston. Boxes with handkerchiefs, tablecloths, napkins, bureau runners, with initials stamped in pale blue, all carefully wrapped in white tissue. As boxes containing new work arrived; others, carefully packed, were heading northeastward to Evanston with completed work. Mother's pay was calculated by the number of initials she had embroidered. The more boxes with initials to embroider, the more pay.

I don't know when Mother began this annual employment. It could have been years earlier, perhaps closer to the beginning of the Depression years. We had moved to Augusta in September of 1938, right after I had started fifth grade. Although the country was beginning to work its way out of the Great Depression, I doubt that salaries of Methodist ministers were increasing very rapidly, so Mother needed to do this work to supplement Dad's income. Just as Dad worked a large garden and Mother canned jar after jar for the winter—to live beyond the subsistence level or thereabouts.

I wouldn't be surprised if Mother had been doing this most of my life, but I knew she had been doing it since at least the early 1930s, when we were at the height of the Depression. Parishioners couldn't give to the church money they could not earn. And if the church didn't receive the money, well, we had to do without.

Mother did not learn to embroider from Gramma. Buttons, patches, and darning most likely, but not embroidery. That came a bit later.

In about May of '09 (pronounced "ought-nine"), Mother completed grade school in Republic, Michigan. But instead of going on to the high school, that tall, two-story building by the pond along the railroad tracks, she headed south to Illinois, to Chicago, to become "nurse girl" (now called an *au pair*) for a well-to-do Jewish family. After a time, the family moved to New York. They must have been well-to-do because, after a few years with the family, she traveled with them across the United

States to the Pacific in an entourage of at least three large touring cars, one towing a trailer with tents and the paraphernalia needed to maintain the family.

When the family was in New York, the grandmother lived with them. Evenings, after the children were in bed, Mother spent time with the grandmother. From her, Mother learned to embroider.

It was the money Mother earned embroidering for the Lace Shop that made the difference between "getting by" at Christmas time and having enough to buy presents for Paul, Dad, and me.

That's how a Jewish grandmother gave us Christmas every year.

The Family Inventor
BY FAYE MILLER

In this story, Faye Miller celebrates her father's spirit of invention . She is a Soleil Lifestory Network teacher. She lives with her husband and their teenage children on a family farm in Freeman, South Dakota. Faye is completing her college degree and has dedicated herself to helping Dakota farm women explore and record their lifestories.

As a self-sufficient Minnesota farmer, Daddy had learned how to weld and fix almost any kind of equipment. He was always tinkering in his shop, and as I look back on his activities during my childhood, I now realize how very creative he was.

Daddy was an inventor. None of his inventions were ever patented, but that didn't matter—they were family projects.

His unique ideas provided solutions for problems that arose. Take, for instance, the first year we raised cucumbers for the Gedney Pickle Company. I was in junior high school at the time, probably in 1964 or 1965. Daddy thought raising pickles would be a bonding family experience that also would bring in additional needed income on our farm.

As soon as the decision to grow them was made, his mind went into creative overtime—what kind of contraption could he make that would ease the labor of cucumber picking? I didn't pay too much attention to his activities until one day he called us out to look at our new "cuke" machine. It looked odd, but the more we studied it, the more ingenious it seemed.

The implement was comprised of a bare frame, an axle, a motor, a steering wheel, and four used wheels rescued from old trailers. Dad had fashioned two platforms that extended out from each side of the machine. They were long enough for two people to lay on them on their stomachs. The apparatus was close enough to the ground so that, lying on our tummies in "complete comfort," we could inspect each plant for perfect-sized cucumbers.

We were five in our family, so Dad made it turn out exactly right with five spots—one person to drive and two on each side. The platforms we lay on were modified in such a way that our heads had support, but the corner of each person's platform was angled to allow room for our arms to move comfortably. Dad had thought of everything.

He had rigged up a conveyor belt on each side of the machine, underneath us and perpendicular to our bodies. As we picked the cucumbers, we put them on the conveyor belt, which dumped them onto another belt, and finally into a huge bag behind the driver. The amazing thing was that the contraption and the set up worked!

Our maiden trip through the field was quite an event. It was early in the morning, since it was cooler then. Each of us "pickers" donned gloves, ready to start. We knew we had the deluxe-model cucumber machine when we discovered that Dad had covered each of the wooden platforms with thick foam mats.

My brother Lauren, who is six years younger than I am, was designated as the driver. Daddy warned him to drive slow so we would have enough time to look through the foliage. Mostly he did a good job, but we sometimes felt he had lucked out with the driving gig. Since he had to drive so slowly, he spent a lot of time singing and throwing too-big cucumbers to our constant companion, Poochie, who would run after them like they were giant dog bones.

Turning around was a big challenge because of the lumbering nature of the machine, so Dad would have to take the controls at the end of each row. Every so often, Lauren would yell "full bag," and we would stop. Dad would shake down the bag, tie it up, set it in the row, and position a new bag.

Because we started in the early morning, dew was a problem. Our gloves would get soaked. We'd either put up with it or change gloves. My younger sister, June, hated the way her wet hands turned into white puckered flesh. The scratchy vines some-

times caused rashes on our arms too, but we persevered. The patch was probably about one-half to three-quarters of an acre and would take us about three to four hours to pick, working on alternate days. Mom always brought a jug of icewater and cinnamon graham crackers for rest time, all the while encouraging my sister and me as we grew tired.

I can still see Daddy, a man of average build, sporting the crewcut he wore his whole adult life. He was even-tempered, even when one of us kids did something not smart out in the patch—or in life, for that matter. His parenting style reflected his personal faith in God.

Daddy didn't attend college, but he was a person who constantly enjoyed the challenge of learning on his own. He always maintained he was shy by nature (which we kids thought was funny because he could initiate a conversation with anyone), but he had trained himself to be gregarious and at ease with people.

We picked cucumbers for at least four years, and we kids usually got a portion of the money earned, which was incentive enough for next year.

Eventually, as each summer came to a close, the cucumber plot dried up, and with it, the cash opportunities for the year. The plot brought in some needed income and provided rich memories as we worked together as a family.

That's what Daddy had hoped for.

My Grandfather's Gift: A Story of Moishe Levin

AS TOLD TO VICTOR W. VORON

Soleil Lifestory Network teacher Victor W. Voron has adapted Turning Memories Into Memoirs® to create memoir and Photo Scribe programs for groups in Philadelphia. He is the co-author of this story with Moishe Levin, whose voice is the protagonist's. Moishe Levin's photo appears on page 225.

In 1918, my family and I lived in the city of Kiev, which was then part of Czarist Russia. Pogroms, in which Jews were killed for who they were and not what they did, were not the only threat we faced. We also lived with the constant fear of starvation. The pangs of starvation drove me and my family to scavenge for food everywhere, even in garbage cans. We would take home scraps of food and wash them as best as we could.

Only five years old, I didn't realize then that the scarcity of work for Jews meant that we didn't have enough money to buy food. All I knew was that I was always hungry. That hunger stayed with me day and night, constantly occupying my mind. The need to eat and to satisfy my hunger drove me to the danger of eating garbage. As a result, I became deathly sick with typhoid fever, a killer disease.

I became weak, and my stomach ached with pain. Soon, my body burned from the heat of the fever. I lay in bed, still, unable to move. I was constantly thirsty. There was nothing I could do but lie there and suffer through the effects of the fever.

I was scared.

Most of the time my room was quiet, but occasionally I could hear a low, muffled crying. The tears were from my mother trying hard to hold back her grief and sorrow that she might lose me.

One day, as I lay in my bed burning with fever, I saw the

Angel of Death appear before me. He held out his hands, his right hand reaching for me, his left gesturing for me to grasp his hand.

"Moishele! Moishele!" I kept hearing my mother calling to me, begging me not to leave her. I was tormented with pain and fever, but I held on to life. The spark of life inside me struggled to keep from being extinguished.

My mother, Esther, and my older brother, Herman, had also had typhoid fever but they were not as infected as I was. Our doctor expected them to survive. But he said to my mother, "Mrs. Levin, Moishe will die. There's nothing more that I can do for him." Back then, doctors didn't have the knowledge about typhoid fever and the miracle drugs they have today.

My mother, still weak from the fever herself, continued to take care of me the best way she knew how. She believed I would survive and never gave up, hoping for a miracle.

My *zadeh* (grandfather), Erev Froim, loved me. He was my *tatteh* (father) while my father, Jake, was in America, working hard and saving money so the rest of us could emigrate there. *Zadeh* was a pious man, tall, with a red beard. He was full of life and love. We would play together. Often he would sit me on his shoulders and give me a ride through the house. I would pat him on his full head of red hair and kiss him. I loved him dearly.

My *zadeh* believed in miracles, too, and in divine intervention. Later, my mother told me what he did for me.

One day, with tears rolling down his face and red beard, my *zadeh* prayed to God to spare my life. I remember seeing my pain reflected on his face. His eyes were red from crying. He felt that asking was not enough. He said to God, "Dear God, spare my Moishele. He's young, a good boy with the future before him. Spare his life. Take mine instead."

And so my *zadeh* struck a deal with God, and slowly I improved and the fever subsided. The Angel of Death went away from me, and I no longer saw him.

But weeks later, the Angel of Death returned for my *zadeh*. Again, the angel held out his hands, this time to my *zadeh*. My *zadeh* grasped the Angel of Death's hands and so he left us, knowing that his request and prayer had been answered.

Zadeh, rest in peace. Thank you for the gift of life. I love you!

The Early Years

The stories we remember about ourselves tell us a lot about how we perceive—or how we prefer to perceive—*who we are.*

Since much of what has happened in our lives has been engulfed by oblivion, we must ask ourselves, why does a particular memory (often of a seemingly unimportant thing or event) survive? Why *this* memory and not some other?

Lifewriters often find that it is because *this* memory strikes an emotional chord that has continued to resonate—for good or bad. We keep playing this archetypal chord until we "get it right." Like the character in Bill Murray's film, *Groundhog Day,* we relive that experience like a broken record until understanding frees us to move on.

Lifewriting is an opportunity to gain insight into shaping forces so we can respond the next time as we have not been able to before, finally allowing a conclusion—sometimes years later!—to unfold. Three-quarters of a century before she took the Turning Memories® workshop, Roseanna (p. 56) watched as her father's funeral cortege pulled away from the train station. "For years, the sound of a train whistle has always made me feel sad," she said.

Writing may allow you to hear the train whistles of your life and to creatively deal with the feelings that arise when memories come rushing down the track!

For some, memories corroborate a family myth, and in repeating them, we not only affirm our need for reassurance and guidance but strengthen our bonds to the family itself. Or, the opposite is true. In exploring a memory in writing, we may hope to end the family's hold on us—whether it is a tight noose or more like a loosely-tied apron string.

Stories in this section delve into the time before adulthood. These writers share the foundations of their lives, the era when they were learning "the rules." Sally Johnston is a little girl again, basking in unconditional love. Yet, some part of her feels uncomfortable that she was so happy when her beloved uncle was so miserable. Renee Cassese remembers the lessons of ballet class with fondness—and a sense of something missing. Judith Stough writes of the experience of blended families before that term was invented and conveys her thanks to a mother who insisted she maintain connection with her "other family." Linda Miller revels in her childhood exuberance and in the unique opportunities that were hers—and yet she sounds a winsome note for the normative youth she did not have and for the enduring mark its lack left on her life. These writers gain access to their "train whistles" and become more fully themselves.

The Little Girl and the Foot Soldier
BY SALLY QUINN JOHNSTON

During the last years of World War II, my uncle, Kenneth Delvin Brumbaugh, my mother's youngest sibling, was 18 and an infantryman fighting in Europe. He was living in dank foxholes in the freezing mountains of northern Italy, with Germans shooting at him. I was a toddler—growing into a little girl—and spending many wonderful nights with my grandmother on a farm nestled snugly in the laurel hills of western Pennsylvania.

Ken had spent the summer after his high school graduation on the family farm, mowing hay, giving fodder to the cows, and harvesting grain for the coming winter. When the days grew shorter, he got on a train in Dayton and went to Fort Meade, Maryland, where he reported for duty. Then duly inducted and earning $20 per month, he continued on to Fort Benning, Georgia, for training. After that, he traveled to Camp Patrick Henry, Virginia. From Camp Henry, he left on a transport for Europe—and the war.

Ken had never been on the ocean before and was seasick on the troop ship for 21 days. Only when the voyage was over and he got off the boat in the Mediterranean did he and his fellow soldiers learn where they were going.

A certified Soleil Lifestory Network teacher living in Gray, Maine, Sally Quinn Johnston has taught in public schools in Pennsylvania, Connecticut, and Maine for over 30 years. She has conducted workshops in creative writing, TESL and Myers-Briggs Preference Types.

Meanwhile, I was back home, where my world consisted of two farmhouses, Belknap church, and an occasional trip to Dayton—a circuit of about three miles. After lunch, I'd go down the grassy hill from our farm and cross the dusty, lower road to my grandmother's place. When I arrived, Grandma might be writing a letter or handsewing. We'd listen to her favorite soaps on the radio—*Stella Dallas* and *Just Plain Bill*—while we drank tea with sugar and lemon. When the soap operas were over, Grandma and I would walk across the wooden bridge and up the winding dirt road to the schoolbus stop to meet my brother, Randy.

In November of 1944, my uncle Ken reached Naples, Italy. He was in the 88th Infantry Division, which was part of General Mark Clark's 5th Army. Ken had heard that Italy was warm and sunny, but it wasn't warm and sunny where he was stationed. In fact, the winter of 1944 to 1945 was unusually harsh. When it wasn't freezing, it was raining and the soldiers were ankle-deep in mud. Once in a while, Ken would get lucky and sleep in a tent; mostly he slept in a foxhole on wet, cold ground or on cement if he found an old building.

At my family's farm, after dinner and a hectic playtime with my big brother Randy and my little brother Jerry, I'd mention to my mother, "Grandma wants me to spend the night."

I would stare into my mother's eyes, hoping she would agree.

My mother would decide to check with Grandma. We were on the same party line, accessed by hand-cranked wooden telephones on the wall. Grandma's ring was one long and one short; ours was two longs. Nanny Myers the operator at the central switchboard in Dayton was one exaggerated long, but we didn't have to bother Nanny to call between our house and Grandma's apartment.

They might talk for a while, and of course, Grandma always said yes! After Mother was sure Grandma would have me, I'd pack my little-girl pajamas and toothbrush in a brown paper bag and head down the hill. However, I would never wear my pajamas when I slept over. I'd borrow one of Grandma's silky gowns, short on her but dragging behind me as I pranced around. My favorite one was a baby-blue gown with white trim. Grandma would undo my auburn pigtails and brush my hair. Oh, I felt like a princess there.

Meanwhile, at the war front, Ken lived and slept in his ODs (olive drabs), a field jacket, a helmet, a scarf, and combat boots, as well as anything else he could find to help him stay warm. His unit moved north, into rugged mountains. On the way up the mountain, at a farm owned by a family named Mussazzino, there was a stone wall about three-feet high and three-feet wide with a trough built in the top. The water came down out of the mountains, down the trough, down and then across the valley for about two miles until the flow emptied into the Vozturna River. The water was ice cold but the soldiers washed in it.

"There'd be maybe a dozen guys on my left and more on my right, all in the same water as it went by," Ken said later.

After they got up in the mountains, he never got to wash with water as he only had snow to rub on his face.

"We didn't smell too good," he remembers of that time.

At Grandma's, before I could eat the bedtime snack she had prepared, she would wash my hands by lathering up hers, then caressing first my right hand and then my left between her two soapy palms. "Let's have a snack before we go to bed," she'd say. Usually she would slice apples or make uncooked applesauce by slicing an apple in half and scraping a table knife along the pulp until the skin was hollow and the dish held fresh pulp and juice.

For Uncle Ken and the men of the 88th Infantry, food was always cold. They ate C-rations or dissolved some bouillon cubes in water, but nothing was eaten hot. "I can't remember having anything to drink except water from a stream or maybe some cognac," Ken recalls. "I couldn't keep warm. Period."

They didn't have any radios and seldom saw the commanding officer, so Ken knew little about the conflict that was going on. All he heard were rumors from other guys—mostly that the war was going to last for 10 years or even longer.

Back on Laurel Hill, every evening was like a slumber party for two. Grandma and I might listen to *Amos and Andy* on the radio or she might read to me. She always had handwork to do and would teach me how to make stitches as she sewed. Her hands were quick and nimble with her needle; mine were both tiny and clumsy. Sometimes she'd rub hand cream on my chubby little feet, and if I stood beside her on the window seat, she'd wrap her loving arm around my legs as I watched the neighbors go by on the single-lane road.

What Ken got to watch were the icy mountains. "In the Apennine Mountains, I was in the same foxhole for 17 days. The snow and ice were so bad. We were in a holding position. You couldn't show yourself during the day." They were under sniper fire. "As a result, my feet stayed wet, and I got trenchfoot. The soles of my feet just started to rot."

Back home, Grandma would get down on her knees beside the bed to say a prayer for Ken and his brother, both fighting in the big war. When we climbed into her high bed, I'd settle down easily. I've never slept as contentedly as I did those nights in the 1940s with the war going on half a world away.

In Italy, Ken was waiting—for sounds, for relief, for letters from home. He got mail often. "I got a letter from a girl in Dayton every day," he said. The mail and rations came up by mule train, and some nights, he could hear the mules' hooves on the ice. Unfortunately, the Germans would hear them too and would lay a bunch of mortars in. Many of those nights, the Americans lost all the mail and all the rations.

Ken slept restlessly, wrapped in a dark wool blanket that had "U.S. Army" stamped in the corner. He never thought the war would be over or that he'd come home. "I thought we were animal fodder for the war," he remembers.

Ken was a white American boy with German and English heritage but "I fought beside the 442nd, the Jap outfit, and the 92nd Buffalo (a Negro outfit). Another bunch, Gurks from South Africa, were assigned to us. They all, every one of them, were the best," Ken says, paying tribute to his buddies.

After the war, returning soldiers couldn't keep their Army-issued rifles. "No one wanted them anyway," Ken said. They were glad to be rid of the guns. Ken's fascination, however, was for the foreign-made weapons he had confiscated. He sent two guns home by wrapping a German Luger and an Italian combine with a bayonet in an Army blanket and hiding them in his duffel bag. They would have been confiscated had they been found, but with hundreds and hundreds of bags coming through, customs officials could only conduct spot-checks. Ken's guns made it through the checkpoints, but it had taken some conniving.

He hid another gun in a German canteen that had a heavy covering. "I took the cover off and split open the canteen at the seam. I took an Italian Beretto all apart, wrapped the parts in handkerchiefs, and put them inside. Then I squeezed the canteen back together and put its cover back on. I mailed that from Naples," Ken explains. Over a year later, the package made it to the farm.

After VE day, Ken's unit boarded a Merchant Marine ship for the return trip to the States. It was another rough crossing for him. He remembers thinking that the Nazis hadn't killed him but seasickness might! After being sick again for 17 days, he arrived at Camp Zee, Virginia.

When they got back to the States, the men in his unit weren't discharged as they had hoped. Instead, Ken and his fellow soldiers were put on another ship headed to the Pacific and Japan.

■ ■ ■

When the war finally ended, Ken came home on the train. I missed Uncle Ken's homecoming because I was wounded in my own battle—with a glass piggybank. While Mom and I sat two blocks away in the doctor's office, others welcomed the returning hero and his train to Dayton.

"I had some things to work through after I got home, but not like some guys," he told me later. "One simple thing for me was when a phone would ring. It just scared the hell out of me. That lasted for a long time."

Jerry, my little brother, was enthralled by the guns and the conflict with the Nazis. Once, when he was about 3 years old, we were in the parlor of the big house as Ken cleaned the guns he had mailed from Italy. With boyish enthusiasm, Jer asked him, "Did you shoot anybody?"

Ken hesitated. "Oh, I hope not," answered our gentle giant.

Ken admits that they went through hell at times, but after visiting Normandy with Randy and Jerry in 1995, he said, "I'm thankful I was where I was, in the mountains of Italy. I feel for anyone who made that Normandy landing."

As a little girl, watching Uncle Ken put medication on his feet or change the dressings, I remember thinking, "How odd to sleep with your boots on!" I had no concept of what he had been through, or how our lives had been so different during the war.

Ballet Shoes

BY RENEE CASSESE

Late summer breezes swirled the leaves as Mom and I walked to the bus stop. In a pink vinyl case with a gold clasp and a picture of a ballerina on the front, I carried a pair of black ballet shoes with elastic straps and a pair of black patent leather tap shoes with black ribbon ties. Every week, I cleaned and shined those tap shoes using butter and a soft cloth. The metal taps on the toes and heels were like medals of honor that pounded out my importance.

The bus came and swallowed us up into its cool interior. Sitting under the harsh fluorescent lights and surrounded by faded advertising posters, we rode from Levittown to the depot in Hempstead, where the bus spit out its passengers like extracted teeth.

Renee Cassese is a Soleil Lifestory Network teacher in Seaford, Long Island, NY. She holds an MA in Education. "Ballet Shoes" is from her memoir.

Mom and I walked two blocks to DaSilva's Dancing School, where I studied ballet, tap, and acrobatics. I was five years old. Mom left me in the studio while she went to the waiting room to watch with other mothers as the group of little girls followed the lead and directions of the instructor. There were two teachers, Mr. DaSilva and Pat, a female teacher. Since I was more comfortable around adult women, I always hoped Pat would be our instructor for the day. This particular time she was.

The dance studio was a huge room with two walls covered in mirrors. Along the long wall at the back ran a wooden *barre*, which we used for practice.

First up was ballet. Pat led us through the five positions known to all ballerinas. We forced our legs into proper alignment and molded our arms and hands into graceful curves, while visions of Swan Lake played in our minds. All the girls wore pastel-colored leotards and tights. Pat, the teacher, was dressed in black. Her tall lanky body made poses I aspired to.

We learned *pliés* and turns and leaps. Then we went to the *barre*. I held on with one hand, raised the other like a swan's neck above my head, and stretched out one leg, resting my foot on the *barre*, arch curved and toes pointed. In time to classical music and taps of the teacher's baton, I touched my forehead to my knee, over and over again.

Pat attentively watched over her charges. Periodically, her gentle hand would re-adjust the arc of an arm or the position of a back. Then we turned simultaneously and stretched out the opposite leg.

After ballet came acrobatics. We did somersaults and cartwheels. We lay prone on the floor and touched our toes to the backs of our heads—a simple feat for five-year-old girls.

Then we would stand against a wall. When my turn came, Pat would lift one of my legs and then the other so I could kiss my knees. I excelled at this exercise, though now I can barely raise my leg parallel to the floor. The ease with which I did that then paralleled the ease of life for a five-year-old girl in the 1950s.

Last came tap lessons. Oh, the wonderful sound of those metal taps on the polished wood floor! The music was brisk and the crisp words "*Sherappe*, ball, change" kept us moving in sync.

When the lessons were over, we tucked away our ballet and tap shoes like precious jewels. As I sat on the floor putting on my saddle shoes, I gazed across the studio to a spot above the *barre* on the back wall. There, hanging by pink satin ribbons, was a pair of pink toe shoes. No pan of gold could have beckoned me more. I coveted them. I lusted after them. I wanted them.

Each week I would stare at them as my eyes glistened over like dew on roses. I wished I could take them home. I wanted to wear them and dance like the *prima ballerinas* in all the ballet books I read.

This day my envy did not go unnoticed. Pat came over to talk to me about those precious satin shoes with the wooden boxes in the toes. The shoes were a size four, way too big for my tiny feet, but Pat promised me that when my feet were big enough she would give the toe shoes to me and teach me how to balance on their tips.

Walking back to the bus depot that day in the silver blue dusk, I should have been happy, but I wasn't. As we waited for the bus, I was overcome with sadness. Perhaps sensing this, Mom took me into a gift shop, where I spied a Ginny doll with a pink satin dress and tiny pink shoes on her plastic feet. Mom bought me the doll. I held it tightly all the way home on the bus.

Outside the window of the bus rose the golden orb of the moon. It was huge. Deep craters etched a face into its surface. It frightened and seduced me at the same time. Shivers darted through me every time I looked at it. But each time I turned away, its crafty eyes lured me back for another peek.

I watched as it followed us home. Later it peered into my bedroom window, listening to my dreams. In the morning it was gone, but my longing remained. I can still feel it to this day.

The ballet shoes I wanted so badly were never to be mine. As an adult I wear a size four shoe, but those satin treasures are long gone, as is DaSilva's Dancing School and the teachers who fed my dream of being a *prima ballerina*.

Zoot Bosh!

BY LINDA MILLER

I have never let my schooling interfere with my education.
—Mark Twain

"*Zoot bosh!*" we yelled at the driver—"hurry up!" Once again, he had thrown the car into a power turn, knocking all of us off-balance, our books and papers flying. As we sped away, our small worried faces peered out the rear window at the narrow lane and the crowd of curb-to-curb angry men, waving their arms, shouting, and advancing in our direction. Our driver raced expertly through what has been acknowledged as the world's most chaotic driving environment, never hitting any of the people, donkeys, camels, carts, street vendors or other cars that crowded the streets of Tehran. Inside the car, my heart was pounding from a combination of terror and excitement. I was never sure whether we were going to get away. Maybe our car would break down, I thought, or a group would come from behind and trap us in the narrow street. My plan, if caught, was to try to pass for Persian! I actually imagined I could speak enough Farsi (Farsi—Persian—is the language of Iran) to get by, and with my dark hair and eyes, I hoped I could fool them. Of course, that would only work if they didn't notice my American accent and fair Irish skin and if they ignored the fact that I was a passenger in a vehicle from the American Embassy with a bunch of American kids and an Iranian chauffeur. Narrow escapes and wild rides were just part of going to and from school for us.

> A former police officer, Linda Miller is a certified Soleil Lifestory Network teacher who offers lifewriting workshops and other memoir services under her company name, PastForward Memoirs. Linda lives and works in the Minneapolis area.

Daddy made his career in the military. As we followed him to various assignments, I learned that home was not a specific location, it was where your family and your belongings were. Once the familiar furniture was in place and our pictures were hanging on the wall, I was home, no matter where in the world we were.

The summer between second and third grade, Daddy left for his new assignment as a cryptographer in the office of the military attaché of the American Embassy in Tehran. My mother, sister and I joined him just after Thanksgiving, and I continued third grade there.

These were tumultuous times in Iran, and there was considerable political turbulence and unrest as the Soviets and the Americans competed for influence. The Shah was overthrown and street fighting—riots, as we called them— were common occurrences. Instigated by Tudeh Party (communist) agitators, these riots could be quite anti-American in tone. These were the same folks who plastered our front door with "Yankee Go Home" stickers nearly every night.

The Community School in Tehran, located on Ghavam Sultaneh Street, had slightly more than 200 students then. It was commonly called the "American School," I suppose, because it was run by Presbyterian missionaries from the United States who had had a presence in Iran since the 1830s. The school had been started to educate children of the missionaries, who had been home-schooled or sent to Europe. Iranians and foreign students were enrolled as well, and by the time I was there, only a few of the students were missionary children. Classes met Monday through Thursday and on Saturdays. They were taught in English, but we all studied French and Persian, too. With the exception of the Americans, most of the students spoke two or more languages.

Someone once called the Community School "a laboratory of democracy at work." Besides the American kids, there were many students from prominent Iranian families and children  from Europe, Asia, and the Middle East, whose families were living temporarily in Tehran. Their parents were diplomats, exiles, professionals, military or oil industry personnel, etc. We represented 28 nationalities and eight religions, yet we studied and played beautifully together, barely aware of the differences between us or of the tensions among many of our countries. Christians, Jews, Moslems, Zoroastrians, and Sikhs blended with no problems. Officially, each student's religion and nationality was respected, although the school curriculum included Christian chapel services and Bible study. Above the school entrance, in beautiful Persian calligraphy, were the words from the Book of John, 8:32, "You shall know the truth, and the truth shall make you free."

We all learned the United Nations pledge of allegiance to our individual countries and flags and we sang the United Nations hymn, the "Song of Peace," set to music by the Finnish composer, Jean Sibelius.

THE UNITED NATIONS PLEDGE
*"I pledge allegiance to my country, and to the United Nations of which it
is a part, one world brotherhood of peaceful nations,
with liberty and justice for all."*

The year after we arrived, the school moved across Tehran to a site on Khiabane Zhaleh, Kucheh Mareez Khaneh (Hospital Drive), near Jaleh Street. The new school was an old Presbyterian missionary hospital. Farah Diba, who became Queen of Iran, had been born there. Used as a military hospital during World War II, it was eventually returned to the missionaries to be used as the school campus. The large, shady compound had several buildings, a church, walking paths, and a pond teeming with tadpoles.

 The new school facilities were a big improvement, but there was a downside. It was located at the end of a dead-end street in a dangerous part of the city where unrest and riots were particularly common. My parents worried. Good thing they never knew that some of us occasionally slipped off campus and into the Tehran streets to shop. Our mission was to buy colored erasers, which we needed for our collections of eraser shavings!

I ventured into theater that year. I thought the story of Cinderella would make a great play and found other kids at school who thought so, too. Of course, not all of them were sure who

Cinderella was, but that didn't stop us. We set about writing the script, selecting the actors, designing the set and costumes and holding rehearsals. I found that I could easily get all of us out of class to work on this by being somewhat honest and saying we had to work on "the play." Each teacher assumed we were involved in a school-sponsored theater production. We had an exciting, productive time for a couple of weeks until my teacher, Mrs. Stephanides, and others found our absences from class excessive. They began to check into who was in charge of the play and were so surprised to discover that it was me! The play was not a school-sponsored event, and of course, there was no adult supervision. Needless to say, the show did not go on.

In America that fall, Eisenhower was running for president. Soon, a gang of American boys started "terrorizing" us on our school grounds. Concealing themselves in the bushes, they would jump out, grab unsuspecting passers-by and threaten to beat them up unless they responded correctly to the question, "Do you like Ike?" When they captured me, I took a wild guess and said I liked Ike. That must have been the right answer because I was released unharmed, though shaken. "Who the heck was Ike?" I wondered.

Fourth grade was the first time I can remember having a "boyfriend." I latched onto Stefan, who was from one of the Soviet countries and was several years older than I. I think it was a rather one-sided relationship, but he tolerated my constant presence well. I stuck to him like glue while he and his friends hung out or played soccer. I remember him as being tall (well, I was only nine years old!), dark and handsome, with a great accent. Looking back, I see that my real motive might have been to gain a protector from those scary "Do you like Ike?" terrorists.

One of the highlights of the school year was Parents' Day, which was held in the spring, just before the end of school. We performed for the parents and other guests, singing in differ-

ent languages and dancing national folk dances, wearing country-specific costumes. Each class represented a country, and so we learned unfamiliar songs, dances, and national dress.

In the spring of third grade, my class was in the Russian group for Parents Day. We sang *"Ochi Chernye"* (Dark Eyes) and danced a Russian folk dance. I can still sing that song in Russian. The event was held outside in the school compound. We rarely had to worry about being "rained out" in Tehran.

I left the Community School behind after fourth grade when my family returned to the United States. Americans were flooding into Iran then, their numbers eventually reaching 70,000. The American Embassy asked the Community School to take responsibility for the education of all American children in the city, but the new principal suggested that it might be time for the Embassy to start its own school. The year we left Iran, the new school for Americans opened. I am so grateful I was there before that happened!

The Community School prospered and grew, continuing to serve both international and

Iranian children in Tehran for many more years until the Islamic Revolution forced its closure. The last class graduated in the spring of 1980. Those who attended the school never forgot the experience and, although former students are living all over the world, we have a reunion every two years to renew friendships and remember those school days in Tehran. Of course, the reunion is not held in Tehran, but that is the goal for sometime in the future.

■ ■ ■

During the two years after we left Iran, I attended four different U.S. schools. Near the end of sixth grade, we left the U.S. again, this time heading to Helsinki, Finland, where Daddy began a two-year tour of duty. That fall, my sister Carol and I enrolled in the English School, a private Catholic School. As in Iran, the tuition was paid by the Embassy but transportation was not provided. Finland was, and still is, one of the safest places on earth. Kids walked or used public transportation to go to and from school. In contrast to Tehran, it was always a calm and peaceful commute.

More often than not, when we moved, it was mid-year, and I invariably missed some key concept in one subject or another. I spent a lot of time trying to "catch-up." I learned to live with the feeling of always being an outsider, of continually making and losing relationships and of expecting all things to come to an end. Connections have been elusive ever since (my sister, my brother and I are all divorced). But I'm convinced my sense of adventure, the attraction to danger that I occasionally indulge in and my penchant for traveling off the beaten track all come from these early-life experiences.

Attending a private Presbyterian school in Islamic Iran, a Catholic school in Lutheran Finland, plus six U.S. public schools, all before eighth grade, made for one mixed-up kid with large gaps in learning. For example, my math is terrible. Really terrible. But thanks to the Tehran Community School, I can spell *hieroglyphics*!

I apparently was somewhere else when Americans my age were learning American history. I probably don't know enough to pass the test given U.S. immigrants applying for citizenship. Instead, I learned about Persia's history: its ancient capitol at Persepolis and about the great Persian kings, Darius and Cyrus. I learned to speak enough Persian and Finnish to be mis-

understood. I know the story of the great Finnish military hero, Mannerheim, and the music of Finland's famous composer, Jean Sibelius. I know a little about the Finnish national epic, *Kalavala*, and a lot about their lovable storybook characters, the *Moomintrolls*. I have a sort of Catholic/Anglican/Presbyterian understanding of Christianity and a pretty good grasp of the origins and history of Islam. I have seen the crushing poverty of the Third World, lived in a country where life hasn't changed in hundreds, if not thousands, of years, and where transgressions of the law could result in brutal public punishments. I never witnessed a beheading, thank God, but I remember hearing that they were carried out in Tehran when we lived there. I have had wonderful friends from other cultures and faiths. I have ridden camels, eaten unidentifiable foods, gone swimming in the Caspian Sea, looked out from behind a *chador* (the head-to-toe veil worn by Iranian women.), given money to beggars, and run from rioters. None of this would have happened if I had spent those years in one town, one neighborhood, and one school.

I consider myself lucky to have had such an exciting, unique and useful education.

Summer Train Rides
BY JUDITH G. STOUGH

Every summer from the mid-1940s to the mid-1950s, my mother and stepfather put me on a train to visit my natural father and his extended family in Tennessee. My parents were divorced when I was three. There was no legal requirement that I visit him, but my mother thought it was important for me to know my father's family, explaining that they were "good people."

As summer approached each year, my mother and I would have numerous discussions about the upcoming train trip. Using my powers of persuasion, I would explain to her why I didn't want to visit a father I did not know, as well as the many other unknown relatives. But despite all my reasons to avoid the trip, my mother always won the argument.

Judith Stough is a retired educator who lives in northern Virginia. She is working on a novel as well as writing her memoir from which this excerpt is taken.

When the day of my journey finally arrived, my suitcase would be packed with freshly ironed summer cottons. My mother would prepare a brown-bag lunch for the trip. Then, too soon, we would be off to the station. My mother, stepfather, little brother and I would stand on the station platform and watch the big, black steam engine approach. The closer the train came, the greater my feeling of dread grew, until sometimes, it exploded into tears.

The train would finally screech to a halt with a last belch of white smoke. With hugs from everyone and my mother's assurances about how much fun I was going to have, I was handed over to the conductor. My mother always asked him to look out for me during the trip and told him that my father and my aunt would meet me at my destination. As the train pulled out, I waved and waved until my mother, stepfather, and little brother shrank to the size of three, tiny dots on the horizon.

The four-hour train ride from southwest Virginia to eastern Tennessee bombarded my senses with new sights, smells, sounds and textures. As I settled into my seat, I could feel the rough, hard woven straw seat on the backs of my bare legs. Every time I moved, it scratched me. Because of the summer heat, I stuck to the seat, and when I got up, the imprint of that straw patterned the backs of my knees.

Gazing out the window, I could see the reflection of a little girl with large, brown eyes and dark, brown pigtails tied with blue ribbons. Dressed in a blue gingham dress, wearing black-patent Mary Janes with white anklets, she returned my gaze. Usually, she was not smiling.

A cacophony of noises accompanied the train as it snaked through the lush, green farmland and rolling hills of southwest Virginia into eastern Tennessee—loud hissing from the release of the steam into the smokestack and the brake pistons, sharp, metallic clanging as the wheels bounced over the rails, and long, mournful groans as the train lumbered up steep grades. The best sound of all was the shrill note of the train's whistle as we came to railroad crossings and approached stations.

My train trips were always in the summer, usually in July when it was very hot, so the train windows would be lowered several inches. The idea was to circulate air, but the result was often a barrage of cinders and smoke blowing through the window from the smokestack. I would go to the ladies' room many times to wash cinders from my eyes. This acrid cloud would make my eyes water, and its smell would linger on my clothes and in my hair.

One of the pleasurable and interesting parts of these train trips was watching the scenery go by. The train never went very fast, so I was able to get long looks at red barns, at cattle grazing, at farmers mowing hay, at children, and sometimes older people, waving from their front porches. I especially liked waving back to the children. We would wave until we could no longer see each other. I wondered as the train slowly moved through those small, rural communities: Who lived there? Were there little girls like me? Had they ever ridden a train all by themselves? Did they have a father and another family they had to visit each summer?

The names of the towns always intrigued me—Rose Hill, Dryden, Ben Hur, Ewing. I especially liked to hear the conductor coming through the train announcing the stops. He always seemed to draw out the last syllable—Ben Hur became "Ben Hurrrrr." Then as passengers boarded he would shout, "All Aboarrrrd!" He seemed to enjoy saying these names as much as I enjoyed hearing them.

As the train neared my destination, Cumberland Gap, I became aware once again of that feeling of dread. Coming into the station, I saw the two familiar figures, my father and Aunt Florence, on the platform. My father had black hair like mine and wore a brown fedora, a dark blue suit. He held a cigar in his right hand. Aunt Florence also had dark hair; she wore a cotton, flowered housedress and clutched a large pocketbook against her chest. They would sometimes shade their eyes from the late afternoon sun with their hands as they scanned the horizon for the approaching train.

After the train came to another squealing, lurching stop, the conductor, placing a small set of steps in front of the train steps, would set my suitcase on the platform and carefully help me down. Another summer visit would begin.

As the years went on, my attitude began to change, and even though I never really knew my father very well, I did establish strong connections with other members of the family. I came to realize that these summer train trips were a gift to me from my wise and courageous mother. It was through them that I came to know and love my other family and to form lifelong relationships which developed and grew during the soft, sultry summer days my cousins and I rode horses, climbed through hay lofts, waded in creeks, milked cows and spent many hours under the spreading branches of ancient shade trees eating candy from my father's store—"The Confectionery," as it was called then.

My summer train rides, which began with reluctance and dread, ultimately became a symbol of motherly wisdom, self-discovery and family connection for me.

Coming of Age: Adolescence

Lifestories provide an opportunity to affirm and celebrate—to write the equivalent of a monument to you and your life. The writers whose stories appear in this section came to important self-realizations; their stories celebrate the decisions that altered the course of their lives. Two tell of an adolescence lived in the 1930s and are heavy with the trauma of the Great Depression. Adolescence then was not characterized by freedom and disposable income! As Gertrude Laliberté's reveals, the responsibilities of adulthood began years sooner at the time than they do today.

Often, as these writers recall their adolescence, they remember—with gratitude—a special person who offered them a different model than their families could. In New York City, Dortha Faulls met a Sunday School teacher who changed her life. As she puts it, "I will never forget Dot Mehring," for she showed Dortha the way to fulfillment and a life of meaning.

Others celebrate the resounding impact of a life experience which itself provided strong mentoring. A medical emergency handed Gertrude Laliberté the model she needed to escape the low-paying, boring work her parents were caught in, the only life they could envision for her. Decades later in a less bleak adolescence, Carole Glass learns from observing a harried employer about the kind of choices she must make in order to fashion a life as the adult she wants to become.

These literary monuments celebrate important turning points in their writers' lives, moments of self-recognition that become landmarks on the personal maps of their life's journey. In erecting them, these writers reaffirm and share how they have recognized and met the challenges we all face in choosing life paths consistent with our essential values and needs.

My Teacher, Dot Mehring

BY DORTHA FAULLS

Born in Missouri, Dortha Dust Faulls grew up in New York City. Like her mentor, she was a teacher. She wrote this story in one of the very first Turning Memories Into Memoirs® workshops in 1990. Dortha is the youngest in this photo of her family, pictured here soon after they arrived in New York.

My Sunday School teacher, Dot Mehring, stopped me at the head of the stairs as I was going up to join the class. Miss Mehring was tall, statuesque, and wore thick glasses. In class, I always listened to her every word. Her low-pitched voice seemed to constantly say something important.

I always sought to please her, and now she would be disappointed with me.

Sunday school was already over for the week, and she told the other girls to continue on down. She leaned against the wall and pulled me to her side. She put both arms around me.

"What's wrong?" she asked.

It was the time of year to change the hour on the clocks and nobody had done it at our home the night before. Until now, I had had a perfect attendance record and I didn't want to lose it. But I was late. Would this mean an absence on my record?

I was immobilized, hardly able to speak. Finally, I said, "I'm late."

As soon as I had told her, "I'm late," I realized the tense was wrong since the class was already dismissed. I should have said "was"—"I was late."

"It doesn't matter," she said. "Next Sunday, you'll be on time."

We walked down the stairs, her arm around me, and I was in heaven again. Because the mistake had not been mine, I was allowed to keep my perfect attendance record—and Miss Mehring was not angry with me.

She had inherited some money from her parents and was able to provide our class with many special experiences we would not have had otherwise. Our parents could hardly afford to raise us, let alone do for us what she enjoyed doing. She took us to our first Broadway show in New York. She took us to visit International House where many foreign students lived. We went to a Chinese restaurant and ate with chopsticks. She took us on picnics and cookouts.

One day, she took us to a corner drugstore for ice cream sodas. Another girl's brother, Jimmy, who had recently started college, was with us. It made a big impression on me: to think that this boy, whose sister I knew, was actually going to college!

Dot Mehring never once said to me, "You should go to college", but she somehow imparted to me the resolve to do this, against many odds. This dynamic woman took the place of something—someone—that was missing in my life. No one in my family had ever gone beyond high school, and Miss Mehring had a master's and a doctorate from Columbia University!

That summer, Dot Mehring toured Europe. She sent a postcard to each girl in her Sunday School class. I cherished mine for months, perhaps even years. At the time, I was so intent on saving my nickels and dimes for a trip of my own that I overlooked the significance of the card she had selected for me. It was a picture of "Big Ben", the huge clock tower in London.

She may have meant to show me the importance of knowing the correct time. But I really think she wanted to remind me of our shared moment, that Sunday when I had been so late.

My cache of nickels and dimes never gave me a trip to Europe, but I did manage, with financial help from an uncle, to go to college.

I will never forget Dot Mehring.

Little Did I Know
BY GERTRUDE LALIBERTÉ

Little did I know that America's involvement in World War II would steer me towards the selection of a fulfilling and financially-rewarding career.

In September of 1939, I entered Lewiston (Maine) High School without an immediate or long range career goal. I enrolled in the commercial course, believing that office work would be my future. My parents' lives had been full of uphill struggles due to illness and financial difficulties. Their existence had revolved around work and family, making of these a strong ethic. Their lives made a deep, lasting—and negative—impression on me. I felt strongly that my life must somehow be different, but I wasn't sure how.

When I was a teenager, because I had no other model and because I needed to earn my keep, I continued the desperate pattern of work they had taught me. I worked my way through high school doing odd jobs. They were monotonous, demeaning and unchallenging. Between 1939 and 1943 therefore, I spent vacations and weekends hulling strawberries at a commercial packing company, picking string beans at a farm, affixing labels to bottles at the Gin Distribution Company. I hand-packed donuts at Lepage's Bakery, sold candy at J.J. Newbury's and cosmetics at F.W. Woolworth's. I babysat for a local family and worked as a spinner-

Gertrude Laliberté held a B.S. in Nursing (Boston College) and an M.S. in Nursing Administration (The Catholic University of America). She was an active community volunteer with many organizations during her retirement. She died in 2000.

cleaner at the Hill Mill. I was a tack puller at the Clark Shoe Shop, a rod examiner at North American Philips Electronics. These jobs provided no challenge—except putting up with the sights, the sounds, and the smells!

There were positive effects to all of this, however. I realized, if I could survive these years of menial work, I could survive anything! My resolve to find a challenging life's work that would provide both stimulation and adequate compensation was strengthened. I vowed to seek a future free of my parents' struggles, a future that would be personally and financially rewarding. I wanted also to be able to ease my parents' problems and help them have a life of greater ease and comfort.

In early 1940, I still had no clue as to a career direction or a course of action to accomplish these career goals. But an unexpected appendectomy that summer turned my life around.

I spent three weeks in the hospital and observed the nurses at work. Their skill, compassion and positive attitudes inspired me to join their ranks.

I mulled over the idea: how could I ever finance three additional years of study after high school? It didn't seem possible, so I continued with the commercial courses, and nursing became a dormant goal. I believed I had no alternate escape than office work—until World War II came to my rescue!

Following Pearl Harbor and the declaration of war, my idea of becoming a nurse resurfaced. I could follow my brother's patriotic example and be of service to my country if only I could find the financial resources to put myself through nursing school.

In 1942, an Act of Congress was passed creating the U.S. Cadet Nurse Corps. The program's purpose was to prepare additional military nurses for service. As soon as I heard about it, I went to a local hospital for more information. It seemed possible that I would qualify.

When I returned to high school for my junior year, I switched from the commercial course to a special one created for those of us who were preparing for the Cadet Nurse program. I dropped typing, bookkeeping and stenography and took up instead Latin, biology, chemistry, algebra and college English.

In September 1943, at the beginning of my senior year, I was accepted into the first class of the U.S. Cadet Nurse Program and entered St. Mary's School of Nursing. The government paid all my educational expenses and provided a monthly stipend of $10 the first year, $20 the second, and $30 the third year. After graduation, the cadets were obligated to serve a minimum of two years in one of the branches of the military service.

The academic and clinical programs were accelerated in order to ready the cadets for mobilization within eighteen months. We carried an intense schedule: six days a week, we began our clinical work at 7 AM. At nine, we had four hours of classes, then back to the nursing units until 7 PM. We were expected to absorb and retain information and skills rapidly during these twelve hour days.

I was proud to wear the Cadet Nurse uniform: slate gray woolen suits with bright red epaulets, and modified French berets for the winter, pin-striped light gray and white uniforms for the summer.

Because the war ended in Europe in May 1945 and in Asia in August, I did not need to continue with the accelerated program, and I graduated only in June 1946. Though I was happy that the war was over and that men and women were coming home to continue with their lives, I was disappointed that I would not be fulfilling my military obligations.

I entertained the notion of joining the Army Nurse Corps nonetheless, though the idea was distressing to my mother. She had worried and prayed long enough over my brother's well-being, she insisted. She wouldn't, couldn't, go through that again. At last, in the face of her opposition, I gave it up.

Years later, I discovered the reason for my mother's persistent objections to my joining the army. My brother had written many letters to her admonishing her at any cost to keep me from joining any military branch at all. I felt quite let down by this brother whom I had supported and prayed for during his life-threatening service in the South Pacific.

The seed for my career selection was planted by a medical emergency; the incentive and financial backing were provided by World War II, and now I had accomplished my goals: to be a nurse and to be able to help make my parents' lives more comfortable. It was the public however, who benefited from my professional services over the next thirty-six years, rather than the military forces, as I carried out my life of challenging, satisfying work. I do believe that the public has been well-served and that my government-funded education has been fully repaid.

My First Job

BY CAROLE GLASS

Crash! There was the loud, harsh sound of metal striking wood, then a hush before multiple voices screamed, "Mommmm!"

Mrs. Wahlensack stopped in the middle of her sentence, turned, and rushed down the hall to the closed door. Quickly, I followed behind her.

She opened the door, and as I peered over her shoulder, seven pairs of eyes stared back at me. The room, once an elegant study, was filled with children. They appeared to be fine but needed an adult to settle a dispute. Two were riding tricycles, another on roller skates circled books and toys scattered on the hardwood floor. As Mrs. Wahlensack tried to calm her children, they began to tug at my leg, jump up and down, and call out my name. The baby-sitter was here!

That the first time I went to the Wahlensack house, I was stunned by the sight of seven small children all in one room. They ranged from Joseph, an infant, to Joanne, James, Jane, Jennifer, Jason,

After a career in marketing, Carole Glass has dedicated herself to memoir writing. She lives and writes in Wisconsin.

and to John, who was 9. But I quickly learned the benefits of Mrs.Wahlensack's containment strategy of using the study as a playroom. You knew where the children were. No searching, no counting heads, and the rest of the house stayed relatively in order.

The playroom was a world unto itself, a world ruled by children. They entertained each other, kept some order, and looked after the little ones. But where I came from, jumping off chairs and climbing on windowsills was not allowed. These children had toys but they clung to me. Jennifer, who was 6, had a sweet smile and brown eyes the size of silver dollars. She followed me everywhere. To occupy the kids, I made up games and stories or just used tinker toys to build fanciful structures.

This was my initiation into the world of responsibility (and earning my own money). It was the summer of 1964. I was 14, just graduated from St. Josaphat's, and this was my first real job. The pay was $1 an hour. Until then, the only babysitting I had done was watching my younger brother and sister while my parents went bowling. My main responsibility then was simply to make sure that the house didn't burn down. But, of course, I didn't get paid.

My father did not believe in paying for family chores or in giving allowances. (Requests for spending money required forms in triplicate, two weeks in advance!) So the thought of having my own money was empowering. I could bypass the Bank of Dad and its miserly methods.

Babysitting for the Wahlensacks started as an occasional assignment, for a few hours on a weekend evening. I don't know if it was because the other sitters in the neighborhood refused, or because they actually had a social life or because the children threatened a hunger strike, but soon Mrs. Wahlensack was asking me to babysit all day, two or three days a week. I did this for the whole summer. At times, it kept me from going swimming, biking or just hanging out with my friends, but I felt important. I learned that having authority could be both fun and profitable.

I would walk up the hill to the Wahlensack's house, alternately imagining myself to be Mary Poppins or Ethel Kennedy. But their story was not a fairy tale. Mr.Wahlensack was in the

Air Force and often out of town. He looked handsome in his uniform, but when he drove me home at night in his red VW bug, he didn't say much. Mrs. Wahlensack looked tired and older than her husband. She dressed plainly and gave few instructions. I never knew where she went while I was taking care of her children.

For all the energy bursting from the children's playroom, the rest of the house had an odd feeling of emptiness. To serve the kids peanut butter sandwiches, I often had to wash some of the dirty dishes in the sink.

September came. I started high school, and the Wahlensacks moved away. I may have missed out on a few trips to Nelson's custard stand with my friends that summer, but I had instead a taste of the independence that having my own money could bring, and perhaps more importantly, I had a chance to try on someone else's life.

Over the years, I have often thought about Mrs. Wahlensack and her seven children. Babysitting for them was when I first realized that life doesn't always turn out like a Nancy Drew novel. I also realized that I needed to think hard about my future. At 14, it seemed like the whole world stretched out in front of me. Not only would I have to make some choices in life but I would need to think about their consequences, too.

Adulthood

In adulthood, we live with and live out the choices we have made. If we are lucky, we have long years to do so. In this section, we read how the selected lifewriters have adapted and created their lives. Their stories portray them at moments of decision-making when change was the order of the day. In each case, the lifewriters record how they were able to make choices that allowed them to live with humor, determination and hope.

Young adulthood is characterized by pursuit of an identity, a mate and work that can become a career. In the first selection, we observe how Bill Boyle learned that romance alone would not be enough to make a lasting marriage for him.

In the modern world, work plays a big part in our lives. My grandfather once told me that "the man who finds his job in life is a lucky man." For most men, it dominates the years between school and retirement. Increasingly, it does so for women, too. In this section, Mary Ellen Elwell writes about her struggle to bring her youthful idealism into line with the reality she encountered as a graduate-student social worker. Pam Burton, an international marketing consultant, writes about finding her job—and becoming a "lucky woman" in her prime.

In her mid-adulthood, too, Robbie Peterson ter Kuile shares the anguish of trying to support her mentally-ill sister—and then struggles to live with the knowledge that her most dedicated and heartfelt effort won't make a difference. Her search for meaning in the face of irrationality is one we all can identify with.

Winnie Easton-Jones writes as a woman who chooses instinctively to remain present to a moment of great crisis—the death of her beloved husband—and does so with dignity. Her reward is a full experience that leaves her able to carry on.

Love, work, family, achievement, loss, survival: the choices vary, the patterns are many. In these stories, we learn how these lifewriters have responded to some of life's biggest demands.

Twisting and Turning
By William R. Boyle

Bill Boyle became a certified Soleil Lifestory Network teacher in 2002. He and his wife, Linda, worked together preserving people's personal and family histories. Bill developed lung disease as a result of using now banned carcinogenic building materials in his hobby of renovating old houses. Sadly, his memoirs were left unfinished when he died in 2004.

I felt many pressures to marry by the time I was 21 years old, especially as I had not attended college. I didn't know then that 21 is really too young to get married. There are too many things a young man has not seen, does not know and has not done. But when I was in my early 20s, I was only learning this.

As a Catholic, with all of the belief systems about waiting until you're married, I had an obligation to save myself for my spouse. At the same time, voices from catechism class insisted that I had an obligation to begin a large family, for the love of God and the love of the church.

So I was trying to figure out what I wanted and needed in a spouse. I knew I wanted someone who was a Catholic. I wanted her to be pretty, to be smart, and all that standard stuff. But I had not gotten to the essence of what it would be like to be married to someone. To complicate matters, I was toying with the idea of entering the priesthood and was pondering a celibate life.

While I didn't know what the future would hold for me, I did know one thing: I liked to dance. During my late teens, I went to dances every Friday and Saturday night.

Even after high school and after returning from the Army, I continued to attend dances. Friday nights, I went to the local firehouse in Linwood, Pennsylvania. Bill Haley played there every now and then. This was before he was the "Big Thing." He lived near Chadds Ford, and while building his reputation, he would sometimes perform with the Comets at the firehouse. On the nights he performed, admission would increase from $.35 to $1.00, but he was worth it, as we had an idea he might be really big some day.

Then, on Saturday nights, I would go to Upper Darby to dance to Big Bands. Some featured really big-name musicians, like Maynard Ferguson. The people who went to these were slightly older, more twentyish than high-school age.

I never took anyone. These dances were kind of expensive, and after all, I had these ideas of priesthood—so why date? I could dance with someone I met there.

One Saturday night, Chubby Checker was scheduled to perform. Chubby Checker! Wow! I thought when I found out. I was a twister. I loved the Twist! The Twist was a dance I practiced for a long time. It required a lot of stamina, a lot of vigor, and a lot of wiggling. I had a lot of each of those.

That evening, the dance hall had set up a Twist contest with Chubby. I knew I could win, if only I had a partner to twist with me. Could I find someone good before the contest began? Probably not since the contest was to begin at 11 o'clock that evening, and it was already 9. How could a miracle happen in so short a time?

But, miracles do happen.

I caught sight of one of the most beautiful Irish-looking girls I had ever seen. I did not know who she was or even if she could dance, but I asked her to slow dance. She was so beautiful, with an equally beautiful name—Cathy Jo. I was dancing with a beautiful Irish-Catholic miracle.

We danced slow and we danced fast. After a while, Cathy Jo asked, "Are you going to dance in the Twist contest?"

"I hope so," I told her, and asked if she could twist.

"Yes, it's my favorite dance," she answered, "but I don't think I can win. I just think it would be a lot of fun to dance in a contest."

A Multiple Miracle was in the making. I was dancing with a beautiful Irish girl who wanted to dance the Twist in a contest with Chubby Checker! God only confers these, his most special kind of miracles, on those He really loves. I was living the good life.

A little before eleven, the contest rules were explained. Many sets of judges would be down on the floor eliminating couples. Once you were tapped on the shoulder by a judge, you and your partner were to walk off the floor and join the audience. You were a watcher at that point, not a dancer. It had to be done in that way—efficiently and quickly. There were too many couples to do otherwise. Chubby would be leaving right after midnight so the winner had to be chosen by then.

Eleven o'clock came, and it was contest time. Chubby came out on stage. He began performing his signature number. The crowd roared. Couples began to Twist, and the judges circulated around the hall. They began tapping people on the shoulder. One-by-one, couples were eliminated. We were still so many people on the floor that Chubby had to play his piece again and again. The judges continued to eliminate couples, but still there were many people dancing on the floor.

It was getting closer and closer to midnight. Cathy Jo had not felt the dreaded tap, and neither had I. After a while, there remained only a few couples. Then, we were down to just a handful. We danced, as if in a desperate 1930s marathon dance.

The crowd was huge that night, and it was getting bigger with each judge's tap. People were cheering us on. The really good twisters, the handful of us who remained, were lost in our frantic gyrating activity.

With each beat, we were closer to not getting the tap and to winning. We had danced for almost an hour, and still there was no winner. I may have been thin, but that did not mean I did not have a lot of stamina and stick-to-it-iveness.

It was just a few minutes before midnight, and neither Cathy Jo nor I had been tapped. There were only us and another couple remaining. Boy, the other couple was good. They and several others who had already left the floor were probably better twisters than Cathy Jo and I, but they were more worn out than we were. Finally we saw a judge tap the other couple. I think, with my 135-pound, 5-foot-9 1/2-inches-tall body, I had simply worn them out. They also did not have my newly found Miracle.

Cathy Jo and I didn't get to meet Chubby that night. I can't even remember if we got a prize, but I had already received the prize I wanted.

Cathy Jo and I dated for a year. She seemed all I had hoped for. We shared many values. Being with her made me realize I didn't want a life of celibacy. Her family was rich by my standards, and I liked that.

I asked my dad to take me to South Street in Philadelphia, Jeweler's Row, where I could get a good deal on a diamond ring. Cathy Jo had told me she had always wanted a specific kind

of ring, a marquis solitaire diamond. The bigger the better. Diamonds meant love to her—and size said it all: the bigger the diamond, the more love. I never believed such silliness before meeting Cathy Jo, but her 20-year-old's vision of love had convinced me that ours would last forever—if only she had that special, big diamond!

I got the ring. We became engaged.

One Saturday evening, we were talking about what our life together would be like. What would we do after we were married?

Cathy Jo told me, "When we wake up every morning, I will make you fried eggs, so you can go off to your office."

"But you know I don't like fried eggs," I told her.

"You'll eat them—or you won't get breakfast the next morning," Cathy Jo said with certainty.

After this threat, I started to think. I realized there are more important things than Daddy's money and saving yourself for your spouse. In fact, I realized at that moment that I needed a less-demanding woman than her insistence on what I should eat implied, someone less likely to punish her loved one for not conforming to her demands. I knew you had to be able to live with your spouse in all kinds of situations. I knew I could not marry my once-marvelous miracle.

The next day, our relationship ended after Sunday Mass. I never saw her again nor the marquis diamond solitaire engagement ring.

Even though Cathy Jo and I were not meant to be married, she helped me know something important—that I did not understand much about married life or who would make me an appropriate partner.

I was disappointed to lose Cathy Jo, but I knew would find someone, someday, sometime, someplace. Maybe. The search would continue.

What I Had to Learn
BY MARY ELLEN ELWELL

In my graduate-school field placement in the Children's Division of the Maryland Welfare Department, I was assigned to work with families of children in foster care. Mrs. Peters, the mother of a teenage son and daughter, was on my client list because of her fourteen-year-old Sammy's problems. Sammy had broken into the National Guard Armory and stolen several guns. He was quickly apprehended and charged as a delinquent. Although he had no previous record, he was clearly the guilty party acting alone. The Juvenile Court staff conducted a background investigation to assist the judge, who decided Sammy was neglected as well as delinquent. Instead of being sent to a facility for juvenile offenders, he was committed to our department for community placement. I was assigned to work with his mother as we prepared for Sammy's group home placement where supervision and therapy would be provided.

From Maryland, Mary Ellen Elwell is a retired social worker who spent many years "in the field' before earning a Ph. D. and teaching graduate school. Mary Ellen served at the national level on the boards of several professional associations. With the help of writing coaching, she has been working on her memoirs so as to tell the story of her professional life.

Mrs. Peters, Sammy and his thirteen-year-old sister, Mary, lived in a third floor walk-up apartment. I grew fond of Sammy and his sister as I visited them. They were kids in a bad situation. I wanted to facilitate a happy life for them and to repair the damage caused by their unstable home life!

Mrs. Peters' second husband, a merchant seaman, was usually away. She supplemented the support he sent her by working as a waitress in a local bar. Sammy loved and respected his stepfather who, when he was at home, was the disciplinarian the boy needed. Sammy was furious when his mother, a heavy drinker, brought men into the apartment late at night for sex. On one occasion, when she had come home with a new man, Sammy had pushed her down the stairs, breaking her arm. Sometimes, he would be so angry he would punch holes in the apartment walls. Neighbors reported they had even heard him threaten to kill his mother.

Mrs. Peters admitted she could no longer control her son.

As their family story unfolded and our plan for Sammy progressed, I found I wasn't able to relate well to Mrs. Peters. She often missed office appointments and was generally uncooperative. A small, frail woman, she was a whiner, blaming her fourteen-year-old son for all the family problems. Everything would be fine with her and Mary, she wanted me to believe, once Sammy was taken away. I tried to get her to take responsibility for the trouble her family was experiencing—to see her men and her drinking as family problems—but I made no headway.

Gradually, I became aware that not only was I unable to relate to her, I had grown to strongly dislike her. It was a relief that the agency's plan to place Sammy in an appropriate group home was apparently going well. Perhaps he would find there, away from this mixed-up woman, what he needed to have a happier, better life.

Two weeks after Sammy had left home, Mrs. Peters had an appointment with me. When the receptionist told me she was there waiting, I was surprised. I had expected that she would fail to keep her appointments after Sammy was placed.

"How's he doing?" she asked at the start of our interview. "I'd like to have a visit with him."

"That would be okay," I replied, surprised at her interest in him. I explained the group home's visiting policies and scheduled a visit for that afternoon, wondering if she would really make the effort to follow through. When she left, I escorted Mrs. Peters to the door and watched as she walked slowly away, all bent over, up the sidewalk to the bus stop.

What a disgusting excuse for a mother! I thought. *I should talk with my supervisor about her.* Returning to my office with a wave of strong feeling about this woman and her shortcomings, I suddenly remembered what one of my graduate school professors had tried to hammer into us students: *You'll never be able to help your clients unless you can change the way you feel about them.*

That afternoon, Mrs. Peters had a good visit with Sammy, according to the group home staff who supervised and called with a report. Perhaps there was hope here for this family; perhaps I could change the way I felt about this woman.

The very next morning, I was in for a shock, however, and there would be no follow up on that good visit. Mrs. Peters' body was found in the vestibule of an apartment house some blocks away from her home. An autopsy revealed a very high blood alcohol level and advanced stages of tuberculosis in both lungs. The examination, however, could not determine whether she had been murdered. Instantly, Mrs. Peters was redefined in my mind. She was still an inadequate, neglectful mother but she was also a sick, tubercular alcoholic who may have been murdered. I recalled the image of her, alone and all bent over, walking up the sidewalk to the bus stop, and my frustration about being able to help her as I watched.

Her death posed a practical problem: who could step in to take responsibility for Sammy and Mary? Who would? The father was missing; the stepfather couldn't be reached. Sammy was already placed. Could I make something good of this?—I could place Mary, too, in suitable foster care—a small repayment to Mrs. Peters for all that had happened—and all that didn't.

This case challenged me and my attitudes in ways that took me by surprise. Clearly, I had failed to offer Mrs. Peters basic acceptance. I hadn't come anywhere near understanding her and her life, and for this, I felt terribly guilty. Gradually, I was able to acknowledge that part of my failure was over-identifying with Sammy and Mary. My rescue fantasy was in full force! I wanted to provide a happy life for every child—and some part of me believed I could! I felt despair as I acknowledged this—how could I ever work effectively with children and their parents? Was my chosen field going to prove to be especially difficult and ill suited to me? I was confident of my ability to do the graduate-school academics, but could I master the other work? I had to develop an awareness of how strongly my feelings about clients could influence my ability to help them. I had to accept that impossible goals would unduly burden me as a child welfare worker and keep me from accomplishing the possible.

Working and Living in the UK

BY PAM BURTON

The phone was ringing in the flat when I walked in.

I'd only been in the country a couple of weeks and hardly anyone knew our phone number. *Who in the world could be calling?* I wondered as I ran to answer.

May 11, 1998, was a rare sunny day in central London. About 10 o'clock that morning, I had just walked back to our flat off the Strand from the Oasis, the Council-run (government-subsidized) health club on the edge of Covent Garden. I had been aqua-training in their pool—jogging my laps up and down, ignoring the curious stares of my fellow swimmers. Running in water was part of my rehab. I had developed *plantar fasciitis* on my left foot and could no longer jog every day on concrete or pavement.

"Hello, is this Mrs. Bradley Burton?" a pleasant voice inquired. *How does this woman know my name and this number?*

"This is Donna Richmond of NETg," she continued. "I'm calling for Mr. Roy Sunley, our managing director. He received your brochure in the post from Jack Dilworth of Harcourt General, our parent company. He'd like to meet with you this week if you have time in your schedule."

Are you kidding me? Of course I'll have time in my not-so-busy schedule!

We made an appointment for later that week, and Donna provided directions to NETg using the London Underground, or Tube.

An international marketing consultant with offices in Gloucester, Massachusetts, Pam Bradley Burton attended several Turning Memories Into Memoirs® workshops and joined a Soleil writing tele-group. This story is from her memoir.

She also gave me the Web site address for the National Education Training Group (NETg), so I could do my homework and research the company.

I was really excited–my first *bona fide* UK prospect!

The contact had come about because my dad had been doing some education market consulting with Harcourt General, and being the proud dad that he is, had passed on my Bradley Burton marketing brochure to the folks there. It had made its way across the Atlantic Ocean from Boston to London via Harcourt General interoffice mail, landing on the desk of a decision-maker with a need. And now it appeared that NETg might require my services. *How often does that happen?* I definitely owed my dad something special for this referral. For some reason, I was very optimistic that this was a match destined to be.

Three days later, I took the District-line Tube to Chiswick and a taxi from the station to NETg's offices on Burlington Lane at the Chiswick roundabout. Donna greeted me in the lobby, took me upstairs and settled me with a cup of coffee in Mr. Sunley's office.

Roy Sunley, NETg's vice president of international operations and managing director, was a ball of energy who rushed through the door to greet me. About 5' 9", blue eyes, brown hair, charming and handsome, he recounted the story of receiving my brochure in the mail at the exact time NETg was going through some personnel changes.

"Look, NETg's marketing has never been very strong," he told me as he settled behind his desk. "We're looking at making some personnel changes internally and really want to improve our international marketing effectiveness."

Roy then gave me a detailed overview of NETg's history, organizational structure, sales channels, revenue goals, and current marketing department. A provider of information technology (IT) skills and "soft" skills courseware, NETg was doing about $36 million in international revenue with 50 percent of that from the UK. The parent company, Harcourt General, was expecting—and insisting on—a 30 percent increase in revenue and profits.

Roy continued, "CBT, our major competitor, spends a lot on marketing and is very strong. I keep telling Harcourt we'll need to spend more money on marketing to achieve the aggressive revenue target they've given us."

NETg had been acquired months earlier by Harcourt General, a multibillion-dollar publishing giant, and Roy was learning how to work with the U.S.-based top management, yet run the company as autonomously as possible.

I was sympathetic to his bind. In my previous roles as international marketing director, I was frequently the confidante of frustrated country managers or international VPs who complained about the interference of U.S. management in their operations. Their gripe was that "the Americans" did not understand what's different about doing business in their country, didn't give them enough autonomy, and required far too much time-consuming reporting. I was flattered to be trusted and respected enough to be considered "one of them."

"You're not like most Americans," my international colleagues would observe time and again.

After hearing more details about my international business experience and previous stints living in the UK and France, Roy echoed that sentiment: "You may talk like one of those bloody Americans but you're not a typical one, are you then?"

At the end of our conversation, Roy took me on a tour of all of the departments. I was impressed that he knew every employee's name and had a cheery comment or personal question for each one we met. The tour concluded in customer operations, located in the warehouse where NETg courseware CDs, available in several languages, were shipped to customers all over the world.

It was about lunch time, and since Roy was going out for a lunch meeting, he kindly offered to drop me off at the Turnham Green Tube station.

"Pam, I certainly think you could help us turn around marketing," he said to me. "But really, the decision as to what we are going to do is for my boss, Nige Howarth, to make. The next step is for you to meet with him."

Nige Howarth was NETg's marketing and product development director. He would soon be returning from a business trip. I planned to call the next day to schedule an appointment.

I returned to our flat on John Adams Street very excited. "That's great," my husband Ross said when I told him how real a prospect NETg was. "I'm happy for you."

Ross had accepted a two-year expatriate assignment as managing director for Lee Hecht Harrison UK, a provider of career transition services. We had moved to London in April of 1998. I was doing international marketing consulting and had a couple of clients, including one based in Ireland, so a move to Europe was great for me, too.

Temporarily housed in a much too tiny, boringly modern flat centrally located off the Strand near Covent Garden, we were looking for better accommodations for the length of our stay, and Ross had had some success. "I think I've found the right nest for my Queen (his pet name and term of endearment for me). Can you believe it?—the goddamn real estate people in this country don't work weekends or evenings! So I had to go looking on my own."

Ross was frustrated with the British "estate agents" who made it so inconvenient to view properties. However, he had convinced Sally, the relocation specialist, to take us to four different flats and houses on Saturday.

"And the one I think you'll like the best is very near to NETg," he told me.

I was excited. "Wow, that's great. It took me over an hour on the Tube today."

"It's a little stand-alone house on Somerset Square, a quiet, private square near Holland Park," Ross continued. "An American ex-pat with Cigna Insurance, his wife and two kids are living there now, but they're moving back to New Jersey very soon."

"How do you know all this?" I asked him. *Had my husband become a sleuth?*

He smiled. "I walked all over searching for the addresses of flats on the relocation people's list. I looked in the window and saw this guy washing dishes, so I knocked on the door!"

My husband is very direct and action-oriented. He ended up in a lengthy conversation with the man, giving him on-the-spot career transition counseling. The man, in turn, gave him tips on where to shop in London (places like Costco and Ikea), where to eat (family-friendly restaurants topped his list), and how to circumnavigate British business incompetency (like what to watch out for with Cable & Wireless).

On Saturday we viewed furnished flats in the neighborhoods of Notting Hill and Kensington. One tri-level was next door to a fish restaurant—can you imagine the smell day after day? Others were located in "mews"—renovated stables with lots of character but no privacy. After seeing all, we decided Ross had been right—27 Somerset Square was the very best of the lot. But at $6,000 a month, it was also the most expensive! Thank goodness Ross's expatriate package covered housing.

I was doubly thrilled: we had found a great house and it was close to my future client, NETg.

Helen and Charles

BY ROBBIE PETERSON TER KUILE

Robbie Peterson ter Kuile is a certified Soleil Lifestory Network teacher. She leads memoir workshops in a variety of formats in Tryon, North Carolina. *In the photos: page 255—Robbie is at left, her sister, Helen, is the baby; page 256—Robbie is at the center, Helen is on the left.*

As I enter the psychiatric unit of the large city hospital, a thin, tall man dressed in blue hospital pajamas with dark stubble over his face is pacing back and forth in his solitary cubicle like a caged animal. He looks down at the floor as he paces. He's talking and waving his arms. There's no one else in his sterile, brightly lit cubicle. I'm not close enough to hear his words but I see his lips moving. As the oldest sister of a woman who suffers with paranoia-schizophrenia, I know this man is exhibiting the behavior of someone who's delusional and hears voices that others don't hear.

Looking for my sister, I glance quickly into the other exposed cubicles. Unlike the patients' rooms in the new, modern emergency ward where my sister and I spent ten hours the day before, there are no doors on these patients' solitary cubicles. Here the patients' rooms are formed by white, canvas drapes that divide a large rectangular-shaped ward into small individual, holding areas. Unlike the emergency room where it's noisy and busy with patients, nurses and aides constantly interacting with each other, this ward is quiet and the patients are not free to leave their cubicles. The only concession to patient privacy is provided by the white canvas drapes that hang to one side of each opening. I feel as if I've stepped across a threshold into the Twilight Zone of psych wards from the '60s, where patients never expected to leave once they'd entered.

Two nurses sit with their backs to the lone, pacing man as

they work on their computers at the nurses' desk that is in the center of this small ward. They're too engrossed with recording patient information to pay him any attention.

"I'm looking for my sister, Helen," I inform the nurses as they catch a glimpse of me standing beside them. I'm struggling to keep level a box of Tasty Kreme donuts, and at the same time, hold on to a canvas bag filled with toiletries, a sweat shirt and personal items for my sister. I'm bringing my sister's favorite cream-filled donuts. I am hoping that they will pacify her before she begins the ambulance transfer to a private psychiatric hospital.

"She's in the bathroom preparing to go home," says one of the nurses.

"Going home? How can she be going home?! Yesterday the emergency room doctor determined that she was a threat to herself and should be hospitalized," I point out. The level of my voice rises as a knot forms in my chest. I feel panic as if someone is putting me in a straight-jacket.

"Well, the doctor and the social worker who saw her this morning decided that she's stable enough to go home. She's called her husband to come get her," they tell me matter-of-factly.

"Of course, she's fine," I shout, "after you all have spent the night shooting her up with medicine to calm her down. I want to see the doctor who decided she can be discharged!" My voice reveals that I'm on the verge of becoming as irrational as the patients they guard.

With a look of disdain, one of the nurses picks up the hospital phone and makes a call. She hunches over the phone with her back to me so I can't hear her conversation. While I wait for her to conclude her conversation, I glance around and notice two off-duty policemen whom I hadn't noticed standing on either side of the double doors through which I'd entered the ward.

When the nurse hangs up the phone, she doesn't swivel in her chair to look at me. She simply turns her head and speaks over her right shoulder. "The doctor has left the hospital. The social worker was here earlier, but she'll return once she's done seeing other patients."

"No, that's not good enough," I shout on the verge of stomping my foot. "Yesterday, I was patient and waited eight hours before the social worker came to see me and my sister. I will not be patient today. You'd better get the social worker and a doctor in here immediately."

Now she looks more disgusted but she does pick up the phone and make the call.

It is unsettling to mentally-ill patients for people to display a high levels of emotion. But I'm not thinking about their feelings at this moment. I've waited patiently for a year to find a way to get my schizophrenic sister to a place where she can become stabilized on her medication and learn to make better choices in her daily life.

Yesterday I spoke with the director of admissions of a short-term psychiatric hospital. She told me that Helen's being irrational and not complying with her treatment plan wasn't enough reason to have her hospitalized. She had to be a threat to herself or to others. When I see that, I should call 911 to request that she be taken to the local hospital for a psych consult. If the emergency-room doctors determine that Helen is a threat to herself or to others, then she can be hospitalized against her will until she's stabilized on anti-psychotic medicines.

After that phone conversation yesterday, I took Helen to lunch. She talked nonstop, but her words didn't form a coherent sentence. Following lunch, we returned to the run-down motel where she lives with her husband. Her paranoia surfaced, and she confronted several women. When one of them ran to Helen and threatened to beat her up, I realized that it was time for me call in the police. The police arrived and interviewed Helen. They decided to transport her to the emergency room for a psych consult.

For my sister to be stabilized for the long-term, she needs to be hospitalized for several days or weeks until the medication is in her system. When the emergency doctor was evaluating

Helen, I informed the doctor that a bed for a female patient would be available the next day at Carolina Center for Behavioral Health and that they'd agreed to accept Helen. The emergency room doctor concurred that the city hospital would hold Helen until she could be transferred to the other hospital. At midnight, when Helen was finally asleep, I left the emergency room, confident that I'd arranged a safe plan for her.

Now ten hours later and after a night of restless sleep, I'm back at the hospital. In the emergency ward, I find that the staff moved my sister from a private room in the emergency ward to the hospital's psychiatric ward. While I wait for the nurses to make their second phone call because I demand to see the doctor and the social worker, I lean against the wall, close my eyes and try to breathe deeply to calm myself.

When I open my eyes, I'm looking into the cubicle of the lone man who was pacing and talking to himself when I entered the ward. He has a razor in his hand and white shaving cream smeared all over his whiskery jaws. "Why does a man in a psych ward have a razor?" I ask myself. He appears to be looking into a mirror that I can't see. He's no longer talking to himself. He brings the razor to his cheek, concentrating on the delicate task of shaving.

I turn to the nurses and ask, "Do you have a phone I may use?" My intuition suggests I call the lawyer who is helping me transfer the guardianship of my sister from Darlington County to the county where she now lives.

"Over there hanging on the wall next to that stack of lockers," one of the nurses tells me as she flips her hand in that direction.

I walk to the lockers and the wall phone across from the room of the delusional man. He has finished shaving and is no longer pacing. As I pick up the phone and dial the number, I become aware of someone standing behind me. I turn around and the delusional man who had been pacing back and forth in his solitary cubicle when I entered, the man who has just shaved, is standing about 18 inches from me. He's looking in my direction but he's looking past me, and he doesn't make eye contact with me. I do notice that now he's clean-shaven.

"I'll be off the phone in a minute," I say calmly. I interrupt my dialing to ask him, "Can you wait?"

"Yes," he says as he continues to stare at the wall next to the phone. He's standing as lifeless as a statue with his arms hanging down by his sides.

Because it's so quiet on this ward, the nurse hears his voice. She snaps her head around to see whom I'm talking to, and her nostrils flare when she sees this patient is out of his cubicle.

"He doesn't need to use that phone," she snaps. "Get back in your room, Charles!" she orders. He turns, hangs his head and slowly sulks back to his room like a puppy who can't find anyone to pay attention to him.

When the phone is answered in the office I'm calling, I identify myself and tell the receptionist I need to speak with Mr. Campbell immediately as I'm in the psychiatric ward of the large city hospital with my sister and I need his advice. She puts me on hold.

As I stand holding the silent phone to my ear, I turn and see Charles standing in his doorway still staring at the wall next to me. "Talk to him," that persistent part of me says.

But another part asks, "What can I possibly say to a perfect stranger in a psych ward?"

My impulsive, female sense takes over and suggests something that I say out loud, "You shaved."

"Yes, I did."

"You look good."

"Thank you." A slight smile appears on his face and a small light glimmers in his eyes.

It is only later that night, when my thoughts and I are alone with my anguish at seeing my sister go home to her abusive husband, and I am overcome by the futility of dealing with the mental health system in our country, that the voices in my head form a chorus and tell me, "Think of Charles; think how he responded to your presence on that desolate psych ward. He came out of his darkness and he shaved, hoping that you'd notice him. And you let him know you you did."

The Last Word?

BY WINNIE EASTON-JONES

A certified Soleil Lifestory Network teacher, Winnie Easton-Jones writes and teaches in Rockport, Maine. She is a former French teacher and served as an editor for this edition of *Turning Memories Into Memoirs*. (And yes, she did dye her hair bright red!)

To my darling husband, Howard G. Jones, from his once and forever wife—Winnie.

In the fall, the psychic had told me that Howard would not be here in the Spring. Now it was March 18, 2002, two days before the Spring equinox. Even so, snow was predicted for that evening.

When I had set out to do errands that morning, I forgot my checkbook. I had doubled back to the house, focusing my mind on all I needed to do before lunchtime. When I entered the house, something strange happened. It was as if some super-awareness had picked me up off the track I was on and put me on a different one...stopping me, slowing me down and making me decide to have an early lunch with Howard, to stop my busy-ness and linger with Howard. The psychic, after all, had said Howard would not be here in the Spring.

My husband, halfway to his ninety-second birthday, was ordinarily so meticulous...didn't like sandy feet or eating with his hands. That noon, he was completely out of character, laughing foolishly with me as the juice of the last, shared "Harry and David" gift pear ran down our arms. Then, out of nowhere, came the inspiration to play cards...in the middle of the day! We usually saved that warfare for after dinner. But somehow it was important to be playing now. Even as I won the first game and decided to throw the next one, he started in on a five-game winning streak, intuitively knowing what I had planned and stubbornly refused to go along. He would have none of it! Howard was routing me handily! With each win, his mischievously insinuating chuckle deepened...

"Thought you were going to win that one, didn't you?" he jabbed, relishing being insufferable, and I retaliated by playing furiously without effect!

"Had enough?" he teased, putting on his "gentleman's manners."

We quit.

In the evening, after supper, keeping to the contract he had established ("We don't need a dishwasher... I'm the dishwasher!"), he got everything "squared away" and had returned to his long-suffering game of Solitaire. Meanwhile, I was puttering around in the kitchen, placing the last of the supper things away, humming along with the radio, as Howard played against his strongest opponent, the luck of the draw. Calling out to him from time to time as I worked, I was hurrying to finish so we could play our ritual before-bed gin-rummy games. We had been teasing each other since noon about five games in a row I had been beaten at. Now it was my turn to win and I wanted at it! I was going to cream him!

In the back of my mind were always the psychic's words: Howard would not be here in the spring. Spring was now only two days away. But outside, it was snowing as had been predicted.

As I turned my back for just an instant to reach up to a higher shelf, an enormous crash, a huge thudding sound, exploded. It was as if all hell had broken loose...

I careened through the kitchen, not breathing. Howard lay on the floor. I knelt beside him. His chest was moving... Was he alive or was it just the pace maker? I reached for his wrist but could feel no pulse. Breathe into his mouth! "Howard, Howard. Don't go. HOWARD, WAIT!" I left him only long enough to call for an ambulance, and then I was back beside him. *Breathe some more into his mouth.*

"Come on, Howard. Come on. You've got to hang on, Howard. They'll be here in a minute. Breathe, breathe! COME ON! BREATHE!"

Although it was now snowing heavily, blowing a gale, the ambulance was there within five minutes. The EMTs burst into the house and immediately put Howard on the gurney and wheeled him out into the snow. I turned away and could not watch. *Do something, do something.* I stood immobilized, gripped by the fear which had settled on us for two years, day and night.

My Howard! My Howard!

The local Rockport Police Chief, Mark, called out of his bed by the dispatcher, arrived and stood near me, quietly, respectfully, watching me trying to breathe through my sobs. I pressed my face hard against the window, staring out through the snow at our driveway, at the shadows of the medics inside the ambulance, the motor running. I was trying to understand from the shadows what might be happening to Howard, my husband, my husband, my husband. *Why weren't they driving to the hospital??* I kept clasping my knuckles, praying.

"Is there anything at all I can do for you? Now?" asked Mark.

I did not wish to raise my eyes to him He is very tall, and I felt so very little. I shook my head, "No."

I was so cold.

"When the paramedics stay out there like that ..." he said, shaking his head, "there's usually not much chance, when they don't go on right away to the hospital."

I knew. I knew. I knew. I hadn't wanted to ask, but the psychic had told me and it was happening just as she had predicted....two days before Spring.

It was 11:15 PM, and somehow I knew Howard would not last until midnight.

I didn't even hear myself crying. I looked up at Mark. "Please will you hug me. I need a hug. Please hold me, hold me tight."

He put his arms around me and held me tight as if I were the smallest child who needed help from a kind friend when everything had just fallen apart with a bang.

"Is there someone you want to call?"

I nodded and walked over to the phone. "Georgia. Can you meet me at the hospital? Howard just fell… a heart attack and the paramedics are here…and…."

I couldn't finish.

I followed the ambulance down to the hospital. Even though it was snowing hard now, I drove myself because I wanted to be alone in the car. Mark followed to make sure I was all right. As I parked the car, Georgia walked toward me. Something about the way she looked at me let me know that she had already been in the Emergency Room and it was "done." Her husband, Bill, was one of the E.R. docs, and Georgia held my hand as we walked to the E.R. door.

Our friend, Kathy, was waiting inside, her face welcoming. Her arms around me felt like wings, "I'm just coming off duty from Intensive Care…I'll stay with you,"

I nodded but couldn't speak.

My godmother Millie was there too, roused from sleep, her hair drawn back in a braided bun. Her eyes were very large and sad; hers, a mirror of my face.

"I'm so sorry," Millie said, as she took my hand in hers. She knew what it was all about. Her husband had died just six months earlier, just days before 9/ll.

I tried not to cry.

A nurse led us into a small white room. Three gray chairs, and the stretcher with Howard's body on it. I had seen people as they lay in their coffins, all prettied up, but I had never seen anyone just as they had died. He was turning blue. I leaned across him, put my head on his chest and circled my arms around him, holding him. Memories of holding him or him holding me as we snuggled at night crept into my arms, talking, sharing jokes and songs and visions of what we could make or do, all the fireflies of creativity that circled around us in our love for each other.

It can't be possible that I would never see him again!

I started caressing his forehead, staring at my hand as it stroked his hair. I don't remember what I said…I just kept stroking his hair, stroking his hair as he had done so often for me, calling his name.

"HOWARD, HOWARD, HOWARD."

He was cold. I was not afraid. I just noticed it and kept stroking his face speaking his name softly. I could hear Georgia crying. It was very quiet in the room. He was getting very blue. We were waiting for his daughter to come up from Portland, but it was snowing very hard now, big flakes, wind blowing. The roads were getting slick.

Midnight came and went, and we three stayed, talking quietly about him, his funny jokes, the way he called me "Bladder Eyes," the twenty-six years of loving and standing up to someone I respected.

The twenty-five years' difference in our ages didn't matter. What mattered was the everyday cherished work of making the truth happen, making sure that there wasn't "one thirty-second of an inch of garbage" between us, and the way he used to go up to our bedroom before we got heat in it and warm my side of the bed before I got in. This was his cherished gift to me even if he was down in his basement workshop, smack in the middle of making a prototype model with "all those numbers" running around inside his head. Even when he wasn't at a good stopping place, he'd stop. Taking off his workshop apron, dusting off all the plastic chips, he would climb the two flights of stairs and spread out on my side of the bed, waiting for me to finish my tooth brushing. "I need to make sure that you are warm!"

I never asked for him to do this. It was part of his loving.

Howard's daughter called from Portland. The snow was too heavy, the road was slippery even with the Volvo, and she had heard her father's voice in her head telling her to turn back, especially with his grandson in the back seat and her being five months pregnant.

"I'll be up tomorrow morning, and you get some rest. OKAY?"

"That sounds fine. You're being smart. Take care. I love you." I hung up, thanking God that, by the time she saw her dad, he would be all prettied up, and it wouldn't be so scary.

The E. R. nurse came in, and we let her know that we would be leaving after a while, since Howard's daughter had turned back to Portland. It was late…or early…almost 2 AM.

I don't know how long I held him. It was a long time. I had stopped crooning his name. I just stayed where I was, my head on his chest, my arms around him.

Suddenly, I sat straight up in the chair, stared at his body with fierce determination and started to laugh…and cry…and laugh at the same time. I could feel something was happening. We all laughed…it was so absurd. Did I expect him to sit bolt upright and start arguing with me in all of his very deliberate Welsh rationality?

"YES! I AM GETTING RED HAIR, AND YES, I AM GETTING A DOG! DO YOU HEAR THAT!!"

I started to scold him; "You should NEVER have beaten me at five games of Gin Rummy in a row at lunch today! You should never have laughed at me with your little chuckle as if to say…'Thought you could beat me, huh?'"

I watched his face, remembering his laughter.

I repeated my remarks as if I could get him to answer. "BRIGHT RED HAIR, DO YOU HEAR THAT? BRIGHT, BRIGHT, BRIGHT RED HAIR, AND A HUGE DOG! AN ABSOLUTELY ENORMOUS DOG!!!"

But, there was only silence.

At that moment, all around me, I FELT HIS PRESENCE IN THE ROOM and the energy that comes when someone's thinking something over! I sat very still, listening, listening.

Did I get to have the last word?

Three hours of keening, holding him, speaking truths of his goodness and kindness, recalling his wonderfully, silly remarks…"You're smarter than you look!"… had worked their miracle. I felt as if angels had come into the room and filled it with grace. Rubbing my eyes, I could feel and see and hear this new, quiet truth: Howard and I would manage this new state of affairs, no matter what, just as we had always managed before! I might never see him again, but I would always hear him in my head, thinking, commenting, encouraging, calling "cut that out, Bladder Eyes" as I cried for him, and toasting me as I grew wise. He would be proud of me and our love, and I would hear him over and over saying his wonderful Welsh toast, clinking the glasses three times:

> "Here's to it, and from it, and to it, again…
> If you don't do it, when you get to it,
> You may never get to it, to do it again."

Appendix B: A Reading List for Lifewriters

A memoir writer must become a memoir reader. It doesn't make sense to engage in the creative struggle to write your autobiography but not to read what solutions others have brought to bear on the challenges of lifewriting.

Let the books below be a start for you as you explore the world of memoirs. The list has been compiled from the many books I have read and found useful over the years and from those suggested by colleagues and clients. It is, by necessity, a very partial list.

I like to browse the new book shelf of my local library for new memoirs. I also enjoy exploring used book stores for regional lifestory collections. Often they are the most interesting to read, the most authentic in tone and voice. The on-line bookstores are also a resource as you look for works to inspire and encourage you in your own lifestory writing.

Most of these titles are available through Internet sources and bookstores.

LIFEWRITING WRITING HOW-TO

Barrington, Judith. *Writing the Memoir.*
Blumenthal, Michael. *The New Story of Your Life.*
Daniel, Lois. *How to Write Your Own Life Story.*
Hoffman, William. *Life Writing: A Guide to Family Journals and Personal Memoirs.*
Keen, Sam. *Telling Your Story, A Guide to Who You Are and Who You Could Be.*
Kempthorne, Charlie. *For All Time: A Complete Guide to Writing Your Family History.*
Lomask, Milton. *The Biographer's Craft.*
Nichols, Evelyn and Anne Lowenkopf. *Lifelines, A Guide to Writing Your Personal Recollections.*
Rainer, Tristine. *Your Life As Story: Discovering the "New Autobiography."* Writing Memoir As Literature.
Stone, Elizabeth. *Black Sheep and Kissing Cousins.*
Thomas, Frank. *How To Write the Story of Your Life.*
Roorbach, Bill. *Writing Life Stories.*
Wakefield, Dan. *The Story of Your Life, Writing A Spiritual Autobiography.*
Zinsser, William. *Inventing the Truth, The Art and Craft of Memoir.*

THE WRITING LIFE

Brande, Dorothea. *Becoming a Writer.*
Duncan, Lois. *How to Write and Sell Your Personal Experiences.*
Goldberg, Natalie. *Writing Down The Bones.*
Keirsey, David and Bates, Marilyn. *Please Understand Me, Temperament, Character and Type.*
Keirsey, David. *Please Understand Me II, Temperament, Character and Type.*
Kremer, John. *1001 Ways to Market Your Books.*
Poynter, Dan. *The Self-Publishing Manual: How To Write, Print, and Sell Your Own Book.*
Riso, Don Richard and Hudson, Russ. *The Wisdom of the Enneagram: The Complete Guide to Psychological and Spiritual Growth for the Nine Personality Types.*
Strunk, William and E.B. White. *The Elements of Style.*
Zinsser, Wiliam. *On Writing Well.*

AUTOBIOGRAPHIES, MEMOIRS AND LIFESTORY COLLECTIONS

Adams, Henry. *The Education of Henry Adams.*
Angelou, Maya. *I Know Why the Caged Bird Sings.*
Antin, Mary. *The Promised Land.*
Arlen, Michael. *Passage to Ararat.*
Baker, Russell. *Growing Up.*
Barnes, Kim. *In the Wilderness: Coming of Age in Unknown Country* and *Hungry for the World.*
Bourke-White, Margaret. *Portrait of Myself.*
Brittan, Vera. *Testament of Youth.*
Broyard, Anatole. *Kafka was the Rage: A Green Village Memoir.*
Burns, George. *Living it up.*
Cahan, Abraham. *The Education of Abraham Cahan.*
Campanella, Roy. *It's Good to Be Alive.*
Carter, Jimmy. *Keeping Faith: Memoirs of a President.*
Chao, Buwei Yang. *Autobiography of a Chinese Woman.*
Chaplin, Charlie. *My Autobiography.*
Chernin, Kim. *In My Mother's House.*
Coberly, Lenore. *Writers Have No Age.*
Conway, Jill Ker. *The Road from Coorain.*
De Beauvoir, Simone. *Memoirs of a Dutiful Daughter.*
Delaney, Sarah and Elizabeth. *Having Our Say: The Delaney Sisters' First 100 Years.*

Denison, Isak. *Out of Africa.*

Drinkwater, Carol. *The Olive Farm, A Memoir of Life, Love, and Olive Oil in the South of France.*

Frank, Anne. *The Diary of a Young Girl.*

Douglass, Frederick. *Narrative of the Life of Frederick Douglass.*

Douglass, Karen. *Green Rider, Thinking Horse.*

Durant, Will and Ariel. *A Dual Autobiography.*

Ford, Betty. *The Times of My Life.*

Foster, Emily. *Barjo Restaurant, The Life of Josephine McAllister Stone.*

Franklin, Benjamin. *Autobiography.*

Fuller, Alexandra. *Don't Let's Go to the Dogs Tonight: An African Childhood.*

Gandhi, Mohandas. *Autobiography.*

Gilbreth, Frank and Carey, Ernestine Gilbreth. *Cheaper by the Dozen.*

Gonzalez, Ray. *Memory Fever: A Journey Beyond El Paso Del Norte.*

Grealy, Lucy. *Autobiography of a Face.*

Green, Graham. *A Sort of Life.*

Haizlip, Shirlee Taylor. *The Sweeter the Juice, A Family Memoir in Black and White.*

Haley, Alex. *Roots.*

Hall, Donald. *String Too Short to Be Saved.*

Hargreaves, Jack. *Panning Gold, A Maine Memoir.*

Hayes, Helen. *On Reflection, An Autobiography.*

Hemingway, Ernest. *A Moveable Feast.*

Herriot, James. *All Things Bright and Beautiful* and *All Creatures Great and Small.*

Isaacson, Judith Magyar. *Seed of Sarah: Memoirs of a Survivor.*

Keller, Helen. *Story of My Life.*

Jacobs, Harriet. *Incidents in the Life of a Slave Girl.*

Johnson, Joyce. *Minor Characters.*

Jung, Carl. *Memories, Dreams, and Reflections.*

Keefer, Janice Kulyk. *Honey and Ashes.*

Kerouac, Jack. *Lonesome Traveller.*

Kingston, Maxine Hong. *The Woman Warrior: Memoirs of a Girlhood Among Ghosts.*

Lewis, C.S. *Surprised by Joy, The Shape of My Early Life.*

Linkletter, Art. *I Didn't Do it Alone.*

MacNeil, Robert. *Wordstruck, A Memoir.*

McCarthy, Mary. *Memories of A Catholic Girlhood.*

Mead, Margaret. *Blackberry Winter.*
Monette, Paul;. *Becoming a Man, Half a Life Story.*
Myers, Linda Joy. *Don't Call Me Mother.*
Naipaul, V.S.. *Finding the Center, Two Narratives.*
Nin, Anaïs, *Diaries.*
Neruda, Pablo. *Memoirs.*
O'Faolain, Nuala. *Are You Somebody, The Accidental Memoir of a Dublin Woman.*
Rodriguez, Richard. *Hunger of Memory.*
Sarton, May. *The House by the Sea* and *At Seventy* and *After the Stroke.*
Schwicker, Fred. *Clamdiggahs, Tales of a Town Gone By, A Long Island Memoir.*
Sills, Beverly. *Bubbles.*
Stein, Gertrude. *The Autobiography of Alice B. Toklas.*
Rodriguez, Richard. *The Hunger of Memory.*
Roosevelt, Eleanor. *On My Own.*
Roth, Philip. *Patrimony.*
Washington, Booker. *Up From Slavery.*
Welty, Eudora. *One Writer's Beginnings.*
Wharton, Edith. *A Backward Glance.*
Wilder, Laura Ingalls. *On the Way Home.*
Wong, Jade Snow. *Fifth Chinese Daughter.*
X, Malcolm. *The Autobiography of Malcom X.*
Zabel, Arnold. *Jewel and Ashes.*

WRITING AND HEALING

Adams, Kathleen. *The Write Way To Wellness.*
Allan, Joyce. *Because I Love You, The Silent Shadow of Child Sexual Abuse.*
Baldwin, Christina. *Life's Companion, Journal Writing as a Spiritual Quest.*
Chandler, Margaret. *A Healing Art, Regeneration Through Autobiography.*
DeSalvo, Louise. *Writing As A Way of Healing, How Telling Our Stories Transforms Our Lives.*
Myers, Linda Joy. *Becoming Whole: Writing Your Healing Story.*
Pennebaker, James. *Opening Up, The Healing Power Of Expressing Emotions.*
    Writing to Heal: A Guided Journal for Recovering from Trauma and Emotional Upheaval.
Stone, Richard. *The Healing Art of Storytelling, A Sacred, Journey of Personal Discovery.*
Weldon, Michele. *Writing to Save Your Life, How to Honor Your Story Through Journaling.*

Appendix C: Soleil Lifestory Network Services

I offered my first *workshops* in 1988. Two years later, a participant asked me to be her *editor*. Thus began my work one-on-one with memoir writers. Today, we use telephone and e-mail. In 1992, I distilled my workshop into the first edition of this book, and in 1996, I created the comprehensive *curriculum and training packages* for teachers. In the late 1990s, I discovered *coaching*—a natural extension of my *writer mentoring*. *Tele-classes* and *co-authoring* now complete my offerings to help people to produce the best memoirs they possibly can.

You can, with the help of this book, write interesting, effective memoirs. Tens of thousands have—with no more than what you now hold in your hands. But, if you are a person who enjoys interactive learning, I invite you to put me and my staff on your writing team. Contact me at 207-353-5454 (during business hours—M-F, 9-5, ET) or denis@turningmemories.com. Be sure to visit our websites—www.turningmemories.com and www.memoiruniversity.com—where you'll find free information and writing tips, current workshop schedules and full descriptions of services.

—Denis Ledoux

SERVICES FOR WRITERS
Personal Writing Coaching

As a coach, I am your thoughtful tutor, insightful editor, shameless cheerleader, supportive friend, and at times, infuriating instigator. I help you identify needs and create a benchmarked strategy plan and schedule for achieving your goals. Coaching is a powerful tool that helps both beginners and experienced writers take charge of their writing. As your mentor and partner, I accelerate your learning process, improve your technical skills and keep you on task. You'll find info about how coaching works at www.turningmemories com/coachingwrite.html

WRITING AND BOOK PRODUCTION SERVICES
Editing

Lifestories are our specialty—but we work with all genres. First-time, one-time, and many-time writers find it useful to have another pair of eyes and an active, objective sensibility to review a manuscript at various stages. A good editor will not alter your voice—he'll enable you to communicate more clearly. A good editor will not subvert your storyline—he'll help you to develop its full potential. Look for info at www.turningmemories.com/editingservices.html.

Co-authoring

If you want a written record of your life experience or family history but recognize that writing a book requires more skills, time or energy than you want to invest, working with a co-author is a great option. If you've struggled with or inherit a manuscript and need it completed or polished, consider a co-author. Info at www.turningmemories com/coauthoring.html.

Book Design, Production & Self-Publishing

Whether you envision a family, a regional or a national audience, you deserve a beautiful book. Mastering book design and printing processes has a steep learning curve. We can help you make appropriate publishing choices for your budget and your audience. We design book interiors and covers, prepare photos and illustrations, do all pre-press production and work with the printer (often saving you fees!). www.turningmemories.com/bookproduction.html or contact martha@turningmemories.com.

WORKSHOPS
Turning Memories Into Memoirs® Lifestory Writing

Join us in the Spring or Fall on the coast of Maine for my signature 5-day, in-depth workshop. You'll learn the skills to recall and explore memories and to record them effectively using techniques of good writing. No prior experience is necessary. Classes are limited to 12 or fewer. You'll write three to five finished stories and gain skills and motivation to keep writing. Find current schedules and info at http://turningmemories.com/schedule.html.

Lifestory Writing Retreat

This 5-day session for those *already* writing features supportive, focused peers and literary techniques presented in the context of daily Turning Memories® group editing and discussion. Writing time dominates; I am available for private consultation at no extra cost. Find current schedules and info at http://turningmemories.com/schedule.html.

PROFESSIONAL DEVELOPMENT
Teacher Training and Certification and Affiliate Programs

Soleil Lifestory Network offers professional development for personal historians in its one-of-a-kind Certification Program. The Affiliate Teacher Packages (in whole or in part) provide materials and resources of our international network of lifestory writing professionals. Share your enthusiasm for lifestory writing with people in your region through programs, classes and services. Visit www.turningmemories.com/memoirteachercertification.html.

These books, manuals and professional development resource packages are available at www.turningmemories.com/bookstore.html.

MEMOIR WRITING

Turning Memories Into Memoirs: An Audio Guide to Writing Lifestories
120-minute 2-cassette set, $16.95.
The Lifewriter's Memory Binder
85 + pages, exercises, instruction & forms, project organizational tips & tools, $21.95

MEMOIR PROFESSIONAL DEVELOPMENT

The Editor's Manual: Editing Prose as a Professional
115 pages, CD (adaptable office forms, client handouts), publicity examples & templates, $79.95
Affiliate Teacher Resource Package ($499) includes:
- *Turning Memories Into Memoirs® Presenter's Manual*
- *Turning Memories Into Memoirs® Curriculum Manual*
- *Publicity Templates CD of press releases, office forms, etc.*
- *Copies of workshop text, audiotape, & Memory Binder*
- *Start-up Consultation with Denis Ledoux*
- *Referrals from lifewriters in your area*
- *Listing and profile at turningmemories.com*
- *E-Newsletter updates of your program schedule and services*
- *Eligibility to pursue Certification*
- *Additional discounts on volume purchases, Web Partner commission, Editor's Manual.*

Associate Teacher Resource Package ($379) includes:
- *Turning Memories Into Memoirs® Presenter's Manual*
- *Turning Memories Into Memoirs® Curriculum Manual*
- *Publicity Templates CD of press releases & forms*
- *Copies of workshop text, audiotape, & Memory Binder*

PHOTO-JOURNALING

The Photo Scribe: A Writing Guide, How to Write the Stories Behind Your Photographs
128 pages, exercises, examples, photographs, $16.95
The Photo Scribe's Memory Binder
85+ pages, exercises, instructions & forms, $21.95
How to Write Great Cameo Narratives in Five Easy Steps
How to Write Great MemoryLists in Five Easy Steps
step-by-step instructional worksheets, $9.95 / gummed pad of 100
The Photo Scribe® Teaching Package
a complete class kit for photo journaling teachers, $129 +free shipping within the US